Demand Management Best Practices:

Process, Principles and Collaboration

Colleen Crum
with
George E. Palmatier

J.ROSS PUBLISHING

APICS.
THE EDUCATIONAL SOCIETY
FOR RESOURCE MANAGEMENT

Copyright ©2003 by J. Ross Publishing, Inc.

ISBN 1-932159-01-0

Printed and bound in the U.S.A. Printed on acid-free paper.
10 9 8 7 6

Library of Congress Cataloging-in-Publication Data

Crum, Colleen, 1953–
  Demand management best practices : process, principles and collaboration / by Colleen
  Crum with George Palmatier
    p. cm.
  ISBN 1-932159-01-0
  1. Business logistics. I. Palmatier, George E.   II. Title.

  HD38.5.C78 2003
  658.5—dc21   2003004913

Phone: (561) 869-3900
Fax: (561) 892-0700
Web: www.jrosspub.com

DEDICATION

For Jerry Crum,
who has taught me that, with hard work, all things are possible.

TABLE OF CONTENTS

ACKNOWLEDGMENTS

The writing of a book involves many people in supportive roles. First and foremost are my clients and Oliver Wight colleagues and their dedication to improving demand management practices so that companies can be more financially successful. Then there are those who have encouraged me to put on paper what I have been teaching and coaching for many years. And, finally, there are those who offered encouragement, support, and patience. I will always be grateful for the support of so many during the writing of this book.

Some people deserve special acknowledgment. Co-author George Palmatier originally suggested that I write a book on demand management. As one of my mentors, George has always been generous in sharing his insight on demand management and sales and operations planning. I hope we can continue collaborating for many years to come.

I am indebted to the many people who took time out of their busy lives to review portions of the book. Special thanks go to the following Oliver Wight colleagues: Pete Skurla, who read nearly every page and offered detailed advice and lively opinions about the best practices of demand management; Liam Harrington, who outlined the topics he felt should be addressed in the book; Larry Wilson, who provided a case example for Chapter 6; Dennis Groves, who reviewed the chapter on demand collaboration; and Marc Bergeron and Ron Ireland, who shared their vision of the future of demand management, collaboration, and integration.

This book would never have come to fruition without the support of a publishing firm committed to advancing the knowledge of business practices. I am grateful for J. Ross Publishing and publisher Drew Gierman. Drew offered years of experience about how to successfully write and market business books. He also offered encouragement and patience that enabled me to write the best book I possibly could.

I have been especially blessed by the support of family and friends. My parents, Jerry and Vivian Crowell, sisters Kathleen Crowell and Constance Pepper, grandmother Lucille Conover, and parents-in-law Bob and Gladys Crum have been wonderfully supportive with their encouragement. Our Friday night group of friends has offered not only encouragement but the battery-charging respite of fun and laughter. Many thanks to Judy Wytock, Jerry and Susan Holsclaw, Rick and Virg Towner, and Kevin and Carol Honkomp. Special thanks, too, to Suzy Stockdale for always believing that I could write a book and encouraging me to do so.

Many years ago, my husband Jerry and I talked about life goals. A goal of mine was to write books. Despite battling cancer, Jerry has done everything he possibly could to give me time to research and write this book. This book would not have been completed without Jerry's "wind beneath my wings."

Colleen Crum
In an airplane en route to Toronto, Canada

THE AUTHORS

Colleen Crum is a managing principal with the Oliver Wight Companies. She has assisted many companies in implementing sales and operations planning, demand management, and forecasting.

Colleen has been involved in the food industry's supply chain management effort. She participated in the development of *ECR: Road Map to Continuous Replenishment,* published by Canadian food industry trade groups in 1995. The publication documented the best continuous replenishment practices in Canada, addressing logistics, distribution, transportation, and resource planning.

She co-authored with George Palmatier the book *Enterprise Sales and Operations Planning,* published by J. Ross Publishing.

George E. Palmatier, a consultant and educator with the Oliver Wight Companies since 1986, is recognized as a leading expert in integrated sales and operations planning. He helped to pioneer one of the first applications of sales and operations planning as vice-president of marketing at Bently Nevada Corporation, now part of General Electric. Based on this experience, he co-authored a book, *The Marketing Edge: The New Leadership Role of Sales and Marketing in Manufacturing.* The premise of the book — that sales and marketing have an essential role to play in developing manufacturing strategies — has helped to drive an increasing number of companies toward using sales and operations planning as an integrated management process.

George has transferred his knowledge to hundreds of companies that produce or market all types of products, from services to soups to satellites. It is this experience as a practitioner, educator, and coach that he imparted in the book *Enterprise Sales and Operations Planning,* published in 2003.

ix

ABOUT OLIVER WIGHT

Throughout the world, the Oliver Wight name is synonymous with many widely adopted operational methodologies. Oliver Wight is a global firm of consultants and educators who specialize in value chain excellence and change management for businesses and professionals in the fields of manufacturing, procurement, logistics, and distribution. Since 1969, Oliver Wight has been a thought leader in manufacturing — creating the disciplines of Material Requirements Planning and Manufacturing Resources Planning and pioneering the use of Class A business process best practices.

As part of its commitment to help organizations achieve operational excellence, Oliver Wight began publishing best practice standards and criteria in the form of what is known as the ABCD checklist. Oliver Wight authors also have published many books on best practices that are now considered classics and seminal works in their field. Oliver Wight's commitment to help companies through consulting, educational courses, books, and other media still continues today.

Oliver Wight has maintained its leadership role at the forefront of change with the creation of new methodologies and the introduction of best practices that fit the needs of today's — and tomorrow's — companies. Oliver Wight consultants and educators are located throughout the world. Company offices are located in New London, New Hampshire, United States; Gloucester, United Kingdom; and Sydney, Australia.

Oliver Wight previously introduced the mechanics of sales and operations planning and demand management in the best-selling and ground-breaking books entitled *Enterprise Sales and Operations Planning: Synchronizing Demand, Supply and Resources for Peak Performance, Orchestrating Success: Improve Control of the Business with Sales and Operations Planning,* and *The Marketing*

Edge: The New Leadership Role of Sales and Marketing in Manufacturing. The sales and operations planning and demand management processes are now best practices that are becoming basic management fundamentals necessary for success in today's economic environment. Experience has shown that operational excellence requires a blend of people, process, and tools — in that order. Software alone cannot be the sole driver of a company's success. Today's technology tools are dependent on strong processes, and an effective sales and operations planning and demand management process is essential to the successful implementation of any integrated management system such as enterprise resources planning and supply chain management.

Oliver Wight and J. Ross Publishing are pleased to introduce the Integrated Business Management Series of best practices and innovations. *Enterprise Sales and Operations Planning: Synchronizing Demand, Supply and Resources for Peak Performance* and *Demand Management Best Practices: Process, Principles and Collaboration* are the first two books in this new series. These books demonstrate how to successfully implement these processes to achieve the operational performance required to remain competitive today and in the future. The series is dedicated to the pioneering efforts and innovative spirit of the late Oliver Wight and his mission of helping companies achieve new levels of excellence that yield competitive advantage and superior profits. Additional information on these and future titles in the Integrated Business Management Series is available on the J. Ross Publishing web site at www.jrosspub.com.

ABOUT APICS

APICS — The Educational Society for Resource Management is a not-for-profit international educational organization recognized as the global leader and premier provider of resource management education and information. APICS is respected throughout the world for its education and professional certification programs. With more than 60,000 individual and corporate members in 20,000 companies worldwide, APICS is dedicated to providing education to improve an organization's bottom line. No matter what your title or need, by tapping into the APICS community you will find the education necessary for success.

APICS is recognized globally as:

- The source of knowledge and expertise for manufacturing and service industries across the entire supply chain
- The leading provider of high-quality, cutting-edge educational programs that advance organizational success in a changing, competitive marketplace
- A successful developer of two internationally recognized certification programs, Certified in Production and Inventory Management (CPIM) and Certified in Integrated Resource Management (CIRM)
- A source of solutions, support, and networking for manufacturing and service professionals

For more information about APICS programs, services, or membership, visit www.apics.org or contact APICS Customer Support at (800) 444-2742 or (703) 354-8851.

Web
Added
Value™

Free value-added materials available from
the Download Resource Center at www.jrosspub.com

At J. Ross Publishing we are committed to providing today's professional with practical, hands-on tools that enhance the learning experience and give readers an opportunity to apply what they have learned. That is why we offer free ancillary materials available for download on this book and all participating Web Added Value™ publications. These online resources may include interactive versions of material that appears in the book or supplemental templates, worksheets, models, plans, case studies, proposals, spreadsheets and assessment tools, among other things. Whenever you see the WAV™ symbol in any of our publications, it means bonus materials accompany the book and are available from the Web Added Value Download Resource Center at www.jrosspub.com.

Downloads available for *Demand Management Best Practices: Process, Principles and Collaboration* consist of templates for measuring forecast accuracy and organizing monthly demand review for reaching consensus on the demand plan.

INTRODUCTION

Thirty years ago, demand management within most manufacturing companies was minimal at best or nonexistent. In some cases, demand was forecast, but it was not common for the forecast to be used to drive financial projections or production rates. Only in rare circumstances was demand information communicated by customers to their suppliers.

Today, companies and supply chains are developing whole new models for managing demand. Companies are using the demand plan to drive their supply and financial plans, which is causing demand plans to be updated monthly, rather than quarterly or annually. Customers and suppliers are collaborating to communicate demand information (monthly, weekly, and even in near real time) and develop tactics to capture sales.

As a result, the roles, responsibilities, and best practices of demand management are changing and continuing to evolve. The purpose of this book is to document the principles and best practices of demand management. It focuses not only on today's best practices but on what the authors believe will be the best practices of the future. In doing so, we hope that you will not have to "reinvent the wheel" in implementing demand management in your company and supply chain. We also hope that the experiences and practices presented in this book will stimulate your company, and the supply chains in which you are a partner, to continue to improve your demand management processes.

Today, there is a greater realization of the value of — and need for — competency in planning, communicating, influencing, and prioritizing and managing demand. What is driving and enabling this new attitude toward demand management? Pressure and opportunity.

Shareholders and Wall Street analysts are increasingly unforgiving when sales revenues and profits are less than what has been promised. It is well recognized that inaccurate demand forecasts result in unwanted inventories and supply glitches that compromise customer service, sales, and financial performance.

Customers are also more demanding and less forgiving of their suppliers. They expect delivery performance, product availability, and responsiveness to continuously improve. Some customers are as bold as one U.S. automaker in demanding cost reductions from their suppliers.[1] Some customers, particularly in the retail industry, are mandating that their suppliers implement standards of best practices for demand collaboration and replenishment.

For suppliers, it is becoming increasingly more difficult to achieve customers' performance expectations — including price expectations — without an accurate demand forecast and effective demand management. Cost, cash flow, and profit pressures do not permit the extensive use of inventory to dampen the effects of an unreliable forecast.

Opportunity is also driving a greater awareness of the need for effective demand management. More and more executives recognize the financial benefits for all supply chain partners when inventory and waste are flushed from supply chains. They also recognize that without mechanisms for forecasting and communicating demand plans, it is extremely difficult to reduce inventories and supply chain costs.

Today, many companies, particularly in the consumer goods industry, are implementing demand collaboration as part of their efforts to reduce the amount of capital required to support supply chains. The vast majority of companies in most industries are at least beginning to explore whether collaborative trading partnerships are beneficial, and if so, what is required to partner successfully. They are finding that successful collaboration starts with effective internal demand management processes that are integrated with their company's supply and financial planning processes.

All of these changes — some might call them advancements — alter the landscape for those who work in sales, marketing, and product/brand management. Instead of operating as functional silos within an organization, decisions are increasingly based on the impact on the organization as a whole. The objective of integrated business management is twofold:

1. To ensure that the demand, supply, and financial plans are synchronized and executed as planned
2. To ensure that decisions with regard to demand, supply, and products will yield the best financial performance for the company

Some companies view their internal integration efforts as a prerequisite to being an effective trading partner. The thinking is: Let's get our own internal house in order before we begin collaborating with our customers and suppliers.

As a result, an increasing number of companies are focused on developing demand management as a core competency.

The advantages of effective demand management throughout the supply chain have been talked about for many years. An article in a prominent business magazine observed in 1996:

> So far, supply chain partners have cooperated only over the short term, via orders. What they need to do is get their overall forecasting and planning systems integrated for a long-term view. If everybody can agree on a forecast and stick to it, you don't have to be changing your production schedules back and forth. That's the way to get better margins.[2]

Why haven't more supply chains integrated their demand planning processes for a long-term view? To do so requires greater competency in three areas: integration of business processes, people development, and information infrastructure.

Too many times, companies futilely search for the "silver bullet," usually information technology, as a painless way of forecasting. Yet, information technology alone does not yield an accurate forecast or ensure effective demand management.

Effective demand management requires a competence that goes far beyond expert use of statistical forecasting software or communicating demand schedules via the Internet or electronic data exchanges. Information technology cannot replace those human qualities so essential to managing demand. True competency in demand management comes from human judgment, integrated business processes operated by knowledgeable people, and skillful execution.

The importance of demand management motivated the author to write this book with George Palmatier. We helped to implement demand management as part of an integrated business management process in our place of employment more than 20 years ago. As industry pioneers in this effort, we experienced firsthand the benefits of an effective demand management process tied to an integrated business management process. We found that this model for managing and operating the business gave our company a competitive advantage that it has sustained more than two decades later.

As consultants, we became disciples for elevating the importance of demand management in industry. Once again, we were pioneers in helping hundreds of companies to implement best practices for demand management as part of an integrated business management model.

Through these experiences, we have learned many lessons along the way. The primary purpose of writing this book is to share these lessons.

With advances in information technology and electronic commerce, these lessons are more important today than ever before. Demand information can be communicated at increasing speeds throughout the supply chain, yet success is not predicated upon the mere communication of demand information. Success is dictated by:

1. The reliability of the demand information
2. What company managers and trading partners do with the information; that is, how the demand information enlightens decisions and drives actions

We recognize that the demand management process, whether it is operating well or not, impacts most functions within a company as well as supply chain partners. Therefore, this book is written with many people in mind.

For the senior executive of sales and marketing, this book demonstrates the key principles and best practices of demand management. It enlightens these executives on where they should focus their time and attention in operating their demand management processes and what results to expect.

For forecasters, demand planners, and demand managers, this book provides insight on how to apply best practices in developing a demand plan. It also shows how to reduce uncertainty of demand, reach consensus internally on a demand plan, and collaborate with customers and suppliers within a supply chain.

For managers and planners in the supply organization, this book gives a perspective of what is realistic to expect from a demand plan and how decisions on synchronizing supply and demand are most effectively made.

For supply chain managers, this book presents the fundamentals for developing more reliable demand plans and schedules. It also shows what is necessary to build successful trading partner relationships for demand collaboration.

Finally, for presidents and general managers of companies, this book demonstrates how effective demand management contributes to sales revenue growth, lower inventories, increased profit margins, and shareholder value. Oftentimes, the demand forecast is blamed when the supply organization does not execute the supply plan. Just as frequently, the sales and marketing organizations claim that it is impossible to forecast. This book gives the president and general manager information that will prevent "pulling the wool over their eyes" and defines what is reasonable to expect from a demand management process.

It is our hope that the lessons shared in the book will stimulate improvements on how demand management is applied in your company and in the supply chains in which your company operates. At the end of each chapter, questions will be asked to help you determine how to implement the lessons from the book. We hope this book will spur a whole new generation of thought on how to utilize demand management to improve company financial performance.

QUESTIONS

1. Review Figure 1. Where would you place your company's demand management process in this figure?
2. To determine whether there is a need to evolve along the continuum shown in Figure 1, ask yourself and others within your company:
   a. Does the production planner or master scheduler develop the forecast because the organizations responsible for sales and marketing do not generate forecasts?
   b. How frequently are supply glitches caused by customers not ordering what was predicted and in the time frame that was predicted?
   c. Does a demand review take place in which those responsible for sales and marketing management agree on a demand plan that is then communicated to the supply organization?
   d. Are the demand, supply, and product plans for the next 18+ months reviewed each month by the senior executive team? Are the plans synchronized each month during this senior executive integrated business management review?
   e. Do your customers communicate their order schedules and future demand plans on a regular basis? Are these plans incorporated into your company's internal demand plan?

No Forecasting	Forecasting Internal Sales and Marketing Only	Communicate Demand Plan to Supply Organization	Demand Plan and Supply Plan Synchronized Through Integrated Business Management Process	Demand Collaboration with Supply Chain Partners

Evolution of Demand Management

FIGURE 1 Evolution of Demand Management. Whereas forecasting of demand was almost nonexistent 30 years ago, today demand management continues to evolve.

This book has free materials available for download from the
Web Added Value™ Resource Center at www.jrosspub.com.

PART I: FUNDAMENTALS OF DEMAND MANAGEMENT

2

WHAT IS DEMAND MANAGEMENT?

The following conversation was overheard at a client company:

> *Forecaster to supply planner*: "Why didn't you use the demand plan numbers as the basis for the production plan?"

> *Supply planner to forecaster*: "Because I don't trust the forecast."

> *Forecaster to supply planner*: "But the demand plan is what customers, the marketing people, and the sales organization have told us that customers are going to buy."

> *Supply planner to forecaster*: "I still don't trust the forecast. It's never right."

The example above illustrates some of the common frustrations that surround demand management. The forecast, or demand plan, often is the subject of much debate and distrust, especially by the supply and financial organizations. Roles and responsibilities are frequently confused. How involved the sales and marketing organizations should be in developing the forecast, or demand plan, is also the subject of debate.

Why the debate, confusion, and resulting frustration? Demand management is frequently not thought of as a process. The development of the demand forecast is seen as an event rather than as part of a larger process. When forecasting is treated as an event — something that must be done once per month, for example — the accuracy of the forecast inevitably suffers. When the forecast is chronically and significantly inaccurate, it is frequently second-guessed or not used at all to drive production rates and financial projections. And when the demand forecast is not utilized, those responsible for providing input into the forecast see their efforts as a waste of time. The quality of the forecast inevitably suffers, which perpetuates the belief that the forecast cannot be trusted.

How does one get out of this unproductive loop? By adopting a broad view of demand management. The narrow view that demand management consists solely of forecasting inevitably yields mediocre results. This chapter introduces some basic concepts of the broad view of demand management. The purpose of introducing these basic concepts is to provide a foundation for the principles and concepts presented in the remainder of the book.

A first basic concept to grasp is that demand management embodies much more than just developing a forecast of demand. According to Philip Kotler, a respected thought leader on marketing management, demand management involves influencing the level, timing, and composition of demand.[3]

Kotler makes two key points about demand management. First, demand management is the responsibility of the marketing organization (he considers the selling function part of the marketing function). Second, the demand forecast is the *result* of planned marketing efforts. Planned marketing efforts should not just stimulate demand but should influence demand so that a company's objectives are achieved.[4] My colleague and co-author George Palmatier calls this "Marketing with a Big M."

This book presents the best practices of demand management. The broader view of demand management is a best practice. Why? Compare the results of companies with a narrow view of demand management to those with a broader view. Companies with the broader view almost always realize greater benefits from the effort. The benefits of demand management are detailed in Chapter 3.

The broader view of demand management drives companies to better understand their customers and their markets. In the authors' experience, when there is keen, insightful understanding of markets and customers' expectations of products, services, and pricing requirements, companies develop more accurate demand forecasts. Marketing and sales executives also use this understanding to better position the company in the marketplace. In short, this broader view makes a company a stronger competitor and gives it an edge in the marketplace.

So what is involved in implementing a broader view of demand management? The broad-view model of demand management (Figure 2) consists of the following elements:

1. *Planning demand*, which involves more than just forecasting
2. *Communicating demand*, which includes communicating the demand plan to the supply and finance organizations and, increasingly, to supply chain partners

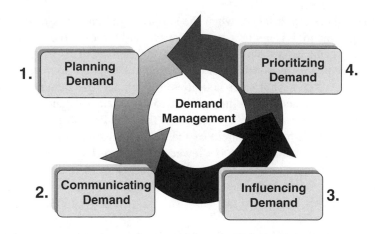

FIGURE 2   Demand Management Process Model — The Broad View (Copyright Oliver Wight International)

3. *Influencing demand*, which includes marketing and selling tactics, product positioning, pricing, promotions, and other marketing and sales efforts
4. *Managing and prioritizing demand*, which includes managing customer orders to match available supply

This is a far more robust process than simply developing a demand forecast. Each of the elements influences the others. By integrating the four elements with supporting processes and information, the most complete view of demand is achieved. And when there is a comprehensive view of demand, the accuracy of the demand forecast improves. (Each of the four elements of demand management will be discussed in detail in subsequent chapters.)

Integral to a broader view of demand management is an understanding of the term *demand forecast*. According to the American Production and Inventory Control Society, the definition of a demand forecast is simply *an estimate of future demand*.[5]

Note that the definition states a forecast of future *demand*, not *shipments*. This distinction is frequently confused. It is not unusual for companies to base their demand forecasts on shipment history, especially when the supply organization is tasked with the forecasting function or when demand history is not available. Use of shipment history almost always ensures less accurate forecasts. Shipment history does not take into account when customers wanted the product to be delivered. Customer-requested delivery dates and actual shipment dates usually do not match, as most companies are not 100 percent effective at delivering products according to customers' requested delivery schedules.

In the authors' experience, when the supply organization is responsible for forecasting demand, it is not unusual for the demand forecast to be biased toward the supply organization's ability to produce and deliver. This is especially the case when the people responsible for developing the forecast do not have knowledge of the marketing and sales activities. Remember, the demand forecast is the result of sales and marketing efforts to stimulate demand. This is why demand management must be viewed from the broader context of marketing, rather than solely from the context of the supply organization.

When demand management is viewed in the broader context, it must be operated as an ongoing process (note that the arrows in Figure 2 show a continuous process). Marketing and sales management must actively participate in the process. In fact, marketing and sales should own and lead the process. This is a best practice.

A key responsibility of marketing and sales management is to reach consensus on a demand plan. The decisions made in reaching consensus turn the forecast — an estimate of future demand — into a demand plan. The distinction is that the plan becomes a commitment to conduct the marketing and sales activities necessary to achieve the plan. These activities include influencing, managing, and prioritizing demand.

In short, the consensus demand plan is an agreement to execute. When there is a commitment to execute — and measures to determine execution performance — the accuracy of the demand plan improves. And with that improvement comes greater trust of the demand plan.

In examining why some companies are more successful than others in operating their demand management processes, one common difference between success and mediocrity becomes obvious: whether marketing and sales management actively participate in the process or whether they delegate the responsibility to others lower in the organizations. Astute marketing and sales executives realize that demand management processes involve not only agreeing on forecasting numbers but on ensuring that the marketing and sales tactics are executed to stimulate demand in the first place. These executives are adroit at using the demand management process as *their* management process. Roles, responsibilities, and accountabilities for the demand management process are discussed in detail in Chapter 9.

As more and more companies integrate their business processes, communicating the demand plan to other functions in the organization becomes critical. How demand information is communicated and the timing of that communication can no longer be casual or informal. Those responsible for developing the demand plan must communicate in terms that make sense to the supply and financial organizations.

Figure 3 illustrates the communications challenge. Note the line "Measure" in the figure. The marketing and sales organizations often think of demand only in terms of sales revenue. The production and logistics organizations think of demand in terms of unit volume and item-level mix, as do the product development and customer service organizations. The financial organization, of course, is interested in sales revenue and gross margins.

There are different users, or customers, of the demand plan, as shown in Figure 3, and it is essential to talk their language. The demand plan is not just developed for internal sales and marketing consumption. It should be used to drive supply planning and financial planning. Consequently, the person responsible for developing the demand plan is also responsible for communicating in meaningful terms to all customers of the demand plan.

Many finance organizations create their own financial projections independently, which results in financial forecasts that are different from the demand plan. Use of an independent financial projection is often motivated by the desire for revenue projections to closely approximate the revenue promised in the business plan. This practice is the antithesis of integrated business management. It often hides the issues and problems that, if unresolved, actually prevent the company from achieving the promised revenue and profit performance in the business plan.

Sometimes finance executives, in their zeal to drive their companies' financial performance, forget a fundamental business principle: sales revenue is the result of delivering something of value to customers. As Peter F. Drucker observes:

A company makes shoes, and no financial man understands that. They think money is real. Shoes are real. Money is an end result.[6]

Because sales revenues are the result of demand for products and services, the financial projections should be based on anticipated demand. By the same token, products and services that must be produced are driven by demand. Therefore, supply projections also should be based on the demand plan. These are best practices, and integration techniques that enable using the demand plan as a driver of supply and financial plans are discussed in Chapter 14.

Integration is now reaching beyond company walls, and members of supply chains are sharing demand and sales information. Point-of-sale data, as well as demand schedules and future projections of demand, are being communicated routinely by customers to their trading partners. This process is called collaboration. The Internet and electronic data exchange are being used to automate the exchange of information among supply chain partners. This activity is frequently referred to as customer linking.

	Sales	Marketing	Production	Logistics	Product Development	Customer Service	Finance
Product information	Product family	Product family by territory Product family by customer	Product SKU	Product SKU by location	Product family	Product SKU	Product family by division and corporation
Measure	Units and $	Units and $	Units	Units	Units	Units	$
Horizon	Up to 12–24+ months	12–24 months	12–24 months	12–24 months	12–24 months	12 months	1–5+ years
Interval (frequency of communication and updates)	Monthly	Monthly	Weekly and monthly	Weekly and monthly	Monthly	Weekly and monthly	Monthly

FIGURE 3 Customers of the Demand Plan (Copyright Oliver Wight International)

Collaboration and linking change the roles and method of work for those responsible for planning demand and supply. They also change decision-making boundaries. The challenge and the opportunity of collaboration and linking are discussed in detail in Chapter 13.

This chapter has introduced definitions of basic concepts of demand management. Each chapter of the book addresses a common question, issue of debate, or best practice of demand management. Exposing the questions, controversies, doubts, and successes of demand management has a purpose. It provides the business context of demand management. In the authors' experience, when people understand the concepts, the logic, and the reasoning for demand management, they are infinitely better able to apply demand management successfully in their corporate cultures.

SUMMARY OF BEST PRACTICES
FOR DEMAND MANAGEMENT

1. The demand management process involves more than just forecasting. It encompasses planning demand, communicating demand, influencing demand, and managing and prioritizing demand.
2. There is the recognition that demand is the result of marketing and sales efforts.
3. The focus of demand management is to generate demand in a way that meets the company's goals and objectives.
4. Demand forecasting accuracy is dependent on the understanding of the markets and customers' expectations, as well as the company's ability to execute marketing and sales tactics.
5. The demand forecast is based on future expectations of demand, not future shipment expectations.
6. The demand management process is an ongoing process, not a periodic event.
7. The consensus demand plan represents a commitment by the marketing and sales organizations to execute the necessary marketing and sales activities to achieve the plan.
8. Marketing and sales management own and lead the demand management process.
9. The demand plan is communicated in terms that are meaningful for the supply and finance organizations.
10. The demand plan is used as the basis for developing the finance and supply projections.

QUESTIONS

1. The demand management process is most effective when it is the responsibility of which function(s) in the organization?
2. What does the demand management process involve, according to Philip Kotler?
3. What are the four elements of the broad-view model of demand management?
4. What are the advantages of a broad view of demand management, rather than the narrow view?
5. What is the definition of a demand forecast?
6. Why should a demand forecast or plan be based on customer-required delivery dates rather than shipment dates?
7. What is the difference between a forecast of demand and a demand plan reached by consensus?
8. In what terminology do the following functions view demand?
   - Sales and marketing
   - Product development
   - Supply organization
   - Customer service
   - Financial organization
9. Why should the supply and financial plans be based on the demand plan rather than vice versa?
10. What does collaboration involve?

ACTIVITY

Contact the customers of the demand plan. Ask each customer how they prefer to view the demand information, including unit of measure and time horizon. Document their preferences and use their input to structure the communication of the demand plan.

3

IS DEMAND MANAGEMENT WORTH THE EFFORT?

Clients frequently express disappointment that their statistical forecasting tools do not predict future demand with a high degree of accuracy. Their distress is heightened because they want the ability to develop forecasts with little human intervention. After all, suppliers of forecasting software have led them to believe that this is possible.

Effective demand management — and accurate demand plans — require the leadership and participation of the sales, marketing, and product organizations and the operation of a regular, routine process. Many executives ask: Is it worth the effort?

This is a legitimate question. After all, now we are talking about investing not just in information technology but in people as well to operate a demand management process. Sales and marketing executives legitimately want to know why it is necessary to deploy valuable human resources to perform all four elements of demand management. Their position often is: Why can't we just use a statistical forecast, or let the supply organization forecast for us? Barring that, why can't we just reach consensus on a demand plan? Why must we also influence and manage demand?

To determine the worth of demand management, it is necessary to look at the consequences of an ineffective demand management process:

■ When customers order more product than has been forecasted, product is not available to fulfill demand. That means inadequate customer service, resulting in a delay in sales revenue at best or a loss of sales revenue at worst.

- When customers order more product or different product than has been forecasted, the supply organization often must change priorities. Changing priorities usually requires ineffective and inefficient expediting. This results in higher costs and lower margins, which reduces profitability.
- When customers do not order as much product as forecasted, product is built unnecessarily. That means increased inventory and associated increases in carrying costs, which in turn reduces profitability and restricts cash flow. Frequently, this unneeded inventory becomes old and obsolete, resulting in inventory write-offs and reduced profitability.
- When customers do not order as much of one product as forecasted in a capacity-constrained environment, precious capacity may be wasted building the wrong mix of products. When a company builds the wrong product in a tight capacity situation, it cannot build the products that could otherwise be sold. This increases costs and reduces revenue.

Maddeningly, the above situations typically occur simultaneously.

What happens when product cannot be shipped when customers want it? Usually, the salesperson or account manager tries to intervene to ensure that the product is available for his or her customer. Salespeople spend valuable time competing against each other for product for their customers. Those who lose spend additional time explaining to their customers why product is not available. These gyrations take time away from the task on which salespeople should be primarily focused — making the next sale.

If the order is significant enough or the customer important enough, the vice-president or director of sales often feels compelled to intervene. This takes time away from the primary focus of the sales executive — positioning the sales organization to make the next significant sale.

Ironically, in too many companies the sales organization has enough time to expedite orders caused by inaccurate forecasts, but will not take time to provide input that would have prevented the imbalance in demand and supply from occurring in the first place. Case in point: A pharmaceutical manufacturer embarked on a supply chain management implementation that encompassed enterprise resource planning (ERP) as well as distribution planning and logistics management. The project team worked diligently to develop a demand management process and sales and operations planning process as part of the implementation.

The company's marketing management readily embraced the demand management concepts. Sales management was less enthusiastic, especially upon learning it would need to communicate its sales plans on a monthly basis. Sales management refused to communicate its sales plans and assumptions as part of the process.

The demand management process was implemented during a downturn in business. It became a common excuse to blame the marketplace and customers for an inability to predict sales. Likewise, when sales materialized, the supply organization was criticized for not having the inventory or the manufacturing responsiveness to ship orders when customers requested.

Had the sales force provided input on its sales plans and its customers' product needs, the demand management and sales and operations planning processes would have ensured that:

1. Product was available when it was anticipated that customers expected delivery, and/or
2. The sales team would have known when there were supply problems and could have made more realistic promises to its customers.

It was observed that sales management and salespeople spent more time chasing orders within the supply organization and soothing customers than it would have taken to communicate their sales plans and assumptions in the first place.

The company successfully implemented the ERP system from a technology point of view. The processes to optimally operate ERP, including demand management, were never fully implemented.

The impact of the ineffective demand management process was great. The company did not achieve its sales targets or profit goals and inventory skyrocketed. The president of the company and vice-president of sales were eventually replaced.

This experience drives home a point: The authors have never seen a company that could predict demand with a high degree of accuracy without participation from its sales and marketing organizations. Conversely, we have seen many companies significantly improve their financial performance and market position with a robust demand management process that includes:

- Input from their sales, marketing, and brand/product organizations
- A demand consensus review meeting, conducted monthly by sales and marketing management
- Communication of the consensus demand plan to the supply organization for synchronization
- A process for managing demand uncertainties and forecast inaccuracies as they become known

It is not unrealistic to expect the demand management process to contribute to improving a company's financial performance and market position. In fact, this should be a process performance measurement.

As stated earlier, inaccurate demand forecasts result in increased inventory. Think about the impact of inventory on capital. At Stone Apparel, for example, inventory accounts for 60 to 70 percent of its capital.[7] An effective demand management process, which included the sales organization working with customers to obtain point-of-sale information, enabled the company to reduce the percent of capital consumed for inventory.

A food manufacturer is another example. The company originally intended to buy a forecasting software tool. In exploring available software tools, it became apparent that the tool alone would not solve its forecasting problems.

In addition to investing in forecasting software, the company's management elected to concurrently implement a demand management process and sales and operations planning process. The demand management process would improve forecast accuracy. It would also establish a mechanism for agreeing on a demand plan each month and communicating it to the supply organization. The sales and operations planning process would ensure that the demand and supply plans were synchronized each month and that inventory, lead time, and pricing tactics were to the company's best advantage.

Figure 4 shows the company's improvement in forecast accuracy for three product lines over a 12-month period. The significant improvement in forecast accuracy resulted in a 6.5 percent, or $800,000, reduction in finished goods inventory in the first year. After implementing an ERP system and process in which the demand plan was integrated, the company achieved the following further improvements in the first year of ERP operation:

■ Reduced finished goods inventory by $2.8 million
■ Reduced raw material inventory by $600,000
■ Reduced obsolete inventory by $400,000

Without a doubt, improved forecast accuracy drives inventory reduction and increased inventory turns. It is not a coincidence that a newsletter on inventory reduction, the *Inventory Reduction Report*, devotes a considerable amount of space to articles about demand management and forecast accuracy.[8] A perusal of the articles on these subjects over a five-year period reveals that companies with effective demand management processes reduce inventory a minimum of 20 percent.

Inventory Reduction Report also periodically publishes inventory benchmarks by industry SIC code. These benchmarks include inventory to sales turnover, inventory to cost of goods turnover, days of inventory, and inventory

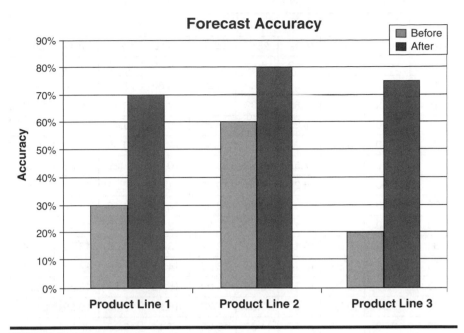

FIGURE 4   Forecast Accuracy Improvements

to working capital. The benchmarks are useful in determining what it takes to become best in class in your industry. As the studies published in *Inventory Reduction Report* repeatedly demonstrate, being best in class in these categories starts with effective demand management.

Gross margin return on inventory investment (GMROI) is another revealing measure employed by Quaker Oats and one of its customers, Oshawa Foods of Canada. Through initial efforts at collaboration and continuous replenishment with Quaker Oats, Oshawa Foods increased inventory turns from 14 to 32. At 14 turns, the GMROI was $4.42 per case. At 32 turns, the GMROI was $11.37 per case — nearly a 300 percent increase in profit margin per case.[9]

Figure 5 shows a GMROI table developed by the Canadian joint grocery industry's continuous replenishment initiative. To achieve this and other gains, it was acknowledged that continuous replenishment efforts need to be integrated at three levels with category management: (1) forecast/demand management, (2) tactical planning and execution, and (3) financial review.[10]

With greater interest in supply chain management, the impact of inaccurate forecasts on business entities throughout the supply chain is becoming increasingly visible. Case in point: Cisco and its contractors and suppliers. Despite warning signs that sales of telecommunications gear were going flat, Cisco did

Turns	Margin								
	20%	22%	24%	26%	28%	30%	32%	34%	36%
14	3.50	3.95	4.42	4.92	5.44	6.00	6.59	7.21	7.88
16	4.00	4.51	5.05	5.62	6.22	6.86	7.53	8.24	9.00
18	4.50	5.08	5.68	6.32	7.00	7.71	8.47	9.27	10.13
20	5.00	5.64	6.32	7.03	7.78	8.57	9.41	10.30	11.25
22	5.50	6.21	6.95	7.73	8.56	9.43	10.35	11.33	12.38
24	6.00	6.77	7.58	8.43	9.33	10.29	11.29	12.36	13.50
26	6.50	7.33	8.21	9.14	10.11	11.14	12.24	13.39	14.63
28	7.00	7.90	8.84	9.84	10.89	12.00	13.18	14.42	15.75
30	7.50	8.46	9.47	10.54	11.67	12.86	14.12	15.45	16.88
32	8.00	9.03	10.11	11.24	12.44	13.71	15.06	16.48	18.00
34	8.50	9.59	10.74	11.95	13.22	14.57	16.00	17.52	19.13
36	9.00	10.15	11.37	12.65	14.00	15.43	16.94	18.55	20.25
38	9.50	10.72	12.00	13.35	14.78	16.29	17.88	19.58	21.38
40	10.00	11.28	12.63	14.05	15.56	17.14	18.82	20.61	22.50

FIGURE 5   Gross Margin Return per Dollar of Inventory Invested (Annual GMROI)[10]

not decrease its demand forecasts. Telecommunications products accounted for 40 percent of Cisco's sales revenues. When demand slowed, Cisco's inventory ballooned to more than $2.5 billion, an increase greater than 100 percent in six months. Cisco's sales growth during the same six months was 25 percent. Cisco's suppliers also suffered from producing based on optimistic demand forecasts. Solectron's inventory increased from $1.8 billion in February 2000 to $4.5 billion in December 2000. Flextronics' inventory more than tripled from $469.8 million at the end of 1999 to $1.73 billion at the end of 2000. The industry as a whole ended up with $467.1 billion of annualized business inventory accumulation in 2000, a buildup that has been described as "having many economists gasping."[11]

When evaluating whether demand management is worth the effort, consider, too, the flip side of the above-described situation. What is the cost of supply chain glitches when product is not available to fulfill demand? Certainly, sales revenue is delayed and customers may be lost to a competitor better able to fulfill demand. For example, it is estimated that out-of-stock situations cost the consumer goods industry between $7 and $12 billion in lost sales annually. An industry observer for *Consumer Goods Technology* magazine calls this "an astounding figure when you consider that the industry's supply chain has one trillion dollars in inventory at any given time."[12]

Supply chain glitches also impact shareholder value. A four-year study of the impact of supply chain glitches on shareholder value showed that companies' stock prices fell an average of 7.5 percent when a supply glitch was announced. The average reduction in stock price was 18.5 percent when measured two quarters before and two quarters after the announcement.[13]

This brings us back to our original question: Is demand management worth the effort? Let's look at the investment required to support a demand management process:

■ A well-designed and -operated process typically requires an hour or two per month of marketing and sales professionals' time.

■ The investment in a full-time demand manager(s) is needed to develop the demand forecast, propose a demand plan, communicate the consensus plan to the supply and financial organizations, and manage uncertainties in demand with the supply organization.

■ Two to three hours per month is required of senior sales and marketing executives for the demand consensus review meeting. Arguably, this is already part of their job responsibilities and is not really an additive cost.

■ An investment in a forecasting tool that ideally integrates with the company's — and increasingly the customers' — planning systems is needed to support the process.

The investment in a demand management process is not hundreds of thousands of dollars. The consequences of a nonexistent or ineffective process, however, can amount to millions — in the case of the telecommunications industry, billions — of dollars. As we have seen, when companies do not perform demand management well, they give up capital, profit margin, shareholder value, customer service, and market position.

Is demand management worth the effort? A better question to ask is: Given today's economic and competitive environment, can you afford not to implement an effective demand management process?

SUMMARY OF BEST PRACTICES
IN THE FINANCIAL IMPACT OF DEMAND MANAGEMENT

1. There is an understanding of the impact of the demand management process on the company's financial and customer service performance.
2. The demand management process is expected to contribute to improvements in the company's financial performance and market position.

3. Metrics are in place to correlate forecast accuracy to inventory and the costs associated with inventory, sales revenue, shareholder value, and other financial measures.
4. Metrics are in place to correlate forecast accuracy to customer service performance.

QUESTIONS

1. What is the impact on financial and customer service performance when customers order more product than has been forecasted?
2. What is the impact on financial performance when customers do not order as much product as forecasted?
3. What are the pitfalls of the sales organization expediting orders?
4. Why is participation by the sales and marketing organizations imperative to the success of the demand management process?
5. What does measurement of the GMROI reveal?
6. What are the financial and customer service advantages of an effective demand management process?
7. What improvements in customer service and financial performance should you expect from a demand management process?

4

PRINCIPLES OF DEMAND PLANNING

The power of demand management is in the process itself — a formal, structured, and routine process in which each element of demand management operates at an optimum level. The elements of demand management are (1) plan, (2) communicate, (3) influence, and (4) manage and prioritize (see Figure 6).

When companies struggle with forecast accuracy problems, it is usually because one or more of the elements of demand management are not in place or not operating effectively. Demand management, in these cases, is superficial at best. The focus is typically on chasing orders to ensure meeting period-end or year-end targets and on expediting orders when the supply organization is unable to deliver orders when customers need the products.

The motivation for these sales activities is to react to a current need, which is the antithesis of demand management. The essence of demand management is being in control of the future by creating demand, influencing customers and the marketplace, and responding to changes in the marketplace. When the demand management efforts of companies are primarily on chasing orders, there is little focus on controlling the future. Not enough energy is spent on creating and influencing future demand, which keeps the company's sales and marketing management in an endless loop of chasing orders.

In this chapter, we will focus on the principles of demand planning. Subsequent chapters will be devoted to each of the other elements of demand management. Specific issues subject to debate or requiring greater clarification, such as multiple views of demand planning, consensus planning, and the role of the demand manager, are covered in later chapters.

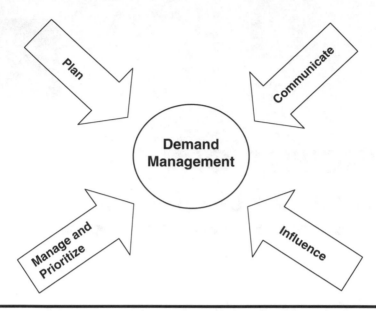

FIGURE 6   Elements of Demand Management (Copyright Oliver Wight International)

Notice that the first element of demand management is planning demand, not forecasting demand, although forecasting is part of planning demand. It is important to understand the difference between forecasting and planning. *Webster's Encyclopedic Unabridged Dictionary of the English Language* provides the following definitions:

Forecast: To predict a future condition or occurrence

Plan: A scheme or method of acting, doing, proceeding, making, etc., developed in advance

Webster's also states that "forecast has much the same meaning as predict; it is used today particularly for the weather or other phenomena that cannot easily be accurately predicted."[14]

The difference between forecast and plan is critical. Forecast connotes a lack of control — something that cannot be predicted with a high degree of accuracy. Plan, however, denotes action arranged in advance, which means that someone is determining and controlling the actions taken.

Too many people have the attitude that demand just happens and cannot be controlled. That is not true.

Think about it. Demand is the result of the actions a company takes to:

1. Develop products or services, and
2. Influence customers to buy those products and services

Some people call these actions demand creation.

Who is in the driver's seat when it comes to creating demand? You are. And if you are in the driver's seat in creating demand, you should be able to develop a demand plan that reflects the anticipated results of demand creation efforts.

Buying behaviors, competitors' actions, and the health of the economy certainly influence the quantity of products and services that are purchased as well as the timing of those purchases. These external factors may be more difficult to control. Actions can be taken, however, to mitigate the negative effects of these factors. This is part of the responsibilities involved in influencing demand. The anticipated results of these and other efforts to influence demand should be reflected in the demand plan.

Some people resist the idea of forecasting, let alone planning, demand. They believe it is impossible to predict future demand with 100 percent accuracy, so why bother? This attitude creates an unrealistic expectation of the demand planning effort.

Consider Peter F. Drucker's view on predicting the future:

> To try to make the future happen is risky; but it is a rational activity. And it is less risky than coasting along on the comfortable assumption that nothing is going to change.[15]

It is also less risky than proclaiming it impossible to predict the future as a justification for doing nothing to prepare for the future.

Instead of becoming overwhelmed because the future is hard to predict, a different mind-set is needed. That mind-set is: In essence, a demand plan is a model. The model is the result of anticipated product, sales, and marketing activities to create and influence demand. Albert Einstein once stated that "all models are wrong, some are useful." The demand plan, while not perfect, is useful for:

1. Validating that the product, marketing, and selling plans and strategies will deliver the expected financial and market positioning results
2. Determining the resources required to produce, transport, and deliver product to customers
3. Developing financial projections of sales revenues, cash flow, and profit margins

It is assumed that a demand plan will not be 100 percent perfect. A demand plan over an 18- to 24-month planning horizon is imprecise and subject to uncertainties. Imperfections should not be allowed to defeat the purpose of demand planning, however. Over time, greater precision can be added to the demand plan. In actuality, demand planning is a *replanning* process. Every month, the plan and supporting assumptions are updated, reviewed, and agreed upon. This is a best practice.

Replanning gives managers greater flexibility and control of the business. Knowing in advance that conditions are changing gives you the advantage of time to prepare. You can monitor the conditions over time and put plans in place to respond in the most timely and profitable manner. You gain the ability to control.

When imperfections in the plan arise, a process for managing these imperfections minimizes the negative impact on customer service, inventory, lead time or backlog, sales revenue, and profit margins. This process, the fourth element of demand management — managing and prioritizing demand, also gives you greater control.

Control starts with demand planning, however. So what is involved in developing a demand plan?

Demand planning is a process of planning all demands for products and services to support the marketplace over at least an 18-month horizon. This process involves updating the product, brand, marketing, and sales plans and assumptions each month and reaching consensus on an updated demand plan. The updated demand plan is communicated to the supply and financial organizations for reconciliation and synchronization. An increasing number of companies utilize a monthly sales and operations planning process to perform reconciliation and synchronization.[16] The synchronization and reconciliation process is covered in detail in Chapter 14 on integration.

Once the demand plan is reconciled and synchronized, and thus approved for execution, the plan is communicated to the sales force. These communications enable salespeople to know what they are expected to sell and what will be available to sell. The effectiveness of communications frequently means the difference between a mediocre and an excellent demand management process. Communications is the linchpin of the demand management process and is covered in detail in Chapter 5.

Figure 7 depicts a best practice demand planning process. As you can see, the demand plan is based on multiple inputs — from the sales, marketing, brand, and product management organizations as well as statistical analysis.

The most frequently used statistical forecasting method is the time series technique. It uses historical data sequenced by time (days, weeks, months, etc.) and projects future demand by the same time sequence. Time series statistical forecasting is a component of the statistical analysis process for supporting demand planning. It is just one part of the input for a demand planning process for good reason. Reliance on a time series statistical forecast alone usually does

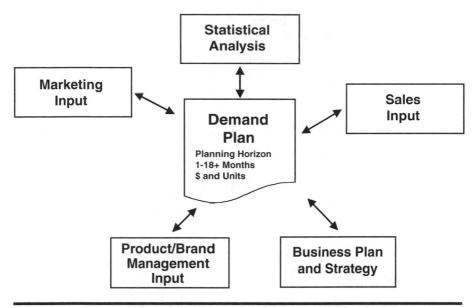

FIGURE 7   Demand Planning Process (Copyright Oliver Wight International)

not yield the most accurate demand plan model. Other statistical analysis techniques also contribute to the demand plan. One such technique, regression analysis for evaluating the impact of business drivers on demand, is discussed in some detail in Chapter 8.

Each of the inputs into the demand plan has its advantages and disadvantages. The advantages of a time series statistical forecast are:

■ It lacks the bias of human judgment, since it is based on historical demand data.
■ It is an efficient method for forecasting a large number of end items.

Most time series statistical forecasting tools use mathematical algorithms to determine the patterns and trends of past demand and extrapolate those patterns and trends into a projection of future demand. The times series forecasting method predicts with a higher degree of accuracy when demand patterns are repeatable and future demand is not changing significantly from past demand. To accurately predict variability in demand, such as seasonal patterns, the time series forecasting method is usually most accurate when there are 24 to 36 historical data periods upon which to base the future forecast.

The next two figures (Figures 8 and 9) illustrate the strength and weaknesses of time series statistical forecasts. The demand history in Figure 8 is highly

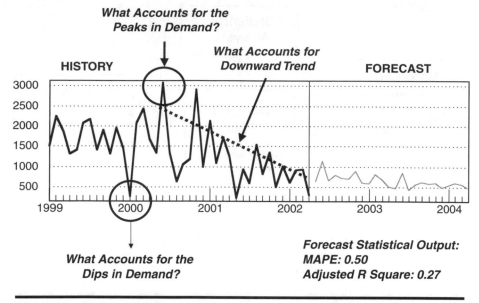

FIGURE 8 Statistical Forecast Model Example — Highly Variable Data without Repeatable Patterns

variable and does not appear to have much of a repeatable pattern. The statistical output provides guidance as to the accuracy of the forecast. The mean absolute percent error (MAPE) in this example is 0.50, or 50 percent. This means that the forecast has an error rate of 50 percent when the forecast numbers are compared to the historical demand numbers. The adjusted R square value is 0.27, or 27 percent. This means that 27 percent of the variation in historical demand is accounted for in the future forecast.

Some might argue that this is an unreliable forecast due to the error rate of 50 percent and that only 27 percent of the variation in past demand is accounted for in the forecast. Others might argue that the statistical forecast could be used as a starting point, and other input is needed to:

- Explain past peaks and dips in demand and whether they will occur again
- Validate the downward demand trend and how long it is expected to continue
- Understand the planned product, marketing, and sales activities and how they will impact future demand

The historical demand data in Figure 9 also have peaks and dips, but these demand patterns appear to be repeated year after year. The statistical output

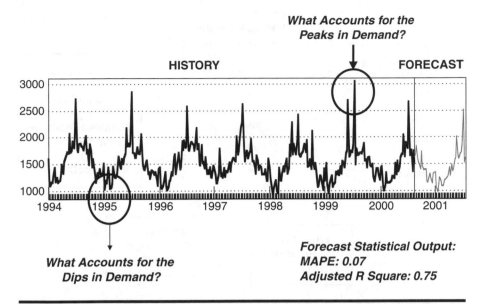

FIGURE 9   Statistical Forecast Model Example — Variable Data with Repeatable Patterns (Example Courtesy of Business Forecast Systems, Inc.)

shows a more accurate forecast than the projection in Figure 8. The mean absolute percent error is 0.07, or 7 percent. The adjusted R square value is 0.75, or 75 percent.

Some might argue that the time series statistical forecast is accurate enough to use as the demand plan. After all, it has an error rate of only 7 percent, and 75 percent of the variations in the historical demand are accounted for in the future projection.

Others might argue that input from the brand, marketing, and salespeople would better refine the model. They might be asked to explain whether:

■ Variations in demand will continue to occur in the same way as in the past.

■ Activities that are planned will cause different demand volume and timing than in the past.

■ Changes will be occurring in the economy, other key business drivers, and with competitors that will impact demand for this product.

With time series statistical forecasting, it is dangerous to assume that history will repeat itself and customers will buy exactly as they bought the previous year. Even if your company does not plan changes in its activities to create demand (which is not likely), your competitors are probably taking actions to

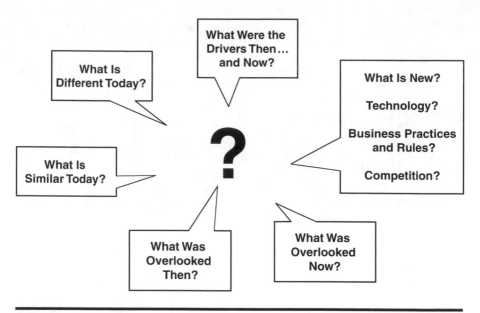

FIGURE 10   Questions to Ask About Demand History (Copyright Oliver Wight International)

increase their market share — at your expense. And even if your competitors are quiescent, the economy and other events can certainly influence whether, and when, customers buy your products. Just look at how home purchases and auto sales are tied to interest rates, for example.

Rather than assume that the past will repeat itself, it is better to ask certain questions about demand history. These questions are shown in Figure 10. The answers to these questions help to determine how much weight to place in the statistical forecast when developing the demand plan.

This is not to say that a time series statistical forecast does not have value. At a minimum, as seen with the examples in Figures 8 and 9, a statistical forecast can be a starting point. When demand is stable and few changes are expected that will alter the volume and timing of demand, the time series statistical forecast may be the most accurate input into the demand plan.

Time series statistical forecasting is also a necessity when a company produces hundreds or thousands of end items. It is folly to develop a demand plan for just a few major product lines. The turmoil caused by not planning the demand for the other products disrupts production. Unplanned demand competes against planned demand for raw material and production capacity. Customer service inevitably suffers, as do sales revenues and profit margins. Consequently, developing demand plans for all products and services is a best practice.

When your product portfolio includes a large number of end items, a planning strategy is needed to ensure that all of the items are adequately planned. A common strategy is to develop an aggregate, or family, plan by product type or category over at least an 18-month planning horizon for consensus planning. The demand plan at the item level can frequently be delayed as late as possible — until raw materials need to be purchased or, if the family uses common materials, until the product must be produced and assembled. The later that you can wait to specify the product mix, the closer in time it is to the actual sale. The closer in time to the actual sale, the better informed your sales organization will be as to what specifically customers will order.

A statistical forecast is of great value for determining the product mix forecast within product families if the mix is not expected to change significantly from the past. Statistical forecasting techniques are frequently used to determine the mix forecast when specific product attributes are not yet known by the salespeople and customers. The statistical forecast, in this case, is validated and revalidated as the salespeople and customers become more informed over time as to the specific products that will be ordered. Whatever is the best method for planning the product mix, the demand plan at the item level must be managed and controlled on a daily and weekly basis. The demand manager and supply manager or master scheduler typically work together to fine-tune the product mix plan.[17]

One view of demand alone is usually not enough to develop the most accurate demand plan, at either the aggregate or item level. The time series statistical forecast provides the historical, or backward-looking, view. Many statistical forecasting tools allow for manual adjustments of the forecast. These adjustments usually have some basis — and that basis is a forward view of anticipated demand.

Alan Greenspan, chairman of the U.S. Federal Reserve Board, has observed that "the best forecast is made with the freshest data."[18] The people with the freshest, forward-looking information reside on the demand side of the business — in the marketing, sales, brand, and product management organizations. These organizations know if new products are going to be introduced and the marketing and sales activities that are planned to create demand for these products. These functions know what advertising, promotions, and price tactics are planned and the anticipated impact these programs will have on demand; they have the earliest knowledge of whether a major customer is being acquired and the expected volume and timing of the resulting sales; and they also have the closest contact with the customers. This gives these functions the most up-to-date information on customers' intentions to buy the company's products and services.

Whereas a time series statistical forecasting tool is looking for repeatable patterns, the forward-looking input from the demand side of the business helps

Inputs	Information	Planning Horizon
Sales	Customer plans Individual salesperson plans Territory/region sales plans Sales strategy and tactics Incentive plans	1–12+ months
Marketing	Market plans Channel plans Promotion plans Pricing plans Monitoring of key economic indicators Business driver analysis and monitoring Competitive analysis	1–18+ months
Product/Brand Management	New product development Product launch plans Product exit plans Product life cycles Product pricing plans Brand and category plans Competitors' product tactics	1–18+ months

FIGURE 11   Forward Input Required for the Demand Plan

to explain the complexities and dynamics of demand. Figure 11 summarizes the forward-looking input that most sales, marketing, brand, and product organizations are capable of contributing to the demand plan.

As with time series statistical forecasts, forward-looking input from the demand side of the business has advantages and disadvantages. The primary advantages are:

- The inputs reflect the most current knowledge about customers, competitors, and the marketplace.
- The inputs are based on what is actively being planned and executed to create and influence demand.
- Customer interaction is involved in sales, marketing, and brand management activities, which provide greater insight on customers' intentions, the strength of your company's relationship with customers, the likelihood of retaining and expanding business with customers, and the probability of acquiring business from new customers.
- Varying and differing perspectives on demand help to reduce bias and prevent blind spots from occurring, which results in a more refined plan.

Some people challenge the wisdom of involving the sales, marketing, product, and brand organizations in the demand planning process. A client in the computer peripheral industry, for example, wanted to base the demand planning process solely on time series statistical forecasting. The attitude was that sales and marketing do not know what they are doing; therefore, why consult them about the demand plan?

The authors find this to be ignorant thinking. The people in sales and marketing organizations certainly are not twiddling their thumbs. They are engaged in activities that will indeed create and influence demand. To cut them out of the process dooms the demand planning process to mediocrity if not failure.

The challenge is in engaging the sales, marketing, and brand management organizations in the demand management process — and in creating accountability for their efforts. This is imminently doable. Methods for obtaining multiple views regularly and routinely are covered in detail in Chapter 8.

This is not to say that forward-looking inputs do not have weaknesses. The most dangerous weakness is bias. Bias comes from a mind-set that is overly optimistic or pessimistic. It comes from having blind spots that shield a person or group from recognizing the true state of reality. In the telecommunications example given in the previous chapter, warnings were communicated that sales for telecommunications gear were going to be flat. Those signals were ignored due to misconceptions about the enduring strength of customer demand.

Bias also occurs as a response to other stimuli such as compensation programs. Case in point: The updated demand plan for a client in the wood products industry reflected a 30 percent reduction in demand. The assumptions upon which the plan was based had not changed significantly, however, when compared to the previous plan's assumptions. External factors impacting the business were also not expected to change. So why the reduction in demand? It turned out that the company was in the process of establishing sales goals for the next year. Of course, the sales force wanted a highly attainable sales target. Its compensation was based on exceeding the annual sales goal; thus the sales plan was reduced to lower the target.

Through the sales and operations planning process, the proposed demand plan was challenged. The assumptions were reviewed and validated. The sales organization was asked to explain the reasons for the 30 percent reduction in demand, given that the assumptions had not changed significantly from the previous month.

In the end, only minor adjustments were made to the previous month's approved demand plan, as it most accurately reflected reality. The sales input was obviously biased by internal activities in setting up next year's compensation program.

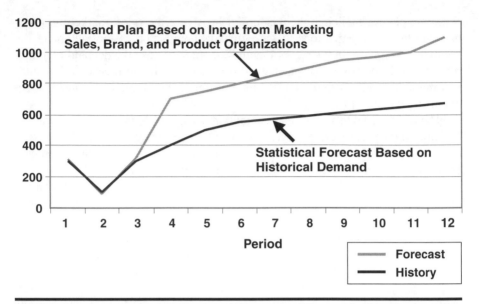

FIGURE 12 Comparison of the Statistical Forecast and Forward-Looking Demand Plan as a Sanity Check (Copyright Oliver Wight International)

This example illustrates the value of utilizing multiple inputs, or views. If the demand plan had been based solely on the sales organization's input, the company would not have been prepared for the true demand that materialized. Multiple views provide varied perspectives that, when scrutinized closely, always result in a more precise plan.

A valuable perspective can be gained by comparing the demand model, resulting from input from the demand side of the business, to the historically based statistical forecast. An example is shown in Figure 12. The time series statistical forecast in this example is significantly lower than the demand plan based on the forward-looking input provided by the sales and marketing organizations.

The demand manager for a client in the mineral mining industry plots the time series statistical forecast against the forward-looking demand plan for each product family every month. When significant deviations occur between the two models, he challenges the sales and marketing assumptions. He asks: What are you doing or plan to do that will cause the volume and timing of demand to be different than the past? Sometimes efforts are not being undertaken to significantly increase demand volume. When this is the case, the demand manager gives the time series statistical forecast greater weight in the demand plan.

This analysis also assists sales and marketing executives in their management efforts. It helps them to assess whether their organizations are taking the proper actions to grow demand and increase sales revenue. It also helps prioritize where to best focus their time and attention on creating future demand.

Comparing the time series statistical forecast to the forward-looking demand plan becomes a "sanity check." It is an effective tool for rooting out bias and ascertaining whether activities and plans are in place to significantly alter future demand, compared to past demand performance. It is one method of ensuring that demand plans are grounded in reality.

The two examples given above — the sales organization reducing its sales plans to gain a more achievable compensation target and using the time series statistical forecast as a sanity check — illustrate another best practice for demand planning: documenting and reviewing the assumptions upon which the plan is based.

In reality, when there are significant errors in the demand plan compared to actual demand, the plan numbers are not what prove to be inaccurate. The assumptions on which the plan is based are usually incorrect and the root cause of the demand plan inaccuracies. Therefore, to improve demand plan accuracy, the assumptions must be documented and carefully reviewed, challenged, monitored, and updated. Documenting and managing assumptions is covered in detail in Chapter 8.

When assumptions are not included as input into the demand plan, the demand numbers should be considered to be lacking validation. An unvalidated plan is always at greater risk for inaccuracies than a plan in which the assumptions have been reviewed and clarified. After all, the plan numbers are the result of the assumptions about demand creation efforts, customer buying behavior, and the state of the economy and other business drivers, not the other way around.

Paying close attention to assumptions has other benefits. It spurs greater understanding of the factors that influence demand, which in turn results in the development of a more accurate demand plan. It also enables the demand side of the business to demonstrate to the rest of the company that it has a firm grasp of the factors that influence demand.

Demonstrating that the demand plan has been well thought out is crucial for the supply and finance organizations to trust the plan. When these organizations trust the demand plan, they are more confident in using the demand plan to drive their projections.

Likewise, when the marketing, sales, and product organizations see that their input is used and useful, they are more diligent in providing input to the demand plan. When the demand side of the business sees that its efforts are helping to make product available when it said it would be needed to fulfill demand, it sees the value of the process. And when it sees the value of its efforts, it is more willing to participate in the process. This win–win creation starts with documenting and validating the assumptions upon which the demand plan is based.

This brings us to two other best practice principles for demand planning:

- The demand plan represents products and services that customers are expected to purchase. It is not restricted by perceived or expected supply constraints. This is commonly called an unconstrained demand plan.
- The demand plan is a request for products and services. It is what the demand organization believes customers are going to buy. The demand organization is committed to executing the demand plan to ensure that customers *do* buy these products and services.

Constraining the demand plan because of supply limitations has several pitfalls. Imbalances in demand and supply will not be visible soon enough to respond and thus usually cannot be addressed quickly enough to accommodate all of the demand. The supply organization will have little motivation to operate more effectively, reduce lead times, and increase capacity if it does not see the need to do so. Inevitably, sales will languish, making it difficult to achieve sales revenue goals and grow the business.

Conversely, the demand plan should recognize that there is probably more market potential than a company is capable of serving. Consequently, the demand plan should only be constrained by the demand organization's ability to create demand and generate sales (Figure 13).

If the demand plan is unconstrained by supply limitations and truly represents the sales the demand side of the business expects and is committed to

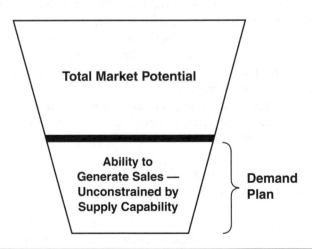

FIGURE 13   The Demand Plan Is Unconstrained by Supply Capability (Copyright Oliver Wight International)

generate, then the demand plan is actually a request for product. It is not wishful thinking. It is based in reality, factoring in the demand organization's ability (and limitations) in stimulating demand and generating the sales.

Thinking in terms of the demand plan being a request for product is an important psychological motivator. Remember the discussion at the beginning of the chapter about the difference between a forecast and a plan? A plan means action, and action means control. If the demand organization has control, it should be able to determine the volume and timing of product that it desires to request to be produced on behalf of the customers.

Consider, too, the risk of forward-looking inputs. They can be biased — either overly optimistic or overly pessimistic. One way to eliminate bias is for the demand organization to ask every month: Is this the product we really want to request? And do we understand that if we request product, we are committed to creating the demand for that product?

These questions provide safe ground for validating the demand plan before it is communicated to the supply and financial organizations. The authors have seen this questioning eliminate the hedging that can occur for selfish reasons such as wanting shorter hurdles for attaining compensation incentives based on sales revenues. Here is how it works:

- If you request the product and do not sell it, you are responsible for the inventory, increased working capital, and reduced profits that result.
- If you do not request the product and do sell it, there will be no assurance that product will be available to fulfill the demand. Reduced or delayed sales revenue will result and customer service will suffer. In many companies, those salespeople who requested product get first priority for that product.

The demand organization is typically not used to thinking in these terms. Members of the demand organization may not recognize that their actions or inactions impact the company as a whole (for example, the cost of building unneeded inventory when demand does not materialize as planned). A focus on requesting product creates greater accountability for the quality of the demand plan and for executing the demand plan. It creates accountability for "doing what you say that you're going to do."

Thinking of the demand plan as a request for product creates a safety valve in another way. It can prevent wishful thinking from taking hold. As George W. Bush has observed, "Wishful thinking might bring comfort, but not security."[19]

At times, there can be pressure to force the demand plan to closely approximate the business plan. This is foolhardy when reality shows that sales revenues are unlikely to materialize at the rate stated in the business plan.

Thinking of the demand plan as a request for product helps executives resist the urge to arbitrarily make the demand plan numbers match the sales revenue numbers in the business plan. It gives them the ability to think through the ramifications of forcing the demand plan to match the business plan. The question can be asked: What are the implications if demand does not materialize as planned in the business plan and we produce to the business plan rate? Of course, the answer is: In addition to lower sales revenues, unneeded inventory is built, resulting in less available capital and lower profits.

Thinking through these ramifications, executives can ask and answer: Do we really want to take that financial risk? Would we be better off producing to the current reality and working to narrow the gap between the business plan and the demand plan? Once the gap is narrowed, then we can produce at the new realistic rate.

As shown in Figure 7, the business plan and strategy is an input into the demand plan. The primary purpose of this input is as a senior management tool.

Think back to one of Philip Kotler's key points on demand management introduced in Chapter 2. Demand creation efforts should not just stimulate demand, but should influence demand so that a company's objectives are achieved. Senior executives on the demand side of the business need to know whether demand creation efforts will result in achieving the sales revenue objective stated in the business plan. A comparison each month of the sales revenue projections resulting from the demand plan to the sales revenue projections stated in the business plan will give them this knowledge.

Figure 14 shows a gap between the sales revenue that will be generated by the demand plan and the business plan objective. The −3, −2, −1 indicate the past three months of history. The 1, 2, 3, etc. indicate each forward-planning period. An 18-month future planning horizon is used in this example.

In this example, the sales revenue that will be generated from the demand plan is less than the business plan objective. Does this mean that the demand plan should be changed to increase the planned sales revenues? Not necessarily, and especially not if the status quo is expected in marketing and sales activities.

The revenue stated in the business plan is a target. The business plan, like the demand plan, is a model; it is not a perfect prediction of a company's financial performance.

Senior executives should be managing to meet the objectives of the business plan. When there is a gap between the demand plan and business plan, as in the example above, it should trigger action to narrow the gap.

The demand consensus review is an excellent forum for reviewing the actions planned to narrow the gap between the demand plan and the business plan objective. This is also the proper forum for determining when the expected results from these activities should be reflected in the demand plan.

$ in Millions

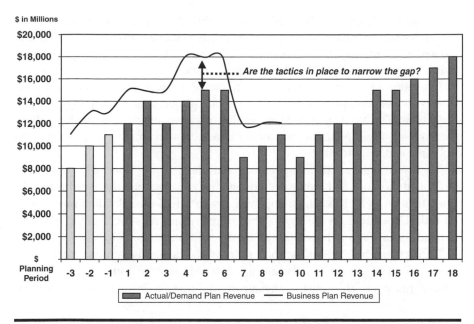

FIGURE 14   Comparison of Demand Plan Sales Revenue versus Business Plan Sales Revenue Objective

Note in the example above that the planning horizon is 18 months. Using a planning horizon of at least 18 months is a best practice. There are several reasons why:

- First, an 18-month or longer planning horizon allows enough time to act when it appears that the demand will not generate the sales revenues stated in the business plan. It also allows enough time to act when demand exceeds your supply capability. In the authors' experience, the time to make significant change to markets, customer base, products, suppliers, and production capacity always takes longer than people believe.
- Second, when you reach midyear, you will have a view of the next year's demand plan. This usually gives executives ample time to ensure that the strategies and tactics are in place to achieve the next year's demand plan. The demand plan thus drives the revenue plan for the annual business plan.

Many companies that use this planning methodology find that developing the annual business plan becomes a nonevent. The work has already been done, and it is usually of higher quality and more reliable than the plans generated in an annual business planning process. After all, the demand plan is reviewed and updated every month. When it is time to create a business plan, it will have been reviewed, refined, and updated six or more times.

One purpose of demand planning is to create as credible a model as possible for driving business plan projections, financial projections, and supply planning projections. The most credible plans result from a replanning process that utilizes a sufficiently long planning horizon to allow enough time to respond to both problems and opportunities.

The updating, or replanning, of demand plans is not a periodic event. It is performed monthly and monitored continuously. Consequently, it requires full-time attention, which is why companies assign a full-time demand manager to the task. Depending on the size of the company and its structure, the full-time demand manager may be supported by demand planners and analysts as well.

The demand manager is the focal point of the demand planning process (see Figure 15). The various inputs into the demand plan are communicated to the demand manager. The demand manager assimilates these inputs, replans appro-

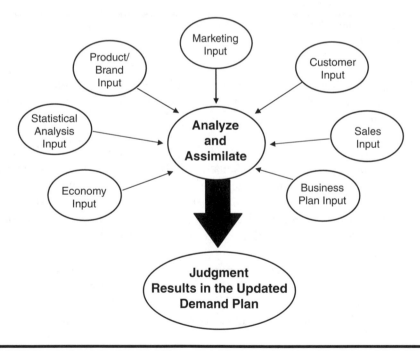

FIGURE 15   Role of the Demand Manager in Demand Planning (Copyright Oliver Wight International)

priately, and proposes an updated demand plan. The updated demand plan and assumptions are reviewed at the monthly demand consensus review.

The demand manager facilitates the communications with the demand organization during the process of updating the demand plan. The demand manager is also responsible for communicating the approved updated demand plan to the supply and financial organization for synchronization and reconciliation. (See Chapter 9 for a description of the demand manager's complete responsibilities.)

The demand manager is not the only person in the demand organization responsible for communications. Communications is the second element of demand management, and it is so important that it deserves its own chapter.

SUMMARY OF BEST PRACTICES
FOR DEMAND PLANNING

1. The demand plan is based on inputs from the marketing, sales, brand, and product organization as well as statistical analysis.
2. There is recognition in the demand, supply, and finance organizations that the demand plan is a model and that all models are wrong, but some are useful.
3. The demand plan is used to validate that the product, marketing, and selling plans and tactics will deliver the expected financial and market position results.
4. The demand plan is used to drive the financial and supply projections.
5. The demand plan is updated at least monthly.
6. An aggregate demand plan and item demand plan are developed monthly. Both plans are communicated in units and resulting sales revenues by time period.
7. The assumptions upon which the demand plan is based are monitored, reviewed, and updated at least monthly.
8. The demand plan is not constrained by supply limitations; it is only constrained by the demand organization's ability to create demand and generate sales.
9. The demand plan is considered a request for product by the demand organization. The demand organization recognizes the financial and customer service impact when the demand plan is inaccurate.
10. The demand plan and business plan are not arbitrarily forced to match. Projection of the revenue generated by the demand plan is compared each month to the sales revenue objective stated in the business plan. Senior demand executives focus on the strategies and tactics required to narrow

any gap between the demand plan revenue and the sales revenue objective in the business plan.

11. A full-time demand manager is assigned to support the demand planning process.

QUESTIONS

1. If you were to design a demand planning process, what would be the most important elements to include in the process?
2. What is the difference between a demand forecast and a demand plan?
3. What are the advantages of a statistical forecast?
4. What are the disadvantages of a statistical forecast?
5. What are the advantages of forward-looking input from the demand organization?
6. What are the disadvantages of forward-looking input from the demand organization?
7. Why is the documentation, review, and monitoring of assumptions important? What do you lose when you do not document and review the assumptions?
8. Why is it advantageous to consider the demand plan a request for product?
9. Why should the demand plan not be constrained by supply limitations?
10. How should the business plan and strategy input be utilized in the demand planning process?
11. What are the risks of arbitrarily matching the demand plan to the business plan objective of sales revenue?
12. Why is an 18-month or longer planning horizon advantageous?
13. What is the role of the demand manager in the demand planning process?

5

PRINCIPLES OF COMMUNICATING DEMAND

A salesperson recognized that the timing for a significant order might be delayed. The customer was waffling. The salesperson did not communicate the uncertainty in the timing to his sales manager or demand manager, however. He knew his company was banking on this order, and he did not want to deliver potentially bad news. He would keep working to close the deal, hopefully within the originally anticipated time period.

A brand manager planned a promotion for a product line. The anticipated increase in demand from the promotion was not factored into the demand plan. The price discount also was not reflected in the sales revenue plan. The brand manager was pleased when the promotion resulted in a 10 percent increase in demand. She was surprised, however, that the demand plan accuracy was criticized in the next month's demand consensus review and executive sales and operations planning meeting.

What do these two case examples have in common? A breakdown in communication. Communication makes or breaks the demand management process. It also is a major factor in enabling companies to achieve their business objectives. When companies struggle with inaccurate demand plans, ineffective communication is often the root of the problem.

Let's review the impact of the communication breakdown in the two examples above. In the first example, the significant order was received four months after the originally anticipated date. Product had been built in advance to ensure that the order could be delivered on time. The company spent money to buy material and build the product when those costs could have been delayed. The manufacturing capacity could also have been used to produce other orders. Ultimately, sales revenues were delayed and less working capital was available for this cash-strapped company.

In the second example, product was not requested to cover the 10 percent increase in demand generated by the promotion. Some of the materials could not be ordered within standard lead time, and expediting charges were paid to procure the materials quickly. Overtime was needed to build the products and some express shipments were required, increasing both manufacturing and transportation costs. These costs, coupled with the lower selling price, resulted in lower than expected profit margins. Despite efforts to ship product on time, the delivery performance was below the 98 percent standard expected by this company's customers.

Why the lapse in communication? There were several reasons. In the first example, the salesperson was not 100 percent certain that the customer would *not* place the order when originally expected. He knew he would be criticized if he told his manager that the order would be late, and he was doing everything he could to bring the order to fruition.

In the second example, the brand manager was not positive about the response rate to expect from the promotion. The salespeople were enthused about the promotion but received details on the promotion later than originally planned. As a result, most of the salespeople had not contacted their customers about the promotion. Thus, the brand manager was reluctant to commit to delivering a specific increase in demand that she could not ensure with a high degree of certainty.

The above reasons for the breakdown in communication are symptoms of a greater deficiency: the lack of a robust communication process. This chapter focuses on best practices for stimulating timely communication that drives sound decision making.

In the examples above, the salesperson and brand manager tried hard to perform their jobs well. The salesperson did not realize, however, that bad news early is better than bad news late. Conversely, the brand manager did not realize that good news early is better than good news late. Unwittingly, the salesperson and brand manager violated the first principle of communication for a demand management process — no surprises.

Uncertainty about when demand would materialize and how much demand to expect clouded the salesperson's and brand manager's judgment about whether or not to communicate. This commonly occurs when processes are not in place to manage uncertainty. Tactics for managing uncertainty are covered in Chapter 10.

Uncertainties must be communicated, however, just as the anticipated results

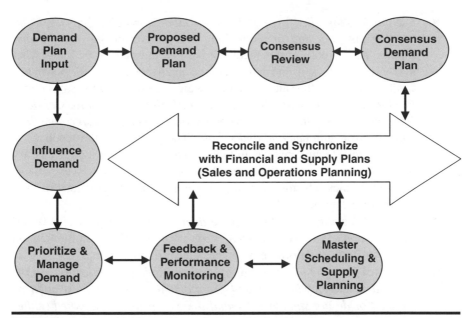

FIGURE 16   Demand Management Communication Process

from efforts to create demand must be communicated. This is not to say that communication is easy. It is not.

Why is communication difficult? First, it requires a structured process for conveying information, assimilating information, discussion, decision, and feedback. Second, many people believe that transmitting demand data is the same as communicating, which it is not. Third, emotion and behavior can stymie communication (e.g., the proclivity to "shoot" the messenger).

Let's discuss a structured process first. Figure 16 illustrates the communication process for demand management. The demand planning process itself is a communication process. It involves communicating input to the demand plan, validating the assumptions, proposing a demand plan, and reaching consensus on the demand plan. The communication process links the demand planning process to the reconciliation and synchronization of the supply, financial, and demand plans through sales and operations planning. It also connects the demand plan to supply planning and master scheduling. The communication linkage with the supply and financial organizations involves conveying demand information in the formats, units of measure, and planning horizons that each organization requires to perform its own planning (see Figure 3 in Chapter 2).

Feedback and performance monitoring are also a part of the communication process and occur at several levels:

■ *Feedback to the sales force of decisions made in reaching consensus on the demand plan and in reconciling and synchronizing demand and supply*: The purpose of this feedback is to let the sales force know what it is expected to sell and what will be available to sell. Performance feedback apprises the sales force how well it is executing the sales plans.

■ *Feedback to the product, brand, and marketing organizations of decisions made in reaching consensus on the demand plan and in reconciling and synchronizing demand and supply*: The purpose of the feedback is to communicate any changes in tactics that were determined necessary for the company to meet its demand and/or business objectives. Performance feedback informs these organizations of the effectiveness of their efforts to create demand.

■ *Feedback from the sales force to the demand manager (and vice versa) when demand does not materialize as planned*: This communication triggers efforts to prioritize, manage, and influence demand.

■ *Feedback from the product, brand, and marketing organizations to the demand manager when demand creation efforts are not executed as planned or do not stimulate demand the way it was anticipated (either positively or negatively)*: This communication stimulates actions to develop alternative demand, supply, and financial plans, if necessary.

■ *Feedback by the demand manager to the master scheduler and supply planning organization when demand does not materialize as planned*: This communication results in actions by the supply organization to alter the supply plan, if possible. It also triggers action by the demand organization to prioritize, manage, and influence demand in order to keep demand and supply as synchronized as possible.

The purpose of feedback and performance monitoring is threefold: (1) to communicate the approved demand plan to the demand organization, (2) to inform the demand organization of the effectiveness of the demand management process, and (3) to alert the sales, marketing, and supply organizations of the need for action.

For the demand organization, action may be needed to prioritize and manage demand — determine which customer orders will get priority over other customer orders. The demand organization may also be called upon to influence demand — close a deal or generate additional demand for a product or service. The techniques for managing and prioritizing demand are discussed in detail in Chapter 7. The interaction with the supply organization when demand does not materialize as planned is also covered in Chapter 7.

The key point about demand management is that it cannot be done well without communication at all levels within the demand organization, with the supply and financial organizations — and increasingly with customers too! The communication process should facilitate the imparting of knowledge and information to:

1. Understand the true state of demand
2. Determine actions that need to be taken to accomplish the company's demand and business objectives
3. Identify actions required to keep demand and supply as synchronized as possible to achieve customer service and financial objectives

If the demand plan is not communicated in the first place or if changes in demand are not communicated, people do not know they need to act until it is too late. Companies are left to deal with the ramifications illustrated in the two examples presented at the start of the chapter.

Communication must be a continuous process. Why? It is rare for demand to be so stable that it can be anticipated with 100 percent accuracy. Customers' buying intentions change. The timing of orders changes. Promotion plans can exceed or underachieve expectations. Product introductions are often late. Competitors are not standing still; they, too, are trying to influence demand in ways that can lower your market share. The economy shifts, and events like changes in regulations, politics, and even terrorism and war can destabilize demand.

Continuous communication is thwarted when no one is designated to manage demand information as it emerges. This is one of the reasons why successful companies insist on a full-time demand manager. The demand manager becomes the communication focal point. The demand manager is responsible for gathering information about the timing, volume, and composition of demand and then communicating that information to the people who need to know so that they can act upon the information. The people who need to know vary, depending on the specifics of the information.

A challenge with all communication is how much detail to communicate, to whom, and when. Companies struggle to communicate the proper level of detail to facilitate action and decision making. There is a tendency to communicate either too much or not enough detail. Let's look at both sides of this coin, starting with not enough detail.

It is not unusual to see only simple demand numbers being communicated. The numbers alone do not suffice, however, and often create confusion. Case in point: the demand consensus review meetings conducted by a leading consumer goods company. The demand numbers for each customer by product family were brought to the demand consensus review. For three hours each month, the sales and marketing executives pored over the numbers page by page. This review, however, rarely extended beyond the upcoming three months.

There was not enough time to examine the projections for the entire 21-period planning horizon. For the sales and marketing executives, the monthly meeting had little value, and they grew frustrated at not having a better understanding of the future demand picture.

As this case example demonstrates, numbers alone lack clarity. Examine the data in Figure 17, for example. What conclusions do you draw from the data? Now look at Figure 18. What does the graphical representation of the data tell you? It takes quite a bit of studying Figure 17 to conclude that demand overall is decreasing over time. With just a glance at Figure 18, you understand that demand is falling.

The information conveyed in Figures 17 and 18 is based purely on numbers, however. Numbers are absolute; demand is nuanced. Neither of the above-mentioned figures explains why demand is decreasing. If you do not understand why demand is falling, it is difficult to know what actions, if any, are required. Decision making is paralyzed. Thus, communication of demand information should be more than simple numbers. Communication of the facts and assumptions behind the numbers should enable clarity and insight.

Then there is the other extreme — communicating too much data and information. Imagine being taxed to review 50 or 60 charts like the one shown in Figure 18 with one or two pages of supporting information for each chart. While this information is based on more than just numbers, it is difficult to distill whether the demand plan is credible or identify potential problems.

Too much information triggers what Richard Saul Wurman calls information anxiety. He observes that:

> Information anxiety is the black hole between data and knowledge.
> It happens when information does not tell us what we want to know.[20]

So how do you ensure clarity and communication of the right amount of detail to provide the insight needed to make sound decisions? Start by defining the information needed to:

- Determine whether the demand plan is based on the reality of the marketplace
- Reach consensus on the proposed demand plan
- Determine whether actions are required to achieve the demand plan and the company's business objectives
- Facilitate the synchronization and reconciliation of the demand, supply, and financial plans

An increasing number of companies use a dashboard approach to review demand information at the aggregate level (see Figures 19 and 20). Advance-

Year	Jan	Feb	Mar	Apr	May	Jun	Jul	Aug	Sep	Oct	Nov	Dec
2001	16,391	39,553	207,322	76,126	84,301	240,654	44,986	73,579	268,836	98,552	90,441	252,741
2002	30,891	40,037	80,·26	90,153	130,452	180,867	61,029	70,463	180,120	100,091	112,294	71,634

FIGURE 17 Demand Data

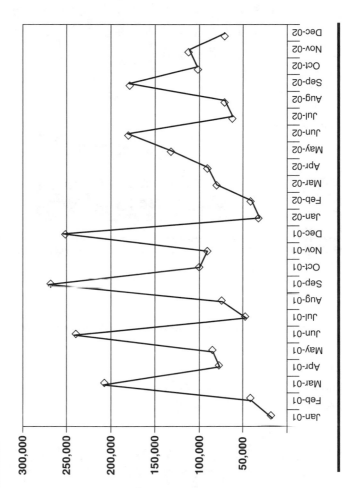

FIGURE 18 Graphical Plot of Demand Data in Figure 17

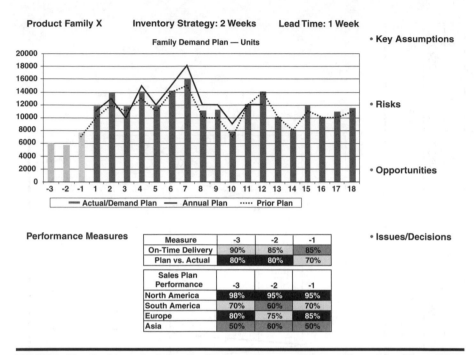

FIGURE 19 Dashboard of Family Demand Plan — Volume (Copyright Oliver Wight International)

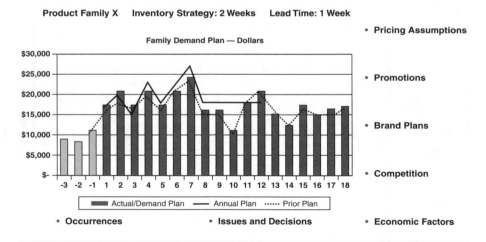

FIGURE 20 Dashboard of Family Demand Plan — Revenue (Copyright Oliver Wight International)

ments in information technology make it possible to develop dashboards of concise information for decision making.

It is the authors' desire to see the dashboard approach become a standard output of all supply chain management and enterprise resource planning software. In the absence of this type of standard output, firms like the Oliver Wight Companies have developed information templates to produce the dashboards. The downside of these templates is that they are not integrated into the planning software. Hopefully sometime in the near future, planning software makers will make these stand-alone efforts obsolete.

Dashboards are part of an evolution of the use of information in business and society in general. Thanks to information technology, less time and effort are needed to obtain data and information. This is transforming the way that managers and executives work. According to Walter B. Wriston, author of *The Twilight of Sovereignty: How the Information Revolution Is Transforming Our World*, much of managers' time used to be spent acquiring information. In the future, managers' focus will change, according to Wriston, who observes:

> They will run the business, which is what they should have been doing in the first place. Managers, no longer forced to devote most of their time to acquiring or moving information, will be able to use information to solve business problems.[21]

That is one purpose of the demand dashboards. The dashboards enable executives to quickly grasp the salient issues and problems. They also enable executives to easily identify when there are no problems. Thus, executives are better able to prioritize where to focus their time and attention. This is sometimes called exception management.

Let's see how this works using Figures 19 and 20 as examples. Figure 19 is a dashboard of the volume demand plan; Figure 20 is a dashboard of the resulting revenue plan, based on the volume shown in Figure 19. The vertical bars show historical demand over the past three months (periods –3, –2, –1) and the future projection of demand over periods 1 to 18. The prior plan line shows last month's approved demand plan. Using this presentation approach, you can see at a glance the changes that have been made in the newly proposed demand plan. Significant changes would require an explanation; this explanation should be part of the assumptions. The annual plan line enables you to compare the proposed demand plan to the objectives stated in the annual business plan. At a glance, you can see whether the proposed plan is in sync or out of sync with the annual business plan objective.

Graphical presentation of the demand data alone is insufficient, however. It does not enable you to understand whether the demand plan is feasible and

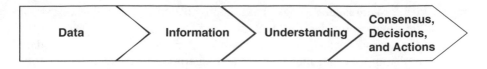

FIGURE 21   Synthesis Process (Copyright Oliver Wight International)

whether there are problems and risks that should be considered. That is why the dashboards include the key assumptions, risks, and opportunities. The assumptions embody sales and customer assumptions, pricing assumptions, promotion assumptions, and brand plan assumptions. Assumptions about competitors' activities and economic factors that influence demand are also included. This information is summarized on the dashboards.

Supporting detail may be needed at times to reach consensus on the demand plan and to problem solve. The demand manager is responsible for anticipating when additional detail may be needed and working with marketing, sales, and brand/product managers to ensure that the additional information is on hand for the demand consensus review meeting. The demand manager is also responsible for identifying and articulating issues and decisions that need to be addressed in the demand consensus review meeting. The demand manager is usually in the best position to identify issues and decisions as all the input into the demand plan flow to the demand manager.

The dashboard approach enables synthesizing and distilling demand information to its essence. It is not intended to filter and hide pertinent information needed to validate the demand plan. Figure 21 depicts the synthesis process.

In order to reach consensus on a demand plan and commit to executing the plan, you need to understand whether the proposed plan is feasible. A review of the assumptions helps to determine feasibility. Highlighting issues to address and decisions that need to be made keeps the demand executives on point. It prevents the demand consensus review from becoming mired in so much detail that consensus cannot be reached on the demand plan over the entire planning horizon.

The dashboards shown in Figures 19 and 20 reveal a gap in the demand plan in periods 4, 7, 8, and 9, compared to the objectives set in the annual business plan. A comparison of the prior plan to the proposed plan shows that the gap has been narrowed. At the demand consensus review, a discussion should ensue about the actions being taken to further narrow the gap. Will the currently deployed and planned actions suffice or are other actions and tactics needed? Any risks in accomplishing the proposed demand plan, and what is being done to mitigate those risks, should also be discussed.

The discussions that ensue from the review of the demand information are part of the communication process. This is where behavior and emotions come into play. The worst behavior that demand executives can exhibit is to arbitrarily change the demand plan numbers to match the annual plan numbers. What does this behavior communicate? It conveys that the demand executives are not seeking a credible demand plan based on reality. It conveys that they have chosen to ignore the impact on customer service and financial performance when credible plans are not developed and communicated to the supply and financial organizations. It also tells those who spend their valuable time providing input to the plan that their efforts are of little value.

When the demand executives question the assumptions, it communicates that they desire to understand the factors that influence demand. Disagreements about the assumptions will arise. When this occurs, consensus needs to be reached on the assumption(s) that is used to generate the demand numbers. The disagreement and any resulting new assumptions should be documented and monitored over time to see which assumptions most closely approximated reality.

Discussion about the assumptions is constructive communication. It creates a better understanding of demand, the marketplace, and the business overall. It also ensures better decision making.

The information communicated in the demand management process and the resulting discussions about this information enable demand executives to make the following types of decisions at the demand consensus review:

- Is this the product we want to request to be produced?
- Are our present tactics for creating and generating demand sufficient or do they need to change in order to accomplish our demand and business objectives?
- How can we best minimize risk?
- How can we best exploit opportunities in the marketplace and our competitors' weaknesses?
- What do we need to do to ensure achievement of the sales revenue goal stated in the annual business plan?

Communication does not stop when consensus is reached on the demand plan. As stated before, the communication process is continuous. As new information becomes known about customers' buying intentions, it should be communicated. When demand does not materialize as planned, the demand manager should be informed. The demand manager uses this information to work with the master scheduler or supply planner to fine-tune the demand and supply plans and keep them as synchronized as possible.

A fundamental principle of communication is that changes in demand are communicated in sufficient time and sufficient detail to economically respond. An economical response frequently requires different efforts to influence demand as well as prioritize and manage demand. In the next chapter, we will look at the best practices for influencing demand.

SUMMARY OF BEST PRACTICES FOR COMMUNICATING DEMAND

1. The first principle of demand communication is to communicate; therefore, there should be no surprises.
2. Changes in demand are communicated in sufficient time and sufficient detail to enable an economical response.
3. Bad news early is better than bad news late; likewise, good news early is better than good news late.
4. A structured communication process is understood and followed to ensure timely communications that drive sound decision making.
5. The structured communication process includes conveying demand information, assimilating the information, discussion, decision, and feedback.
6. The demand plan, along with uncertainties in demand, must be communicated to the demand, supply, and financial organizations for effective decision making.
7. Transmitting demand data is not the same as communication.
8. The communication process links the demand planning process to the reconciliation and synchronization of the supply, financial, and demand plans through sales and operations planning.
9. The communication linkage with the supply and financial organization involves communicating in the formats, units of measure, and planning horizons each organization requires to perform its own planning.
10. Feedback and performance monitoring are critical elements of communication.
11. The communication process should facilitate the imparting of knowledge and information to understand the true state of demand and determine actions needed to accomplish the company's demand and business objectives.
12. Communication is ongoing and continuous.
13. The demand manager serves as the focal point for communication.
14. The level of detail to communicate, to whom, and when are defined as part of the communication process design.
15. Demand information is synthesized and distilled to its essence to enable a quick grasp of the significance of the information and decisions that need to be made.

16. Review and discussion of assumptions are part of the communication process to ensure that the demand plan is credible.
17. When demand does not materialize as planned, communication is required to synchronize demand and supply as closely as possible. This communication involves the demand manager, master scheduler or supply manager, and appropriate sales and marketing managers.

QUESTIONS

1. How would you encourage the demand organization to communicate demand information as honestly as possible?
2. What are the key elements of communicating demand?
3. What are the key linkages of the communication process?
4. Who should receive feedback on the agreed upon demand plan and why?
5. What types of decisions are based on demand information?
6. Why is ongoing, continuous communication of demand information needed?
7. How can the proper level of detail to communicate be determined?
8. What are the advantages of using dashboards to present demand information?

PRINCIPLES OF INFLUENCING DEMAND

The essence of marketing and sales is to influence demand. The reason marketing and sales organizations exist is to convince customers to buy products and services in such a way that supports your company's objectives.

Influencing demand has another facet. Marketing and sales organizations are also responsible for influencing their companies to meet the expectations of customers and markets. Figure 22 depicts the two facets of influencing demand.

The illustration in Figure 22 may appear simple, but influencing demand is not an easy or simple task. To do it well requires structure.

Why is influencing demand not simple? Customers, the marketplace, competitors, and the economy are ever-changing. This dynamic environment conflicts with our natural desire for stability. After all, a stable environment is much more predictable and easier to manage.

Whenever you observe a stable environment, it appears stable only because people are working very hard at continually adapting to changes that occur. Stability, at most, is a temporary condition. One purpose of a structured process for influencing demand is to adapt to changing conditions. This is accomplished through the plan, do, check, and act methodology of influencing demand (see Figure 23). This chapter reviews that methodology and introduces the best practices of influencing demand.

Let's review a case example. At a company where the authors first cut their teeth on marketing, a product was introduced that utilized a new technology for

FIGURE 22   Facets of Influencing Demand

processing information. The new technology enabled customers to output electronic data acquisition signals for graphical presentation. By offering a new technology, we had a potential to expand market share. We also expected that existing customers would replace their older versions of the product line with this new product.

FIGURE 23   Influencing Demand Process

We diligently performed market research and analysis and developed marketing and sales plans for both the product launch and the expected life cycle of the products. We executed the marketing, promotion, and sales plans for the product launch with very few hitches. The product did not sell, however. Sluggish sales were further complicated by product performance issues.

What did we learn from this experience? First, we responded too slowly to signs that customers were not purchasing the product at the volume we originally planned. Second, we underestimated the amount of time it would take for the critical mass of customers to embrace innovation. Third, we did not have a process to routinely review the results of our efforts to influence demand and to replan.

The new product was discontinued, much to our disappointment. We put our learning to good use, however, with the next new product launch. This second product utilized a simpler version of the same new technology (with the performance flaws worked out). One year before launching this second product, we began awareness advertising, paper presentations at conferences, and trade journal articles to introduce the advantages of the new technology. We cultivated customers with a history of being on the leading edge of industry advancements and focused on selling the product to them first. They would become disciples and influence others in the industry to adopt the technology. We identified milestones for when it was okay for the sales organization to demonstrate the new product, first to leading-edge customers, next to companies that were constructing new facilities, followed by customers that were in need of replacing their old equipment, and finally to other new and existing customers.

We conducted monthly reviews to make adjustments in our plans and execution tactics. This enabled us to adapt as conditions changed with customers, competitors, and the economy. The second new product was launched at the tail end of an economic downturn. The pace of the economic recovery was monitored and plans adjusted accordingly.

This second new product was a great success. It contributed to our company's growth and profit objectives, and it satisfied a need in the marketplace.

Where did we go wrong with the first product? At that time, we did not have a structured process for influencing demand. The process we used did not include regular measurements, review, and replanning. We also were in the very early stages of implementing an integrated business management process. Therefore, we did not regularly synchronize and integrate plans with the manufacturing and financial organizations. If we had regularly done so, we would have changed our tactics for influencing demand — and downgraded the demand plan — much earlier.

In essence, we short-circuited the plan, do, check, act methodology for influencing demand. A short-circuited process is depicted in Figure 24. We

Marketing and Sales Strategies and Tactics

Plan

Influencing Demand Process

Act

Do

Check

Replanning Based on Results and Feedback

Execution of Marketing and Sales Strategies and Tactics

Results, Performance Measurements, and Market/Customer Feedback

FIGURE 24 Short-Circuiting the Process

planned well, and we executed well. We did not have a mechanism, however, to check the results, measure performance, and communicate feedback from customers and the market in a timely manner. As a result, we did not replan until it was too late. In the end, we were unsuccessful in influencing customers to buy our product in a way that supported our company's business objectives.

Let's look at an example that shows the importance of not short-circuiting the process. A paper producer reviewed results and performance measurements monthly as part of its demand consensus review. For two months in a row, sales volume and revenue were less than planned. The company measured performance by sales territory, and it became obvious that one specific region accounted for the underperformance. Two salespeople in the region had left the company and had not been replaced. Upon determining the reason for lower sales revenues, salespeople were temporarily redeployed to provide coverage in the territory until the salespeople could be replaced. The hiring process for two new salespeople was accelerated. The company recovered and met its annual sales revenue objective.

The lesson learned from this experience: the value of operating a complete plan, do, check, act process of influencing demand. The director of business development was extremely pleased with how well the process worked. The demand organization identified an execution problem early and fixed it. Prior to implementing this process, the company would have taken at least six months

Plan	Do	Check	Act
■ Develop marketing, brand, and sales strategies and tactics	■ Execute marketing and brand activities for value and demand creation	■ Measure results — market share, volume, revenue, profits	■ Replan based on results and feedback — marketing plan, profit plan, segment plan, channel plan, sales plan, and product and brand plans
■ Plan expected results of tactics to influence demand	■ Execute the sales activities for acquiring, growing, and retaining customers	■ Document and review market/ customer feed-back — value, price, product features, and other factors that influence buying behaviors	
■ Input expected results in the demand plan			
■ Review and reach consensus on the demand plan			
■ Synchronize and integrate the demand plan with the supply and financial plans			
■ Approval to execute the marketing and sales strategies and tactics			

FIGURE 25   Elements of Plan, Do, Check, Act

to recognize and correct the problem, according to the director of business development.

The activities involved in operating a complete plan, do, check, and act methodology are shown in Figure 25. The planning activities integrate with the planning demand, which was covered in Chapter 4.

Execution can be summarized as follows: Do what you said you were going to do in the plan. Results measurements and feedback are needed to understand how well you are executing, identifying execution problems, and communicating marketplace changes. Sometimes execution problems are externally driven by customers, competition, the market, and the economy, as in the case example of the new product launch. Other times, execution problems are internally driven, as in the case example of the company that lacked sales resources to provide the required sales coverage. Finally, the philosophy that nothing is static, including your internal capabilities, customers, the competition, the market, and the economy, is requisite. Therefore, regular review and replanning must be the norm. An annual process of developing marketing and sales strategies and tactics is insufficient. So, too, is replanning strategies and tactics only at crisis points when it is usually too late to effect significant change to your advantage.

So far, we have focused on the process of influencing demand. Now let's highlight some of the principles of influencing demand.

The purpose of influencing demand, as stated before, is to convince customers to buy your company's products and services in a manner that supports your company's objectives. Principally, there are four elements of marketing. In marketing jargon, this is called the 4 Ps — product, price, place (distribution), and promotion. The specific techniques for implementing the 4 Ps are beyond the scope of this book. Two excellent resources on marketing management are *Marketing Management: Analysis, Planning, Implementation, and Control*, by Philip Kotler, and *Market-Based Management: Strategies for Growing Customer Value and Profitability*, by Roger J. Best.

The 4 Ps activities influence the product and customer mix. (Remember Philip Kotler's definition of demand management: "Marketing's main thrust and skill is demand management, namely to influence the level, timing, and composition of demand in the pursuit of the company's objectives."[22]) Composition of demand is the mix. How you influence demand mix takes forethought. The mix needs to support your company's business objectives. This is a best practice.

Case in point: A pet food manufacturer operates with a fixed manufacturing capacity and has no plans to expand capacity in the near future. Before implementing a demand management process as part of an integrated business management process, the company struggled to deliver product on time. Customer relationships suffered as a result. The company also struggled to achieve its profit goals.

The company found that selecting the proper product mix was the key to solving both the customer delivery and profit problems. Selecting the best product mix required a two-pronged approach. First, the company needed to understand what customers wanted to buy and were willing to pay for those products. Second, the company needed to determine what products were most profitable to sell to its customers. Once the company determined what it wished to sell to the market, based on what customers wanted to buy and profit margins, it then influenced customers to buy accordingly. The company was able to make the best, most profitable use of its chief constraint — capacity.

Determining the appropriate mix — balancing customer needs and expectations with the company's sales revenue and profit goals — was a serious task that culminated with the monthly demand consensus review. These meetings took longer than average, sometimes up to a full day. The majority of the meeting focused on reaching consensus on the best mix. Senior marketing and sales managers, and even the general manager at times, participated in the meeting. The company's success hinged on getting the product mix right. As a result, the demand consensus review became a marketing management process.

This approach was highly successful. The company improved customer service and repaired its relationship with customers. The supply organization benefited from the time taken to determine the best product mix; production schedule stability and operating efficiencies improved. So, too, did profit margins.

This case example drives home a key principle of influencing demand: The objective of influencing demand is not purely growth. It is *profitable* growth.[23] This is the reason why profit is measured as part of the check portion of the process. It also is the reason for developing — and routinely updating, or replanning — the profit plan.

There is a flip side to profitability — what customers want, need, and expect. Simultaneously assuring company profits and meeting customers' expectations is a balancing act. Sometimes the two do not go hand in hand.

It is necessary to listen to the voice of your customers — and influence your company to do the right thing for customers. Communicating the voice of the customer frequently falls on the shoulders of salespeople, as they are on the front line with customers. Companies with a market-driven management philosophy regularly and routinely engage the marketing organization and their senior leadership team in gathering information from customers. Some of the marketing techniques that are regularly utilized to determine customers' expectations include surveys and focus groups.

A formal feedback mechanism for understanding and communicating customer expectations, operated on an ongoing basis, is the most effective. It should be part of the process of providing input into the demand plan. An ongoing feedback process is better than waiting for the lost sales report or the loss of a major account to rethink your offering to customers. With an ongoing process approach, you develop a customer-oriented perspective on how to best influence demand. This perspective is known as the 4 Cs of marketing: customer value, cost to the customer, convenience, and communication.[24]

It can be difficult to respond to customers' expressed wants and needs, especially when there is already a firm mind-set about what customers desire. Frequently, companies offer a mule to customers when what they really want to buy is a horse. And then companies get mulish over the need to change their offering. A classic, well-documented example is the slowness of mainframe computer makers in adding personal computers to their product offerings. An example of a company that regularly obtains customer feedback, and uses the information to influence its product decisions, is carmaker Toyota. For every car that is sold, Toyota conducts customer surveys annually for at least five years.

Companies can go to the other extreme as well and try to offer everything that customers want. This approach can lead to financial disaster when products are not priced to generate profit. An Oliver Wight Companies colleague, Larry Wilson, tells of a client that tried to be all things to all customers. Despite efforts to cut manufacturing costs, it was not possible to produce and sell all of the products at a profit. The company embarked on a product rationalization program and decided to discontinue a number of product options. Some people within the organization resisted this decision; they feared that customers would take all of their business to the competition. Indeed, one competitor added to its offering many of the product options that the company had discontinued. In the end, however, the company became profitable. The competitor declared bankruptcy three years later.

Influencing demand, as the last two case examples show, involves more than managing product mix. It also requires managing customer mix. Both product- and customer-oriented views of profits are needed when determining how to most effectively influence customers to buy in the most advantageous way for your company.

Roger J. Best, a professor of marketing at the University of Oregon, offers the following observation about customers and profit:

> Products will come and go; assets will be purchased and consumed; but *the customer is the only enduring asset a business has*. Keeping in mind that the customer is the only source of positive cash flow, it is the responsibility of those in marketing to understand how customers affect a business and its profitability.[25]

In both of the last two case examples, the companies' intent was to retain customers. They understood they could lose customers by changing the product mix, but took pains to convince customers to buy alternative products that were more profitable.

These case examples illustrate another key principle of influencing demand: Influencing demand to meet your company's objectives encompasses tactics that encourage customers to buy alternative products or to delay their purchases. This tactic is frequently called demarketing or unselling.[26]

When companies have fixed capacity and demand is greater than supply, prices are typically increased to encourage customers to delay their purchases. Companies also reduce advertising and promotion spending to cool demand when demand outstrips supply.

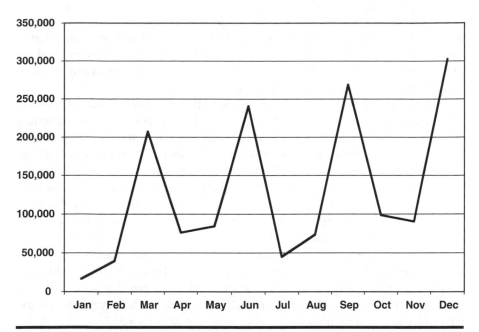

FIGURE 26   Demand History — End-of-Quarter Push

Demarketing also involves redirecting customers to buy alternative, more profitable profits. This is accomplished by increasing prices of unprofitable products, discontinuing unprofitable products altogether, or unselling, that is, convincing customers to buy alternative, more profitable products by touting the advantages of the alternative product.

A note of caution: Efforts to influence demand can change buying behaviors and buying patterns in a detrimental way. Companies often unwittingly influence customers to buy in a way that harms the companies' long-term financial health. The demand history shown in Figure 26 illustrates this point. You can see that demand peaks every three months. Some people label this type of demand pattern a hockey stick. Other people call it the end-of-the-quarter crunch.

What causes this demand pattern? Usually companies are trying to hit the quarterly revenue targets promised in the annual plan or to Wall Street. Customers do not really want to buy as much product as the company needs to sell to achieve the promised sales revenues. Companies, therefore, offer incentives in the form of price discounts or other generous terms to convince customers to buy earlier than planned. Customers comply and reduce their purchases in the following months.

Eventually, customers become trained to wait for end-of-the-quarter incentives before buying, and the demand cycle repeats itself quarter after quarter. This practice of influencing demand becomes a habit that is hard to break. It requires discipline to avoid getting sucked into a short-term mentality of managing the numbers, rather than managing the business.

What is wrong with offering buying incentives to achieve financial targets? If the practice is used only occasionally, it might be useful at times, depending on how steeply prices are discounted to entice customers to buy. Some people may argue that convincing customers to buy so that sales revenue targets are achieved satisfies one element of influencing demand, that is, influencing demand in a manner that supports your company's objectives. In reality, the only company objective satisfied by this practice is the achievement of the sales revenue target. Achieving the sales revenue target usually comes at the expense of lower profit margins and higher operating costs.

When some form of financial incentive is used to entice customers to buy early, Wall Street, the chief executive officer, chief financial officer, and chief operations officer may be temporarily satisfied. This practice almost always diminishes the amount of cash generated through sales, however, and all too frequently leaves a company cash poor over the long term.

Promotions involving price discounts can influence demand in a way that causes both the promoter and the customer to suffer financially in the long run. The long-term financial effects of promotions have been well studied by the grocery industry over the past decade. It is clear that promotions cause spikes or surges in demand that, in turn, cause costly production and shipment surges for the manufacturer. Figure 27 illustrates how the demand variability resulting from promotions is counter to the optimal method for manufacturing product.

Customers may receive a price discount when they opt to participate in promotions, but wittingly or unwittingly they are also accepting additional, less visible costs in the bargain. Promotions usually result in customers spending

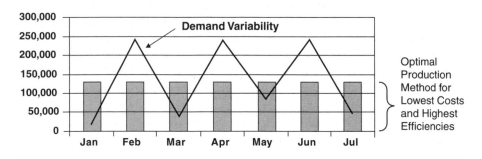

FIGURE 27   Demand Variability Runs Counter to Optimal Production Methods

cash to pay for product earlier than necessary. Customers also incur additional inventory warehousing expenses to store unneeded product. Overall, practices such as promotions that cause surges in demand are estimated to add 12.5 to 25 percent in excess costs in the grocery industry.[27]

This discussion should not be interpreted as saying that all promotions are bad or that encouraging customers to buy earlier than planned to achieve financial goals is always detrimental. The point is this: Do so with your eyes wide open.

A best practice for influencing demand is making sure that the senior executive team understands how efforts to influence demand impact the long-term financial health of the company. One way to gain this understanding is to include profit projections as part of the demand consensus review.

Efforts to influence demand rarely elicit an immediate response. One promotion alone will not cause customers to wait for the next promotion before they buy again, for example. Developing market awareness and presence takes longer than one month or one quarter to accomplish. Creating value in the form of products and services takes more than one month or quarter to accomplish. Likewise, developing market channels and acquiring customers takes time. And retaining customers requires forethought and continuous time and attention.

The length of time required for efforts in influencing demand to bear fruit makes it necessary to have a long-term focus. Senior management needs to be assured that activities are in place that will impact future demand and deliver the desired sales revenues and profits. This is one reason why a planning horizon of at least 18 months is recommended for the demand management process.

In addition to an 18+-month planning horizon, some management teams utilize a dashboard to monitor the status of efforts to influence demand by product line, product family, brand, or category. Figure 28 shows an example of this dashboard. Frequently a traffic light system of green, yellow, and red is used to indicate status in each column. This methodology shows managers at a glance where their attention should be focused. Indicating changes and significant learning helps to facilitate managing by exception — and prevents needlessly revisiting past discussions and decisions. These dashboards are typically reviewed at the demand consensus review meeting.

Despite best efforts to influence demand in a way that meets your company objectives, you will not always be successful. As a marketing executive reminded me years ago, customers are not obligated to do what we want them to do. What happens when customers buy less than anticipated? Conversely, how do you manage when customers buy more than you have capacity to provide? How do you manage these situations in a way that minimizes the negative impact on your company's financial performance? This will be the subject of the next chapter on prioritizing and managing demand.

PRODUCT LINE/BRAND/CATEGORY:				
Planning Activity	**Completion Date**	**Revision Date**	**On Schedule**	**Changes and Significant Learning Since Last Review**
Market Research				
Market Share Analysis				
Customer and Value Creation Analysis				
Competition Analysis				
Marketing Plan				
Pricing Plan				
Revenue Plan				
Profit Plan				

Execution Activities	**On Schedule**	**On Budget**	**Demand Yield**	**Timing of Yield**	**Changes and Significant Learning Since Last Review**
Advertising					
New Product Promotion					
Other Promotion					
Sales Tactics					

FIGURE 28 Marketing Status Dashboard

SUMMARY OF BEST PRACTICES
FOR INFLUENCING DEMAND

1. The purpose of efforts to influence demand is to convince customers to buy products and services in such a way that supports your company's objectives.
2. The process for influencing demand includes influencing your company to meet the expectations of customers and markets.
3. A plan, do, check, act methodology is used in the influencing demand process.
4. One purpose of the plan, do, check, act methodology for influencing demand is to adapt to changing conditions.
5. Regular reviews, measurements, and feedback — at least monthly — are used to adapt as conditions change with customers, competitors, the economy, and your company's internal capabilities.

6. Replanning is regular and routine as part of the demand management process.
7. Execution means doing what you said you would do in the plan.
8. Results measurements and feedback are used to understand how well you are executing, identify problems with execution, and communicate marketplace changes.
9. Growth in demand and revenues is insufficient; the objective is profitable growth.
10. A process is in place for determining the optimum product and customer mix to achieve profitable growth.
11. A formal feedback mechanism is in place for acquiring ongoing feedback from customers and the marketplace.
12. Influencing demand to meet your company's objectives encompasses demarketing and unselling tactics.
13. The senior management team understands how decisions to influence customers to buy early impact profits, operating costs, and the long-term financial health of the company.
14. The demand planning horizon is at least 18 months to enable senior management to monitor and manage the plans and tactics for influencing demand.

QUESTIONS

1. What is the definition of influencing demand?
2. Why must demand be influenced in such a way as to achieve a company's objectives?
3. What are the advantages of a plan, do, check, act methodology of influencing demand?
4. What does the plan step for influencing demand include?
5. What does the do step for influencing demand include?
6. What is involved in the check step for influencing demand?
7. What is involved in the act step for influencing demand?
8. Why is replanning important?
9. What considerations need to be taken into account when determining the proper product mix?
10. What are the four elements of marketing?
11. Why is a formal, ongoing customer feedback mechanism needed?
12. What are the four elements of customer-oriented marketing?
13. Why is profitable growth, rather than growth alone, the objective of influencing demand?
14. What is involved in demarketing and unselling?

15. Give examples of practices in influencing demand that can be counterproductive to a company's financial health.
16. Why is a planning horizon of at least 18 months beneficial?
17. Design a dashboard for monitoring the status of efforts to influence demand.

7

MANAGING AND PRIORITIZING DEMAND

The ability to manage and prioritize demand is like fine-tuning a race car. You must make sure you have the right gear ratio to get the engine power to the tires. If the gear ratio is too low, the tires break loose and you risk blowing the engine. If the gear ratio is too high, the engine accelerates slowly and other cars pass you coming off the turns. When the gear ratio is set correctly, you gain optimum power and handling performance.

The purpose of managing and prioritizing demand is to manage for optimum demand performance — from demand volume, sales revenue, profit, and customer service points of view. This aspect of demand management is often overlooked and undermanaged, often with chaotic and costly results.

Part of the problem is that many sales and marketing executives do not recognize the need to manage and prioritize demand. This lack of awareness is frequently caused by a self-centric focus with little regard of how demand impacts the organization as a whole, company financial performance, and customer service.

Case in point: A conversation was overheard between two salespeople on a shuttle bus at Chicago's O'Hare Airport. They had obviously landed a large order and were very excited about it. One salesperson said he would call and report the sale to his vice-president. The other salesperson asked: "Don't you think we should let the operations people know, too? What if they can't supply the order on time?" The first salesperson replied: "That's their problem, not mine."

This is a shortsighted view. Sure, the manufacturing organization may have been able to make adjustments to accommodate the large order — at the expense of other orders and at a cost that diluted profits. Or maybe only a part of the large order could be delivered on time, at a cost of customer satisfaction and the company's reputation.

The salesperson who wanted to immediately tell the operations organization about the new demand understood the risk involved with the large order. The other salesperson did not perceive a risk to delivering the new large order on time.

Recognizing the need to manage and prioritize demand requires an understanding of some basic business realities:

■ First, as the Greek philosopher Heraclites observed, nothing endures but change. The volume, timing, and mix of demand almost always materialize differently than planned.

■ Second, the supply organization almost always has some form of constraint that makes it unable to produce to the exact volume, timing, and mix of the demand plan.

Given these realities, a process is needed to manage and prioritize demand. This is the fine-tuning that, like that of the race car, ensures optimum performance. Not only must the car be fine-tuned, but someone needs to be in control of managing and prioritizing demand. You would not drive a race car without your hands on the wheel. You cannot achieve optimum demand performance without your hands on the wheel either.

All too often, demand executives relegate how demand is managed and prioritized to others — either to individual salespeople, the supply organization, or both. The result is conflict, reluctant decision making, and marginalized performance.

Who should manage and prioritize demand? This is the responsibility of the managers in the demand organization. Specifically who in the demand organization is responsible depends on the situation and the level of risk. Because responsibility can vary, a clear policy and practice should be agreed upon, documented, and communicated. This way, the demand and supply organizations understand the decision-making process for each situation.

Following are typical situations that require managing and prioritizing demand:

1. During the monthly reconciliation and synchronization process when supply constraints make it necessary to adjust the demand plan in order to synchronize demand and supply

2. When customers buy less than anticipated in the demand plan in a time frame where making changes in the plan have sales revenue and cost ramifications

3. When customers buy more than anticipated in the demand plan in a time frame where making changes in the plan has cost and service ramifications
4. When a one-time, nonrecurring demand opportunity materializes that impacts service to other customers, costs, and profits

Let's review each of these situations as a way of illustrating best practices for managing and prioritizing demand.

An agricultural chemical company had fixed supply capacity for active ingredient that it did not intend to expand in the near future. The company was plagued by high inventory and poor customer service. The demand organization blamed the poor performance on supply constraints and the inability to predict the weather, which resulted in inaccurate demand forecasts. Clearly, demand for agricultural chemicals is dependent upon the weather.

As part of implementing demand management and sales and operations processes, marketing executives reviewed how they currently planned and managed demand. They made the following changes to their process.

First, they developed a detailed volume demand plan each month. They considered this plan their request for product. Recognizing that supply was fixed, however, they prioritized the request for product each month to ensure the proper mix, best customer service, and highest profit. This prioritization occurred during the monthly demand consensus review meeting.

In prioritizing demand, the sales and marketing executives took a global view of demand, rather than allocating a fixed amount of inventory to each region. This approach gave them a new perspective on demand. They learned that when the weather was hot in one part of the globe, it was cool in another part of the globe. These conditions impacted the mix of products required in each region and the amount of inventory to stock in each distribution center.

Second, the planning horizon was expanded to three years. This was the amount of time it would take to increase production capacity for the active ingredient.

Third, the sales organization utilized replanning to fine-tune its sales plans over the entire planning horizon. The salespeople reviewed their previous requests for product and made changes as needed. Sometimes demand increased, sometimes it decreased. When demand from primary customers decreased, this became an opportunity to potentially provide product for customers that were not determined to be a priority during the previous planning period. Of course, the prioritization of demand continued to be based on the best customer and product mix to yield the greatest profit.

Prioritizing and managing demand in *anticipation* of demand — before demand actually materialized — gave the demand organization greater control. The sales organization knew what product was available to sell and the priority for selling the product. The marketing and sales organizations determined where to best locate inventory in distribution centers to serve customer requirements. By replanning and communicating the updated demand plan to the supply organization, demand and supply were better synchronized.

One year after implementing these improvements, the company's performance dramatically improved. Sales revenues and customer service were the highest on record. Inventories were the lowest in several years. These performance improvements were accomplished without making capital investments to expand the supply capability for active ingredient.

This case example reinforces several best practices:

- Managing and prioritizing demand occur whenever it is recognized that the volume, timing, and mix of demand will not be synchronized with the supply organization's capability to deliver the demand.
- Managing and prioritizing demand are not relegated to an individual salesperson or member of the supply organization. They require decision making by the managers of the demand organization. They also require a broad view of the company's strategic objectives, marketing and sales goals, and cost and profit objectives.
- The sooner you identify the need to prioritize and manage demand to match supply, the more options and control you will have over sales revenues, manufacturing and transportation costs, profits, and customer service. This is one reason for using a longer planning horizon and synchronizing demand and supply over the entire planning horizon.

This does not mean that you must decide unequivocally today how to prioritize demand that is anticipated in the longer term. The decision can wait until it is absolutely necessary to commit the resources to produce the demand. For maximum flexibility, decisions should not be made earlier than necessary. For improved operating costs, decisions should not be made later than necessary. The demand and supply organizations should agree upon key decision points for each product family.

In the meantime, much must be done to prepare to make the decision. Scenarios need to be developed on the potential ways to prioritize demand and determine each scenario's impact on sales revenue, profit, cost, and service. These scenarios are communicated to the supply organization so that it can develop its own scenarios. The supply scenarios focus on various ways the demand can be fulfilled and the impact of each scenario on customer service, operating efficiency, and costs.

The actual decision on how to prioritize demand frequently can wait until a point in time when material must be ordered or investment in additional capacity needs to be made. This is known as determining a decision point. Before reaching the decision point, both the demand and supply organizations have time to monitor changes in demand and supply capability and revalidate or change their planning scenarios.

Here is a case example: A client that produced a commodity product had a fixed capacity for a certain product line. The business development organization had been working very hard to increase demand for this product line. It was more profitable than other product lines the client produced. The client's business strategy was to expand sales of more profitable product lines and eventually discontinue some of the less profitable product lines.

The industry operated mostly on annual or multiyear contracts, although there were also spot purchases at times. One of the client's competitors struggled to consistently deliver product on time at a quality the customer required. This particular product was highly profitable for the company to produce and deliver. The customer was interested in shifting its business for this product to the client company, which was one of its most reliable suppliers. The customer would not begin buying the additional product for ten months — after its contract expired with the other supplier. Demand for this product line was seasonal, and the supplier would begin purchasing at the height of the season, which ran from August through November.

Figure 29 illustrates the client's demand plan for this product line. The light vertical bars are the past 3 months of history; the darker vertical bars are the newly updated demand plan over an 18-month planning horizon. The updated demand plan includes the increase in demand from the existing customer. The solid black line shows the previous month's demand plan. The line with the triangles shows the annual plan, which coincides with the fixed supply capacity.

The company did not have to make a decision then, November 2001, on whether and how to prioritize demand to accommodate the new opportunity. Through its sales and operations planning process, the supply organization proposed making alterations at a second production facility to expand its supply capability for this product line. The alterations would include test runs of the product to ensure product quality and operating efficiency. If they started this work in December 2001, they would need five months to accomplish the cost review, engineering, alterations, and testing. Meanwhile, the demand organization would review contracts with customers to determine the certainty of retaining the current business. And, of course, it would continue talks with the customer, who was interested in increasing its purchases with the client.

Through the sales and operations planning process, it was determined that the client would need to decide by May 2002 whether or not demand would need to be prioritized. By this time, the client would know if it was feasible from a cost and facility perspective to expand supply capacity. Thus, May 2002 became

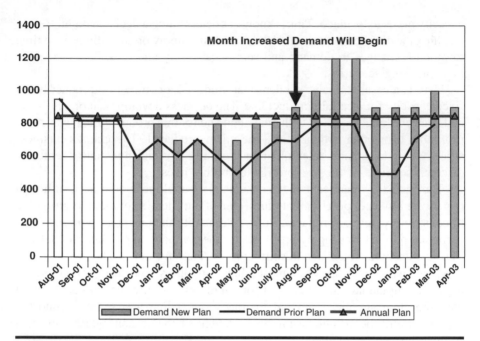

FIGURE 29 Updated Demand Plan

the decision point, which is shown in Figure 30. As part of setting the decision point, the executive staff agreed upon the information it would need to make the decision in May 2002. This provided the demand and supply organizations ample time to develop the information that was required.

Setting the decision point gave the client another advantage. It did not have to commit resources to fulfilling the demand until absolutely necessary. The executive staff wisely recognized that its business was dynamic and changes in demand would occur between November 2001 and May 2002.

In the end, the company was able to increase the supply capacity, and it was unnecessary to prioritize demand. But what if the demand organization had waited until June 2002, when it signed the contract with the customer, to include the increased demand in the demand plan? The supply capacity could not have been expanded until November 2002. The client would have been faced with the choice of (1) accepting the new demand and allocating product to other customers or (2) declining the additional demand. This would have placed the client in a lose–lose position. If product was allocated, some customers surely would have been dissatisfied. If the contract for increased product had been declined, the client would not have expanded sales revenues for this profitable product line.

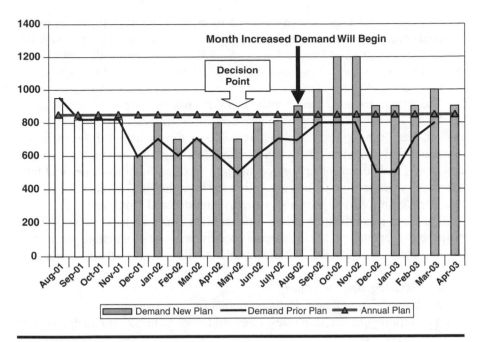

FIGURE 30   Use of a Decision Point

In managing this demand opportunity, the company utilized the following best practices:

- Communicate changes in demand in sufficient time and sufficient detail to economically respond.
- Utilize a planning horizon that is long enough to enable responding to change by increasing supply capacity.
- Do not make a decision until you need to; establish a time point where decisions need to be made and make the decision then. Do not commit resources until it is absolutely necessary.
- When demand and supply are unbalanced in a time frame when commitments *do not yet* have to be made to purchase materials and/or value has not been added to the product, plan supply to match demand.

What happens when demand changes in the near term and materials have been purchased and value has already been added to the product? This situation calls for a different approach than the case above. Instead of managing supply capability to match demand, demand must be prioritized and managed to match supply.

So how do you know which response to make — manage supply to match demand or manage demand to match supply? A best practice is to define stability zones for each product line or family. Stability zones define the appropriate action to synchronize demand and supply. Decision points, or time fences, are used to demarcate each stability zone.

The authors prefer the term "decision point" over "time fence" because many people, particularly in the supply organization, misinterpret time fences as meaning that changes cannot occur inside the point of time where the fence is set. Applying time fences in this manner stifles flexibility to accommodate change and results in poor customer service and loss of sales. Stability zones and time fences are intended to establish *guidelines* for how change is managed. They are not intended to prevent changes in supply and demand from occurring.

Time fences, or decision points, and stability zones go hand in hand. Their purpose is to create stability in material procurement and production, yet accommodate changes in demand. To create this stability requires the following:

- Defining stability zones
- Identifying optimum decision points or time fences
- Defining the decision rules, roles, and responsibilities for each zone and decision point

Figure 31 illustrates the concept of stability zones. Here's how they work: There are typically three zones of time where the cost of change can be differentiated. The first zone of time, labeled firm zone, is the time period when significant value has been added to the product. Change within this time period is costly. Ideally, changes within the firm zone should be minimized because of their cost. When changes in demand occur, demand should be managed to match supply. How the demand is managed and prioritized is the responsibility of the demand organization in consultation with the supply organization, as appropriate.

The second zone, labeled trading zone, is the time period when material has been purchased to support the products planned in this time period. Change within the trading zone is not as costly as within the firm zone because production has not begun or other value has not been added to the product. Ideally, the volume to sell and produce would be fixed, but there is flexibility to change the mix of products within the volume. When changes in demand occur, demand should be managed to match supply. How the demand is managed and prioritized is the responsibility of the demand organization in consultation with the supply organization, as appropriate.

The third zone, labeled free change zone, is the time period when material has not been purchased and value has not been added to the products

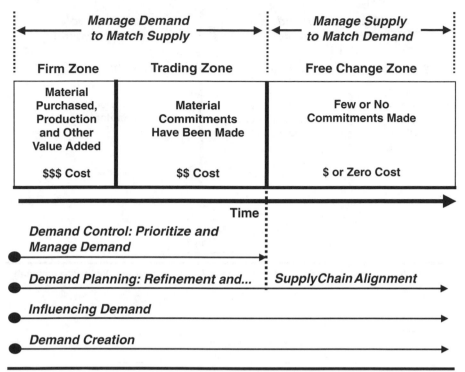

FIGURE 31   Stability Zones (Copyright Oliver Wight International)

planned in this time period. Changes in volume, mix, and timing can be accommodated with minimal financial impact. When there are changes in the demand plan within the free change zone, supply capability should be managed to match the demand. How the supply is managed is determined by the supply organization management in consultation with marketing and sales management, as appropriate.

Using a stability zone approach, the time fence that demarcates each zone becomes a decision point, as shown in Figure 32. These decision points can be a useful tool for the demand organization when updating the demand plan. Thinking in terms of requesting product, the sales and marketing organizations can ask whether they really want to move requested product into the next stability zone (see Figure 33). This way of reasoning helps to validate the timing of anticipated demand and results in greater planning accuracy.

A company that manufactured products to support the construction of oil drilling rigs used this method to improve the demand planning process. The timing of construction for oil drilling rigs can vary widely. The company knew when rig construction was in the planning phase, but was less certain about when

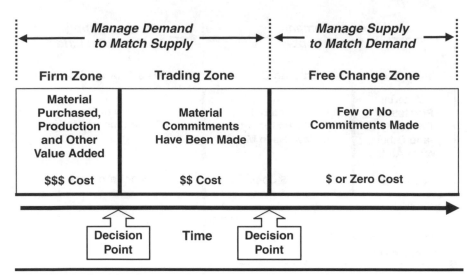

FIGURE 32   Decision Points in Stability Zones (Copyright Oliver Wight International)

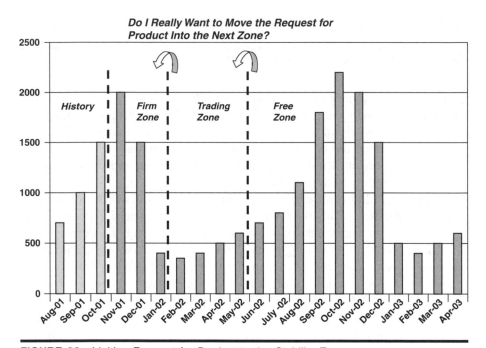

FIGURE 33   Linking Request for Product to the Stability Zones

construction would actually begin and whether the company would win the bid to supply products for the rigs.

Rather than develop a demand plan based on the percentage of certainty in obtaining the business, the demand organization began determining whether the demand should move into the next stability zone. In this way, all of the potential demand remained visible and continued to be managed. Sometimes the decision point would be reached when material procurement was needed to begin. If the company did not yet have a signed contract, the decision was made in the sales and operations planning process whether or not to accept the risk and move the demand into the trading zone. The cost of accepting the risk was well defined and understood. Other times, the company decided not to move the demand into the next, more expensive zone, knowing that demand and supply would be unbalanced. When this was the case, the sales and marketing organization quoted and promised a longer lead time for supplying the product once the order was received. In essence, use of the stability zones in this fashion became a risk management tool.

The period of time for each zone varies from company to company. In the case example above, each zone was many months, extending to a planning horizon of 24 months. For fast-moving goods, the firm zone may be measured in days. The length of time for each zone is dependent upon the time it takes to build product, procure materials, and expand supply capacity.

We have said that change should ideally be minimized in the firm zone. We have also said that the purpose of using stability zones is not to prevent changes in demand from occurring. So how is change managed when more demand than planned materializes in the firm time zone (you sell more product than planned)? Does it mean the unplanned demand cannot be satisfied? Should you be unconcerned, like the salesman at the start of the chapter, and leave it to the supply organization to figure out what to do?

To answer these questions, let's look at the decision-making process for managing change in demand in the firm zone. Figure 34 summarizes the steps involved in managing change when more demand than planned materializes in the firm time zone. First, the demand manager determines whether all of the requested product is going to materialize as planned in the time periods in which the additional demand is requested. If the demand is not going to materialize as planned (both timing and mix), the additional demand can usually be satisfied without disrupting the production schedule. Therefore, demand does not need to be prioritized.

If all of the requested demand is going to materialize, the demand manager next talks to the supply planner or master scheduler to find out whether there is any flexibility in the schedule and material inventory to accommodate the

Questions to Ask and Answer	Action	Decision Maker
Is all of the unplanned demand going to materialize?	If no, de-expedite the demand that will not materialize. If the mix and volume for the unplanned demand match, the unplanned demand can be substituted for the de-expedited demand. If yes, determine whether the organization can accommodate unplanned demand.	Demand manager after consulting the sales organization.
Can the supply organization accommodate the unplanned demand without significantly disrupting production, increasing costs, and increasing lead time?	If yes, the unplanned demand can be accepted. If no, prioritization is required.	Supply manager after consulting with the supply organization and demand manager. Sales management, working with the demand manager, if prioritization is required.
How should the demand be prioritized? (A) Give the customer the option of receiving the unplanned order later than originally requested? (B) Accept the unplanned order and delay other customer orders, thus increasing lead time or backlog?	If option A, the demand manager communicates the decision to the salesperson, who will communicate to the customer. If option B, the demand manager works with sales management to determine the prioritization of the demand. Once the decision is made, the demand manager communicates the decision to the appropriate salespeople, who will communicate to the customers.	Sales management working in conjunction with the demand manager.

FIGURE 34   Steps for Managing When Demand Is Greater Than Planned

additional demand. If there is flexibility, the demand can be fulfilled with little disruption to the production schedule, and there is no need to prioritize demand.

Should there be no flexibility to produce the additional demand in the volume and timing requested, the demand organization has many choices, including the following:

- Fulfill the additional demand later than originally requested
- Fulfill the additional demand when the customer originally requested and delay delivery of other customer orders
- Offer a substitute product
- As a last resort, decline the additional demand

Companies that sell their products through the Web encourage customers to buy alternative products when product is unavailable. This is sometimes called demand conversion.[28] When offering a substitute product, it is important to document what the customer originally wanted to buy. The historical demand database should reflect the true demand (what the customer wanted to buy) rather than the substituted demand (what was available to sell). Otherwise, planning future demand based on history will be inaccurate. You will not have a record of true demand. It is also important to document and communicate any reduction in profit margins as a result of substituting product.

Declining the additional demand is contrary to all our sales training. Sometimes, however, a lost sale is the best decision, especially if the demand is for a noncore product or a product with a low profit margin.

Whichever decision is made, demand and supply must be balanced. As has been observed by Professors Vinod Singhal and Kevin Hendricks, "supply chains create value by reliably and responsively matching demand and supply."[29]

When demand must be managed to match supply, it is a demand organization decision. If the demand organization fails to decide on an alternative, the supply organization will do it for them. When matching demand to supply is left to the supply side of the business, the decision is frequently skewed toward what is most convenient for the supply organization, rather than what is best for the company's customers. The supply organization often provides little advance communication as to how it intends to match demand to supply. As a result, salespeople and their customers do not know in advance that some orders will be shipped late. Customer service suffers, and the demand organization loses control of managing in the best interests of its customers.

Let's discuss the reverse situation. What happens when demand does not materialize in the firm zone as planned (you sell less product than planned)? This situation can potentially cause increased inventory and reduced sales revenue.

Questions to Ask and Answer	Action	Decision Maker
Is any unplanned demand going to materialize?	If yes and the volume and mix match the planned demand that is not going to materialize, substitute the unplanned demand. If no, determine the impact of the demand not materializing on the supply organization and expected sales revenues.	Demand manager working in conjunction with the sales organization.
Can the supply organization accommodate the decrease in demand without significantly disrupting production, increasing costs, and increasing inventory?	If yes and the impact on expected sales revenue is not significant, de-expedite the demand that will not materialize. If no, or the impact on expected sales revenue is significant, determine how to best manage demand.	Supply manager and demand manager working together to understand the impact.
How should the demand be managed? (A) Determine whether orders can be delivered early? (B) Sell the volume to another customer that has not yet placed an order? (C) Create inventory?	If option A, the demand manager works with the appropriate salespeople to determine which orders can be delivered early. If option B, sales management will determine the tactics and actions to generate sales for the needed demand volume and mix. If option C, the demand manager works with the sales management to determine the tactics for consuming the inventory.	Sales management, working in conjunction with the demand manager.

FIGURE 35   Steps for Managing When Demand Is Less Than Planned

Figure 35 summarizes the steps involved in determining the best course of action to take. The demand manager, working with sales, marketing, and supply management, has the following choices to make:

■   Determine whether unplanned orders are expected in sufficient volume, mix, and timing that can be substituted for the demand that did not materialize.

- Determine whether it is feasible or advantageous to ship some orders early.
- If the two options above do not work out, determine whether it is best to de-expedite the supply or build the inventory. If the decision is to build the inventory, tactics will be needed for consuming the inventory.

Communicating as early as possible when demand is not going to materialize as planned is a best practice. It enables de-expediting. When demand is de-expedited, it frees up resources that would have been expended to fulfill the unneeded demand. Those resources can be used to produce other orders. For example, say that demand is less than planned for product A but more than planned for product B. The resources that would have been used to build product A can be used to produce product B, provided that sufficient material is available for product B and both products use the same production resources.

Determining the best alternative when more or less demand is sold in the firm zone involves daily and weekly interaction between the demand and supply organizations. The demand manager takes a lead role in working with the appropriate sales and marketing management, supply managers, and master schedulers to fine-tune demand and supply. This responsibility can be time consuming and is one reason why the demand manager role is a full-time position.

Let's look at how changes in demand are managed in the trading zone. When more or less demand materializes in the trading zone, demand must be managed to match supply. There is more flexibility in how demand is matched to supply than in the firm zone, however. Production or other value has not been added to the product. While it may not be possible to change the volume of demand, the product mix usually can be changed. This gives the demand manager and sales management a greater number of alternatives in solving the problem.

To match demand to supply in the trading zone, the same steps are taken as illustrated above in the firm zone and summarized in Figures 34 and 35. In the case of more demand materializing than planned in the trading zone, the first question to ask is whether the material procurement schedule can be altered. If it cannot be changed, then the choice is whether to promise delivery of the new demand later than requested by the customer or shift other customers' orders for later delivery. In the case of less demand materializing than planned, the choice is whether to influence some customers to take delivery earlier than they origi-nally requested, sell the product volume to another customer, or increase, at a minimum, raw material inventory. Because the trading zone is farther out in time, it also may be advantageous to set a decision point for when to decide how to match demand to supply.

To summarize, the following are the best practices when demand must be managed to match supply:

- Stability zones and decision points are defined and understood by both the demand and supply organizations.
- When demand must be managed to match supply, the demand organization has control over how demand is managed and prioritized. In doing so, the demand organization ensures that the best alternatives are put in place from a customer, sales revenue, and profit point of view.
- The organization recognizes that the intent is to fulfill all demand — even demand that is unplanned. Time fences and decision points are not used to arbitrarily decline fulfilling demand. Rather, the process is used to determine the most effective way to fulfill all demand.
- The organization recognizes that not all customers are equal. Some customers are more important to the business than others. These customers may generate a significant percentage of a company's sales revenues and profits. They may be important to achieving a company's strategic objectives. Sales management takes responsibility for determining which customers will receive product when supply is constrained.
- De-expediting is considered as an alternative when less product is sold than planned. The demand organization is responsible for communicating to the supply organization when there is an opportunity to de-expedite demand.

The use of the above best practices makes change more manageable. Most people do not like change because it creates complications. Stability zones and decision points provide a structure that enables the organization to more readily adapt to change. The zones and decision points are defined in advance. They are communicated to both the demand and supply organizations. The decision rules, and who makes the decisions, are defined and communicated as well. This ensures that the people who are best suited to manage the risk involved in the change make the decision.

If the change can be accommodated without impacting other customer orders, lead time, inventory, or sales revenues, the decision on how to match demand and supply is typically made by the demand manager and supply manager or master scheduler working together. If other customer orders are impacted, the decision on how to manage the change is made by sales management. If lead time, inventory, or sales revenue is significantly impacted, the decision is made by sales and marketing management working with supply management. When significant investment in resources or facilities is required to adapt to a change in demand, the executive team makes the decision, usually through the sales and operations planning process.

How are stability zones determined in the first place? This is a collective decision made by the senior executive staff. Members of the demand and supply organizations work together to reach consensus on the stability zones and decision points. Once consensus is reached, the recommended stability zones are presented to the entire executive team for approval.

If this process is not managed well, it can turn into a wrestling match. The supply organization, of course, wants as much stability as possible; longer firm and trading zones are preferred. The demand organization, on the other hand, wants as much flexibility as possible; shorter firm and trading zones are preferred. The worst approach is to try to reach consensus on generic stability zones that apply for all product lines or families. Most product lines have different material procurement and production cycle times. Unique stability zones should be agreed upon for each product line. Agreement always involves compromise by both the demand and supply organizations.

The supply organization may not be used to working collectively with the demand organization to reach consensus on stability zones and decision points. As Don Swann, a former plant manager and consultant, aptly observes:

> We in manufacturing have had the leverage, prestige, and clout to make what we want, when we want it, despite the ravings of marketing managers and forecasters, and despite the less-than-perfect customer service.[30]

By working together to define stability zones, the supply organization becomes more customer centered. The impact of current procurement and production strategies on customer service becomes more apparent. The definition of stability zones also makes clearly visible a company's ability to be responsive and flexible to changing market conditions and customer needs.

Case in point: The demand and supply organizations at a consumer packaged goods company met to agree upon stability zones. The lead time for procuring packaging for seasonal products was 12 months. Customers, however, were unwilling to order seasonal products 12 months in advance. The long lead time for packaging had been a problem for years. The demand organization, however, never had a forum to demonstrate how long cycle times impacted its ability to both generate sales and develop an accurate forecast of demand.

By working together to agree upon stability zones, the demand organization elevated the need for shorter packaging lead times to the executive level. The executive team approved the stability zones as part of the sales and operations planning process. In doing so, the executive team considered the stability zones from a strategic and tactical perspective. One of the company's strategies was to improve its customer service. Lack of responsiveness and flexibility was a common criticism by customers. The procurement lead times were eventually reduced, and the trading stability zone for seasonal products was shortened. As a result, demand plan accuracy improved.

When procurement and production cycle times are shorter, you do not need to provide an accurate product mix forecast farther out in the planning horizon. As a rule of thumb, it is easier to forecast accurately closer in time than farther out in time. In other words, it is easier to predict what customers will buy 1 month from now than 12 months from now. Customers also predict more accurately what they need to purchase closer in time than farther out in time.

In the case of the consumer packaged goods company, customers were not ready to decide what mix of seasonal products they would order 12 months in advance. Customers knew what they would purchase with much greater accuracy 6 months in advance. Reducing the cycle time for packaging made it unnecessary for the demand organization to provide a detailed demand plan 12 months in advance. This in turn increased the demand plan accuracy.

A particular challenge for both demand and supply organizations is managing abnormal demand. This is demand that is unplanned, yet significant in volume, from a customer that normally does not purchase in that high a volume or from a first-time customer. Often, the customer will not order this product in the same significant volume again. A company's performance in fulfilling the abnormal demand can frequently influence the customer to continue buying the product or other products from the company, however.

For example, a confectioner was asked to supply candy for World Youth Day in Canada. This celebration brought more than 200,000 young men and women to Canada. World Youth Day would not be celebrated in Canada again for many years. Should the company accept the order to supply one million pieces of candy for the celebration? The downside was the disruption to production and the need to replan procurement and manufacturing schedules. The upside was a boost in sales revenue and promoting the company name and its products. After reviewing demand and supply scenarios and determining the *most effective way* of fulfilling the demand, the company accepted the order.

Here is another case example of abnormal demand with a different ramification: A client in the biotechnology industry that made blood test diagnostic kits had lost significant market share to a larger competitor. The competitor offered a less robust product at a lower price. The product was bundled and sold by the competitor with other diagnostic test products. The competitor's product was recalled by the U.S. regulatory authorities, however, because of quality issues.

With the recall, customers were forced to shift their business to other suppliers, creating an opportunity for the client company to regain market share. The question for the client company was not if it should accept the abnormal demand, but how much demand it could supply without sacrificing quality and customer service, which customers it wished to pursue, and how to best position the company to recapture market share.

The demand and supply organizations worked closely together to determine how quickly production could ramp up and the peak demand that could be confidently supplied. This analysis enabled the client to prioritize which customer business it sought to pursue and to make accurate delivery promises. The resulting recommendations were approved by the senior executive team at a special sales and operations planning meeting. In the end, the client company fulfilled most of the demand from its competitor's customers. The competitor decided to withdraw permanently its product, giving the client company a substantial boost in market share.

In both case examples above, the companies had a defined process for managing abnormal demand. The process incorporated the following best practices:

- Abnormal demand is communicated to the demand manager and demand organization management as soon as it is recognized. The order entry, customer service, and salespeople have received training on recognizing abnormal demand and the process for communicating abnormal demand.
- When abnormal demand represents a significant increase in sales revenue and significant risk in supplying the demand, the senior executive team decides whether to fulfill the demand and the most effective way to supply the demand from customer service, cost, and profit points of view.
- To decide whether to accept or decline the abnormal demand, the demand and supply organizations develop alternative scenarios that include expected customer service, cost, and profit margin performance for each scenario.
- If demand must be prioritized to fulfill the abnormal demand, the sales organization determines the prioritization.

In both cases above, the companies already had in place an integrated business management process through sales and operations planning. As a result, the demand and supply scenarios were developed very quickly. The demand and supply plans for an 18-month planning horizon were already available and did not have to be created. It was simply a matter of adding the demand to the current demand and supply plans. This allowed both companies to develop several scenarios and evaluate the advantages and disadvantages of each scenario. The executive team was also well apprised of the current plans, the risks and vulnerabilities contained within those plans, and the company's reliability in executing the plans. Little education on the current situation was required, enabling the executive teams to act more decisively.

Prioritizing and managing demand always involve risk in the form of customer service performance, sales revenue generation, increased operating costs, and profit generation. If you manage the risk well, your company gains greater control over sales revenues, profits, operating efficiencies, and customer service. A structured, well-defined process for prioritizing and managing demand is needed to manage the risk effectively.

The advantages of using a structured methodology for prioritizing and managing demand are significant. The process defines the demand and supply roles in prioritizing and managing demand. When the roles are respected, arbitrary decisions that do not consider the impact on the company as a whole are avoided.

The structured process facilitates fulfilling all demand — even demand that is unplanned. In doing so, the impacts on sales revenues, profit margins, and operating efficiencies are well understood. If it does not make sense to fulfill the demand from this perspective, the organization is not compelled to do so. But declining an order is an exception, not the rule.

Finally, use of stability zones makes visible your company's ability to be flexible and responsive to the marketplace. When unplanned demand repetitively occurs inside the firm and trading zones, it is time to re-evaluate procurement cycle times, manufacturing cycle times, lead time, backlog, and inventory strategies. This evaluation inevitably causes your company to become more customer focused and more in tune to the marketplace.

SUMMARY OF BEST PRACTICES
FOR MANAGING AND PRIORITIZING DEMAND

1. The demand organization is responsible for communicating changes in demand in sufficient time and sufficient detail to economically respond.
2. The demand organization recognizes the need for managing and prioritizing demand and accepts the responsibility to do so.
3. A process is in place for managing and prioritizing demand. This process includes the use of stability zones and decision points and defines decision-making roles and responsibilities.
4. The demand and supply organizations collectively determine the stability zones and decision points for approval by the senior executive team.
5. When demand does not match supply in the time frame when materials have not yet been procured and production or other value has not been added to the product, supply is managed to match demand. It is the supply organization's responsibility to determine how supply is managed.
6. When demand does not match supply in the time frame when materials have already been procured and production or other value has been added to the product, demand is managed and prioritized to match supply. It is the

demand organization's responsibility to determine how demand is managed and prioritized.

7. Stability zones and decision points are used to manage change in demand in the most effective manner. The intent is to fulfill demand — even unplanned demand — whenever possible.

8. Managing and prioritizing demand are triggered whenever it is recognized that the volume, timing, and mix of demand will not be synchronized with the supply organization's ability to deliver the demand.

9. Managing and prioritizing demand are not relegated to an individual sales-person or member of the supply organization. The decisions are made by the managers of the demand organization. The decisions also require a broad view of the company's strategic objectives, marketing and sales goals, and cost and profit objectives.

10. The sooner you identify the need to prioritize and manage demand to match supply, the more options and control you will have over sales revenues, manufacturing and transportation costs, profits, and customer service.

11. Decision points are used to identify when decisions need to be made on how demand will be managed and prioritized. Decisions are not made until they need to be made; resources are not committed until it is absolutely necessary to do so.

12. A planning horizon is adopted that is long enough to enable responding to change by increasing supply capacity.

13. The organization recognizes that not all customers are equal. Some customers are more important to your business than others, and they receive preference when demand must be prioritized.

14. De-expediting is used when demand is less than planned. This creates greater flexibility in fulfilling demand in the most cost-effective manner, especially when supply is constrained.

15. A process is established for managing abnormal demand and developing the demand and supply scenarios needed to make a sound decision as to how to best manage abnormal demand. The organization is trained to recognize abnormal demand and trigger the use of the process.

QUESTIONS

1. You are the vice-president of sales and marketing. Your sales team has worked for more than six months to land an order that will increase volume for one product line by 20 percent. You expect that a contract will be signed with the customer, and the customer will want to start taking delivery of the product in seven months. You believe that this volume of demand will

be beyond the supply capability to produce. Should you accept the order? If not, why not? If you choose to accept the order, how will you interact with the supply organization to ensure that all of the volume for this product line can be produced?

2. How is it determined that, in response to changes in demand, the supply organization manages supply to match demand?

3. How is it determined that, in response to changes in demand, the demand organization manages demand to match supply?

4. What are the advantages of the demand organization determining how to manage and prioritize demand, rather than the supply organization?

5. How would you decide upon firm, trading, and stability zones and their time fences or decision points?

6. Give three examples of how decision points can be used to manage and prioritize demand.

7. What are the advantages of using stability zones to manage changes in demand?

8. Demand is less than planned in the firm zone. You are the demand manager. What actions will you take to ensure that demand matches supply?

9. Demand is greater than planned in the firm zone. You are the demand manager. What actions will you take to ensure that demand matches supply?

10. Give two examples of abnormal demand. What are the characteristics of the process to manage abnormal demand?

PART II:
ISSUES AND
TECHNIQUES

8

MULTIPLE VIEWS
OF DEMAND

When implementing a demand management process, the sales and marketing organizations often resist providing input to the demand plan. Why the resistance? They do not see the value in their participation, and it takes time away from their primary activities.

This resistance has a certain degree of irony. When the sales and marketing organizations do not contribute to the demand plan, they make it harder to achieve their performance objectives. Demand plans are almost always more accurate when they are based on inputs from the sales, marketing, and product or brand management organizations. After all, they work most closely with customers, the marketplace, and new products. As a result, they should have the most accurate information on customers' buying intentions and the forces in play that influence customers to buy.

When demand plans are inaccurate, product is not available to fulfill customer orders because the product was not requested. The wrong product is also on the shelf. Why? Because someone, with less knowledge about customers' buying intentions and the efforts to create sales, made the decision on the demand plan and what to build, buy, and put into inventory. This creates a triple whammy for the sales and marketing organizations — lower sales revenues, disappointed customers, and reduced profits.

The sales and marketing organizations have a point, however. Providing input into the demand plan should not consume a significant amount of time. It also should provide value to their efforts to create and manage demand. These best practices are the subject of this chapter.

How do you devise a process to obtain multiple views of demand without consuming exorbitant amounts of time and while providing value for those who provide input? It takes simplicity, continuous communication assisted by technology, and common sense.

Here is a worst-case example that the authors do not recommend anyone replicate: The vice-president of sales for a pump manufacturer insisted that his organization perform sales planning every month. To do so, salespeople and sales managers were required to complete a lengthy report. The information reported was used as input into the demand plan as well as to communicate the status of efforts to create sales. The selling cycle was long — six months to one year or more — and complex, involving engineering, design, and financial discussions. To reduce the selling cycle, sales management monitored the selling progress, particularly the technical details of the sale. As incentive to report each month, the sales bonus was reduced when the information was not provided in a timely manner.

Every salesperson and sales manager spent *two to five days* each month completing the report and sending it to corporate headquarters. It was not surprising that sales productivity and bookings declined after the reporting process was implemented.

The vice-president's intentions were good. He wanted to demonstrate through his leadership that the sales planning and demand management processes were important. Missing, however, were common sense and simplicity. No one asked the following key questions when designing the reporting process:

■   What is the minimum information that needs to be communicated as input to the demand plan?

■   What is the minimum information that needs to be communicated to provide sales management with an understanding of the progress and any problems in booking sales?

■   What is the most efficient method for communicating this information?

Common sense should have prevailed when salespeople and sales managers complained about the amount of time required to complete the reports. Without a doubt, the primary responsibility of the sales organization should be selling and building relationships with customers. It was not surprising to find that the salespeople and sales managers had poor attitudes toward sales planning and demand management. They saw it as a waste of time that prevented them from making sales. This type of experience sours people on wanting to participate in the demand planning effort.

Providing input into the demand plan does not have to consume inordinate amounts of time. Many companies have devised communication processes so that input can be provided with a minimal amount of effort. Consider the following case example.

A company that produced consumer packaged goods was implementing a demand management process. The sales managers initially opposed being required to provide monthly input into the demand plan. One manager spoke eloquently for the sales organization when he said, "I want my salespeople selling, not completing paperwork!"

Discussion ensued about the responsibilities of the sales organization to the demand planning process. The original intention was for the sales organization to provide input to the demand plan over an 18-month planning horizon. The sales managers argued that they had a reliable view of sales in a one- to six-month window. They had much less knowledge of sales beyond six months. Beyond that time period, the marketing organization had greater influence over demand through its efforts to create new products, bundling options, promotions, and store displays.

The sales and marketing managers agreed that the sales organization would provide input for months one to six in the planning horizon. The marketing organization would provide input for months 1 to 18. A statistical forecast would be generated for months 1 to 18 as well. In addition, some customers provided demand forecasts for months one to three.

Both the sales and marketing organizations accepted responsibility for communicating information when it became known. For instance, if a planned new product introduction for month six was going to be delayed, it would be communicated by the marketing organization. The sales organization would not have knowledge that the product was delayed and therefore sales could be less than planned. Conversely, if the sales organization learned of customers' plans that impacted demand more than six months in the future, it communicated this knowledge to the marketing organization. This gave marketing insight on designing floor displays and other product options to meet the customers' requirements. An elaborate communications system was not needed. The sales and marketing people were well known to each other. They communicated through simple phone calls or e-mails.

As a result of these discussions and agreements, three views of demand were considered in the demand planning process — sales, marketing, and customer input, as well as the statistical forecast (see Figure 36).

The company originally envisioned a demand manager supported by a demand analyst. Sales management, however, did not want to take salespeople away from selling to design the demand planning communication process. A sales planning manager was assigned to fulfill that role. The sales planning manager worked with the sales managers to define the sales information to communicate as input into the demand planning process. It was agreed that demand information would be communicated at a subfamily level in both case

Period	Statistical Forecast Input	Sales Input	Customer Input	Marketing Input
1	10000	15000	20000	15000
2	25000	30000	35000	30000
3	45000	50000	55000	50000
4	10000	5000		7000
5	10000	5000		7000
6	10000	5000		7000
7	30000	35000		40000
8	30000	38000		40000
9	45000	50000		55000
10	65000	60000		75000
11	75000	90000		85000
12	50000	20000		30000
13	11000			17250
14	27500			34500
15	49500			57500
16	11000			5750
17	11000			5750
18	11000			5750

FIGURE 36   Multiple Views Template

units and sales revenue. In addition to communicating the assumptions behind the plan, the sales team would also communicate risks, opportunities, issues, and requests for decisions. Knowing this information every month gave sales managers greater visibility of the status of customer accounts.

The sales organization did not want to "start fresh" in communicating demand information each month. It wanted to communicate only changes from the previous month's demand plan. The sales planning manager developed an information template that he managed on Microsoft Excel (Figure 37).

This approach enabled the salespeople to communicate only new information. If they changed the plan, they documented the new plan number under the New Plan field. If there was no change, they left the New Plan field blank. The same approach was used with documenting the assumptions, risks, opportunities, and issues and decisions. Only changes were communicated.

Sales Input Template

SALESPERSON:
ACCOUNT:

	HISTORY						CURRENT																	
	-3		-2		-1		1			2			3			4			5			6		
PRODUCT FAMILY	PLAN	ACTUAL	PLAN	ACTUAL	PLAN	ACTUAL	PREVIOUS PLAN	NEW PLAN	DEMAND HISTORY	PREVIOUS PLAN	NEW PLAN	DEMAND HISTORY	PREVIOUS PLAN	NEW PLAN	DEMAND HISTORY	PREVIOUS PLAN	NEW PLAN	DEMAND HISTORY	PREVIOUS PLAN	NEW PLAN	DEMAND HISTORY	PREVIOUS PLAN	NEW PLAN	DEMAND HISTORY

LAST MONTH
Assumptions:

Threats:

Opportunities:

Issues/Decisions:

NEW/CHANGES
Assumptions:

Threats:

Opportunities:

Issues/Decisions:

FIGURE 37 Sales Input Template

The salespeople requested that the previous year's demand for each product be added to the template. The demand history was used as a "sanity check." It also was a useful trigger to question why an account was doing significantly less or more business than the previous year.

The template was e-mailed to every account manager each month. They updated it and e-mailed it back to their sales managers as well as the sales planning manager. The sales planning manager then consolidated the various account plans into a sales plan by subfamily. This plan, with the major assumptions, was communicated to the demand manager.

The company realized several advantages from this approach. First, it was easy for the salespeople to communicate the changes in demand for their accounts. Second, sales managers received a concise view of each account, including opportunities and problems with the accounts. This report became a management tool that helped the sales managers identify where they needed to focus their time and attention. In the end, the sales managers, who originally resisted providing sales input, became advocates of the process. They had timely information that enabled them to manage, problem solve, and exploit opportunities, rather than spend their time trying to seek out what was happening with accounts.

Sales management and customer relationship management software tools are available to assist in developing sales plans and communicating sales information for demand planning. This particular company was in the process of installing an enterprise resource planning system, and sales planning software was not yet budgeted for purchase. The company's managers, to their credit, did not let the lack of a sales automation software tool prevent them from developing a process and a method for communicating sales information.

The example above focuses on techniques for making it easy for the sales organization to communicate its input into the demand plan. Similar approaches can be used to facilitate the communication of demand information by the marketing and product/brand management organizations. Bottom line: It should be easy to provide input, and there needs to be a mechanism to make visible the previous month's assumptions and approved plan.

The above case examples illustrate the following best practices:

- To facilitate obtaining input from the sales, marketing, and product/ brand management organizations, the method for communicating input is simple and easy. As a result, the administrative effort to support the process is minimized.
- In developing the demand planning process, the periods in time when sales, marketing, and product/brand management have the most reliable information are considered.

- Available software tools and technology are used to facilitate documentation and communication of the demand input and assumptions.
- The demand information gathered, communicated, and monitored by the sales force helps sales management at the individual, district, region, and headquarters levels. The value for sales management is a better understanding of what is happening in the market, with specific customers, specific salespeople, and specific products. This understanding helps sales management to take appropriate action and ensure that sales objectives are achieved. The better the information and the earlier the information is received, the better the chance that the sales force will meet its sales goals and objectives.
- The demand information gathered, communicated, and monitored by the marketing organization and product/brand management organizations helps them to understand what is happening in the market and with specific products, specific customers, and competitors. This understanding contributes to the knowledge needed to identify customer needs and respond to market trends, risks, and opportunities. It also helps marketing and product/brand management to take the appropriate actions to ensure that the company's marketing and financial objectives are achieved.
- The statistical forecast is used as a frame of reference for providing another view of demand and for comparing with other inputs into the demand plan.

The inputs from the sales, marketing, and product/brand management organizations, as well as the statistical forecast, may not agree, as shown in Figure 38. The demand manager is responsible for consolidating the inputs and developing a proposed demand plan for review and consensus.

If only numbers were provided as input, it would be difficult for the demand manager to make a judgment on the new demand plan. The demand plan numbers must be backed by assumptions and other information about customers' buying intentions, the market, the economy, competitors' actions, and internal strategies and tactics that explain how the numbers were derived. This is a best practice.

The demand manager reviews the various assumptions and information. In doing so, he or she considers whose input has historically been most reliable. One method for understanding whose input is most reliable involves tracking the accuracy of assumptions. Liam Harrington, an Oliver Wight colleague in Europe, utilizes the assumption management template in Figure 39 for documenting assumptions and monitoring assumption accuracy. Under the column titled Last Period, the assumption can be compared to what actually happened. The assumptions about the longer term future are documented by quarters.

Period	Statistical Forecast Input	Sales Input	Customer Input	Marketing Input	Product/ Brand Mgmt Input	New Demand Plan	Previous Month's Approved Demand Plan	Annual Plan/ Target
1	10000	15000	20000	15000		15000	10000	15000
2	25000	30000	35000	30000		30000	25000	30000
3	45000	50000	55000	50000		45000	45000	50000
4	10000	5000		7000		10000	10000	10000
5	10000	5000		7000		10000	10000	10000
6	10000	5000		7000		10000	10000	10000
7	30000			40000		30000	40000	50000
8	30000			40000	5000	50000	40000	50000
9	45000			55000		60000	55000	50000
10	65000			75000	80000	70000	75000	80000
11	75000			85000	90000	80000	85000	80000
12	50000			30000	40000	50000	30000	40000
13	11000			17250	40000	11000	11000	
14	27500			34500	40000	27500	27500	
15	49500			57500	40000	49500	49500	
16	11000			5750	20000	11000	11000	
17	11000			5750	20000	11000	11000	
18	11000			5750	20000	11000	11000	

FIGURE 38   Consolidation of Multiple Inputs into a New Proposed Plan (Copyright Oliver Wight International)

The column titled Degree of Control documents how much control the company can exert over the assumption. A company, for example, has great control over promotions and the products that are launched. It has little influence over the performance of the economy. This is useful knowledge when planning activities to increase demand or alter the timing of demand. It also becomes a bellwether that guards against wishful thinking.

Let's use as an example a company with products that are capital intensive. Sales, in this case, are dependent upon customers' ability to borrow money. Therefore, assumptions about interest rates and money supply should be part of the demand planning input. If interest rates are high and it is difficult to borrow money, the demand plan for capital-intensive products would need to be tempered to reflect this reality.

In the example shown in Figure 39, the sales assumptions were more accurate for predicting the sales volume that would be generated from new products during the last period. The marketing assumptions on economic trend and lift from planned promotions were inaccurate. So, too, were the sales assumptions on revenue and volume from new customers and the customer retention rate.

This tracking approach gives the demand manager, marketing management, and sales management insight on what they know and do not know about customers, the marketplace, and the economy. By focusing on exceptions — the assumptions that were incorrect — they can identify actions for improving the accuracy of those assumptions. In some cases, like the economic trend, a more accurate source of economic indicators could be utilized. In the case of new customers and customer retention, sales management would review the selling tactics to determine additional actions that need to be taken to generate sales from new customers.

Improving the accuracy of assumptions inevitably improves the understanding of customers and the market. This in turn causes the company to improve its marketing mix and sales tactics. The end result is improved accuracy of the demand plan as well as improved competitive position and performance.

Documenting assumptions in this manner also gives additional insight to the demand manager and executives who participate in the demand review and consensus meeting. They can see areas of disagreement among the multiple inputs into the demand plan. For instance, the assumption highlighted in gray in Figure 39 shows disagreement between the sales, marketing, and product/brand management inputs on volume for new products. The disparate views should be discussed during the demand consensus review meeting. In this case, the demand manager should document which assumption input he or she gave most weight to in determining the plan numbers from the conflicting input.

Basing a demand plan on multiple inputs, rather than just a statistical forecast, yields a more robust, more accurate demand plan. Obtaining multiple inputs may not be practical, however, when planning demand for hundreds of end items or stockkeeping units.[31] The above template and practices are intended for planning at the aggregate level. My colleague George Palmatier astutely observes: "No amount of adjustments at the item level will compensate for an error at the aggregate level." The purpose of these techniques is to yield the most accurate demand plan at the aggregate, or family or subfamily, level. Techniques for improving the accuracy of item-level demand plans will be discussed in Chapter 10.

One input that we have not discussed in this chapter is the statistical forecast. What is the role of the statistical forecast in planning aggregate demand? It is

Assumption Management Example

Assumption Management

Product Family: Date:	Degree of Control		Last Period	This Period	Period 3	Period 6	Period 12	Period 15	Period 18
Marketing Assumptions									
Population of users	Some	Assumed	20,000	20,000	20,000	22,000	25,000	28,000	32,000
		Actual	20,000						
Economic trend	None	Assumed	-0.5%	-0.5%	-1.0%	0.0%	0.0%	1.0%	2.0%
		Actual	-1.00%						
Volume from new products	Full	Assumed	10,000	8,000	8,000	12,000	15,000	10,000	8,000
		Actual	6,000						
Revenue from new products	Full	Assumed	$500,000	$400,000	$400,000	$600,000	$750,000	$1,000,000	$400,000
		Actual	$300,000						
Rate of new product introductions	Full	Assumed	1			1			
		Actual	1						
Lift from planned promotions	Full	Assumed	8,000	4,000	2,000	8,000	10,000		
		Actual	6,000						
Competitor activity	None	Assumed	Price discounts	Price discounts	Price discounts	New product & promotions	Promotion		
		Actual	Price discounts						
Market price movement	Some	Assumed	-5%	-0.25%	-3%	-5%	-5%	0%	0%
		Actual	-0.25%						
Market share	Full	Assumed	25%	25%	25%	27%	27%	30%	30%
		Actual	21%						
Profit	Full	Assumed	30%	30%	30%	33%	33%	33%	33%
		Actual	28%						

Sales Assumption

			$200,000	$250,000	$75,000	$250,000	$300,000	$100,000	$50,000
Revenue from new customers	Full	Assumed	$200,000	$250,000	$75,000	$250,000	$300,000	$100,000	$50,000
		Actual	$125,000						
Volume from new customers	Full	Assumed	400	500	150	500	600	200	10
		Actual	250						
Customer retention rate	Full	Assumed	98%	98%	98%	95%	95%	98%	98%
		Actual	95%						
Volume from new products	Full	Assumed	6,000	9,000	10,000	14,000	15,000	12,000	10,000
		Actual	6,000						
Changes in buying patterns	Some	Assumed	None	Wait for new products	Wait for new products	Increased buying	Increased buying	Freer spending	Freer spending
		Actual	Delaying purchases						
Price discounts	Full	Assumed	5%	5%	5%	0%	0%	0%	5%
		Actual	5%						

Product/Brand Management Assumptions

New product launches	Full	Assumed	1			1			
		Actual	1						
Launch delays	Full	Assumed	0	0	0	0	0	0	0
		Actual	0						
New products sales volumes	Full	Assumed	10,000	8,000	8,000	12,000	15,000	10,000	8,000
		Actual	6,000						
New product samples for sales	Full	Assumed	0		1,000	0			
		Actual	0						

- - - - Inaccurate Assumption   [shaded] Disagreement on Assumption

FIGURE 39 Assumption Management Example (Copyright Oliver Wight International)

another view. The demand manager must decide when to give more weight to the statistical forecast over the other inputs in developing a demand plan. A statistical forecast is generally more accurate in the short term and increasingly less accurate further out in time. The historical database, upon which the statistical forecast is based, does not reflect future actions, activities, and economic changes. Thus, it will be less accurate further out into the future.

The statistical forecast certainly should not be ignored. By documenting the time periods where the statistical forecast is more accurate than the other inputs, demand managers will know when to and when not to rely on the statistical forecast. The statistical forecast is also a useful validation tool to help refine the forecast further out in time. As explained in Chapter 4, a comparison of the statistical forecast to the demand plan makes it possible to ask: What are we going to do differently in the future to change the volume and timing of demand?

Another technique for validating the demand plan involves business factor analysis. Business factor analysis is used in the demand planning process in the following ways:

- Identify and monitor key business drivers
- Develop a forecast based on key drivers and other factors that influence either total sales revenue or total sales volume
- Determine the impact of pricing tactics on demand
- Perform a sanity check, by comparing the annual total sales revenue plan to the forecast based on business factors
- Identify turning points, i.e., significant shifts, upward or downward, that are followed by a change in direction[32]

Use of business factor analysis in this manner becomes another view, or another input, into the demand plan. Here is one example of how it works.

To perform business factor analysis, you must first identify factors that influence sales revenue or sales volume. The factors must be quantitative rather than qualitative in order to determine which factor is a key business driver and to yield a statistical forecast. After identifying and quantifying the potential key drivers, a statistical analysis technique, called regression analysis, can be used to determine which business factors most influence demand.

Case in point: An original equipment manufacturer wanted the ability to validate the total sales revenue plan as well as identify turning points in demand. The industry this company served had historic swings of robust business and extended downturns in business. This company's products were used in the facilities that supplied a worldwide commodity.

The company's managers identified more than a dozen factors that they believed influenced their business. There was wide disagreement as to which of

Year	Total Sales Revenue	Consumption	Avg Price	New Construction	Capital Spending
1979	27772	59.1	12.65	77	10345
1980	40899	61.2	14.3	38	22612
1981	66980	63.1	14.85	50	27806
1982	87055	64.5	22.4	71	29103
1983	169543	62.1	37.37	139	39627
1984	309112	60.2	36.67	229	50124
1985	248853	57.8	32.75	175	46223
1986	58619	57.4	30.25	62	12469
1987	67802	58.4	29.83	37	27841
1988	65117	58.5	28.08	49	26907
1989	32088	60.1	16.44	37	13508
1990	21599	61.4	18.21	24	13447
1991	34492	63.2	15.52	17	14269
1992	29538	64.4	18.29	11	10595
1993	54686	65.6	24.42	13	12578
1994	58349	65.5	21.31	12	12036
1995	54509	66	20.55	12	12842
1996	43392	65.8	18.37	9	17098
1997	41426	67.1	17.26	10	22725
1998	53935	68.2	18.46	5	22401
1999	57075	69.9	22.01	8	26397
2000	84781	71.7	20.64	31	28212
2001	83302	74.2	11.6	64	29457

FIGURE 40   Business Factors Example — Historical Information

these factors played the greatest role in influencing the business cycle, however. Using statistical analysis to determine key business drivers stripped bias from the discussion and provided an objective view of the key drivers. Following is a partial look at the analysis.

Figure 40 shows four business factors that were considered. In statistical analysis parlance, the business factors are called independent variables. The sales revenue is called the dependent variable. In other words, sales revenue is dependent on the status of certain business factors, or drivers.

The statistical output of the regression analysis indicates which factors are significant in influencing sales revenue. The p-value indicates how important the factors are in influencing sales revenue. A p-value of 0.05 or less indicates that the factor is important. The statistical output in this case example, shown in Figure 41, indicates three key factors: consumption, commodity average price, and new construction. Capital spending is not important, as its p-value is 0.10.

The R square and adjusted R square statistics are important to consider as well. They indicate how well the business factors explain the variations in the sales revenue. Some people call this a "goodness of fit" measure. An R square and adjusted R square of 0.75 or higher indicate a good model. It means that 75 percent of the variations in the sales revenue are explained by the business factors. In this case, the adjusted R square is 0.93, meaning that 93 percent of the variations in sales revenue are explained by the business factors.

The above explanation of regression analysis is meant as an overview. Detailed technical explanations of regression analysis can be found in most statistics books, some of which are written specifically about business forecasting.[33]

Changes in the key drivers can be monitored over time to identify business shifts, either up or down. By monitoring the changes, it may be possible to identify leading indicators of change. Advance knowledge that change will occur gives companies time to prepare and respond to the change — and at times to exploit change.

Regression analysis also can be used as a forecasting tool to predict sales revenues if the business factors change. This forecast will be most accurate when a leading indicator is available. Otherwise, you are predicting what the business factors will be in the future, and these predictions usually will not be 100 percent accurate.

Using regression analysis as a forecasting tool is an effective method for developing scenarios, especially when there are significant uncertainties about the future. Here is an example, using the three key drivers identified in the example above, of how regression analysis can be used to predict future sales revenue (Figure 42). In this case, the following scenario is used:

- Consumption will increase by 10 percent over the previous year.
- Average price will increase 8 percent over the previous year.
- New construction will increase 15 percent over the previous year.

The formula used to calculate the resulting increase or decrease in sales revenue is shown in Figure 42. This scenario results in an increase in sales revenue from $83,302 to $103,079.

SUMMARY OUTPUT

Regression Statistics

Multiple R	0.97149974
R Square	0.94381175
Adjusted R Square	0.93132547
Standard Error	18561.4597
Observations	23

ANOVA

	df	SS	MS	F	Significance F
Regression	4	1.04169E+11	2.6E+10	75.58791539	5.29996E-11
Residual	18	6201500164	3.45E+08		
Total	22	1.1037E+11			

	Coefficients	Standard Error	t Stat	p-value
Intercept	-221951.82	77654.0389	-2.858213	0.010445454
FACTORS Consumption	2772.63501	1177.819563	2.354041	0.030131219
Average Commodity Price	2345.38519	808.6375373	2.900416	0.009536824
New Construction	842.392315	143.9732764	5.851032	0.000015
Capital Spending	1.23758567	0.714297601	1.732591	0.100267363

HOW TO INTERPRET STATISTICAL OUTPUT

R Square and Adjusted R Square for Goodness of Model:
Greater than .75 means a good model — explains that 75% of the variations in the dependent variable (in this case, sales revenue) are explained by the business factors.

p-Value for Determining the Importance of Each Factor:
Greater than 0.10
   Weak or no importance
0.05 to 0.10
   Moderate importance
0.01 to 0.05
   Strong importance
Less than 0.01
   Very strong importance

t Statistic for Determining Correlation:
±1.75 means correlation is significant.

FIGURE 41   Statistical Output of Factor Analysis

Year	SALES REVENUE HISTORY (Dependent Variable)	BUSINESS FACTORS (Independent Variables) Consumption	Commodity Average Price	New Construction
1979	27,772	59.1	12.65	77
1980	40,899	61.2	14.3	38
1981	66,980	63.1	14.85	50
1982	87,055	64.5	22.4	71
1983	169,543	62.1	37.37	139
1984	309,112	60.2	36.67	229
1985	248,853	57.8	32.75	175
1986	58,619	57.4	30.25	62
1987	67,802	58.4	29.83	37
1988	65,117	58.5	28.08	49
1989	32,088	60.1	16.44	37
1990	21,599	61.4	18.21	24
1991	34,492	63.2	15.52	17
1992	29,538	64.4	18.29	11
1993	54,686	65.5	24.42	13
1994	58,349	65.5	21.31	12
1995	54,509	66	20.55	12
1996	43,392	65.8	18.37	9
1997	41,426	67.1	17.26	10
1998	53,935	68.2	18.46	5
1999	57,075	69.9	22.01	8
2000	84,781	71.7	20.64	31
2001	83,302	74.2	14.5	64

What If Analysis

Predicted Sales Revenue	Predicted Business Factor Values Consumption	Average Price	New Construction	Planning Scenario
103,079	81.62	15.66	73.6	What if consumption increases 10%, average price increases 8%, new construction increases 15% over 2001

	Coefficients	Formula Using Microsoft Excel
Intercept	-221951.8183	(Predicted value for Consumption ∗ Consumption Coefficient) +
Consumption	2772.635005	(Predicted value for Avg Price ∗ Avg Price Coefficient) +
Average Price	2345.385193	(Predicted value for New Construction ∗ New Construction Coefficient) +
New Construction	842.3923151	Intercept Coefficient

FIGURE 42 Using Factor Analysis and Regression Output to Forecast

Some companies routinely use regression analysis to predict their overall annual sales revenue and track changes in key business drivers. Use of regression analysis to forecast sales revenue is sometimes called determining "how big is the bread basket." This prediction can be used as a sanity check, much like the time series statistical forecast can be used as a sanity check for aggregate demand plans. When there are major deviations between the annual plan and the regression-based forecast, the demand manager and executive team can ask for an explanation. The explanation inevitably results in a better refined, more accurate demand plan. It also helps to eliminate bias from the plan.

The demand manager is typically responsible for receiving the various views of demand, ensuring that the statistical analysis is performed, and consolidating the multiple views into a recommended demand plan. In companies that utilize best practices, this is not the final step before the demand plan is communicated to the supply and finance organizations. The next step involves reaching consensus on the demand plan and is the subject of Chapter 14.

In this chapter, we have discussed ways to obtain multiple views, the role of the demand manager in consolidating these views into a proposed demand plan, and use of some statistical tools. In the business factor analysis example, Microsoft Excel was used to generate the analysis. Many other software tools, ranging from Excel to statistical analysis tools to forecasting software, are capable of performing regression analysis.

This book has cautioned that it is unwise to put demand planning on autopilot and rely solely on statistical forecasts. Statistical tools are not a substitute for understanding the market and customers, knowing the marketing and sales activities that are planned to create demand, and forward thinking about the future of the market and customer needs. Statistical analysis can be revealing and should not be ignored, however.

Ultimately, demand management comes down to judgment and execution. Decisions should be made by people who understand the dynamics of the marketplace, not technology. The next chapter addresses the human element of demand management.

SUMMARY OF BEST PRACTICES FOR OBTAINING MULTIPLE VIEWS

1. The process for communicating input into the demand plan is designed for simplicity and to minimize the administrative burden.
2. Periods of time when sales, marketing, and product/brand management have the most reliable information are considered. Time horizons for providing input are defined for each function.

3. Software tools, technology, and other communication methods are used to facilitate documenting and communicating demand input and assumptions.
4. Assumptions and other information upon which demand numbers are based are communicated as part of the demand input.
5. The demand planning process is designed to provide value for those who communicate demand input.
6. The demand manager is responsible for consolidating the demand input and proposing a new demand plan.
7. Assumptions are documented, monitored, and tracked to highlight areas of agreement, determine which information is most reliable, and measure assumption accuracy. When assumptions are inaccurate, actions are taken to improve assumption accuracy.
8. Disagreement about assumptions is discussed at the demand consensus review meeting.
9. The statistical forecast is used as another view, not the sole view upon which the demand plan is based.
10. A process exists for identifying key drivers and for monitoring these drivers for turning points.
11. A process exists for evaluating planning scenarios and the resulting effect of these scenarios on demand and sales revenues.

QUESTIONS

1. How would you design the communication process to reduce the administrative burden in providing input into the demand plan? Address the information that is communicated as well as the means of communication.
2. Should the sales, marketing, and product/brand management organizations all be responsible for providing demand input for the entire planning horizon? Why or why not?
3. How does an effective demand planning process provide value to those who provide demand input?
4. How much importance should be attached to the statistical forecast? Why?
5. How are the assumptions, upon which the demand numbers are based, used to validate the demand plan?
6. What are the advantages of monitoring the accuracy of assumptions?
7. How is the identification of key business drivers useful? What additional insight does this provide?

9

THE HUMAN QUOTIENT

Successful demand management is dependent on the human quotient. Think about the four elements of demand management — planning demand, communicating, influencing demand, and prioritizing and managing demand. People drive these activities.

To plan demand, someone must decide on the plan. Even if only a statistical forecast is used, someone decides whether to use the forecast without alteration or whether there are reasons to change the numbers. When multiple views are used as input into the demand plan, people communicate each view, and someone must assimilate those views into a single proposed plan. When a demand consensus review meeting is conducted, a group of people work collaboratively to reach consensus on the plan.

People are the drivers in influencing, prioritizing, and managing demand as well. People determine the marketing, brand, product, and sales strategies to create value and generate demand. People execute those strategies and tactics. Salespeople sell to people. Even in e-sales, people decide the products and price to offer and how to present the products in a way that will make people want to buy the merchandise. And when it comes to prioritizing and managing demand, this is a pure judgment call. Someone must determine which customers get priority for product when demand outstrips supply. Someone also must decide whether to build inventory or influence customers to buy early when demand does not materialize as planned.

All too often the people factor in demand management is either undervalued or ignored altogether. Companies that recognize the importance of people in the process, and design the process around and for people rather than around and for a software tool, almost always develop a highly successful and reliable demand management process.

Case in point: A multinational company in the telecommunications industry implemented demand management as part of its global sales and operations planning process. The company's leaders recognized that it was becoming increasingly market driven. They needed greater visibility of changes in customer expectations, competitors' tactics, and the market condition in each operating territory. They also needed a greater visibility of their own marketing strategies and tactics and the resulting impact on demand.

The company's leadership team wisely understood that demand management is a competence, just as research and development was a highly regarded competence in the organization. In creating the expectation for the demand management process, the company's leaders asked: What does it take to be competent in demand management? What skills are required, and how do we blend these skills in the brand management and sales organizations?

This approach is in striking contrast to other companies that view demand management as a necessary evil, something that is being imposed. When this attitude toward demand management prevails, usually a low-level administrative person is assigned the task of forecasting. The marketing, sales, and brand/product people are not educated and trained to contribute to the demand management process.

In the case of the telecommunications company, its demand management process was extremely successful. It was implemented across the globe in nine months. In the case of companies that undervalue or ignore the people element altogether, the authors have never seen anything but mediocre or failed processes.

The subject of this chapter is the human dimension of demand management. Understanding the human dimension and developing true competence in demand management starts with understanding the roles and responsibilities of demand management. One of the critical success factors in demand management is how well each role is executed. Success is predicated upon putting the right people in the right roles and creating reasonable expectations of those roles.

Let's review the role and responsibilities of the demand manager. The demand manager is a unique individual in a company. On the one hand, the demand manager must relate well with others in the organization. Because the demand plan is based on inputs from the sales, marketing, and product or brand management organizations, the demand manager needs to understand the demand side of the business. It is helpful to know that customers don't always behave the way we would like them to behave. It is helpful to understand that promotions do not always generate the demand that is intended and the selling cycle can be longer than expected.

Having this knowledge helps the demand manager to ask the right questions of sales, marketing, brand, and product managers — and to speak their language while doing so. When a demand manager knows the right questions to ask, the quality of the information that supports the process is enhanced. This, in turn, helps the demand manager make better informed judgments about the accuracy of assumptions and the volume and timing of demand.

The demand manager also needs to understand the big picture of business, that is, a company is in business to make money, grow its sales revenues, and return financial gains to its shareholders. Through participation in the demand consensus review as well as the sales and operations planning process, the demand manager is exposed to the company's senior leadership. The demand manager thus needs to communicate in their terms, which is usually direct and to the business point.

The demand manager also requires an analytical bent. The ability to perform statistical analysis to forecast, identify trends and seasonality, recognize turning points (up or down) in demand, and monitor changes in the key business drivers is also part of the demand manager's job. In performing analysis, the ability to shape the analytical findings into a meaningful business picture is a critical skill.

Not only must the demand manager understand the demand side of the business, he or she must also understand the supply organization's planning needs. The demand manager is responsible for communicating demand information in a format that enables the supply organization to plan production, fulfillment, and delivery. This means that while the demand manager may communicate with the demand organization and senior leadership team in terms of aggregate demand, sales revenues, and profits, a different vernacular is needed for the supply organization. In order for the supply organization to plan, demand information must be communicated in the form of unit volume at the product item level.

Finally, the demand manager requires a deft touch with people. The success of the demand manager hinges on his or her ability to maintain open, honest communication with virtually every function of the company — from sales and marketing to finance to the supply organization. Increasingly, the demand manager must also have an ability to connect outside the company walls with customers as well.

Open and honest communication is a key element of collaborating with the demand, finance, and supply organizations to solve problems. In fact, the demand manager is usually the bridge between these organizations when there are problems in synchronizing demand and supply.

As described, the job of the demand manager is not an easy task (see Figure 43 for a sample job description). Needless to say, it is a full-time job; this is a best practice.

Increasingly, the demand manager role is being filled by highly skilled, well-rounded managers who are compensated accordingly. Gone are the days when a clerical person was assigned to the task. Figures 44 and 45 are two examples

Position Summary: Recognize and manage customer demand for all products. Develop demand plans for use in sales and operations planning and supply planning. Interact with the marketing, sales, and brand/product organizations to facilitate the planning process.

Duties and Responsibilities
1. Develop the aggregate demand plan and supporting assumptions on a monthly basis for sales and operations planning.
2. Develop a macro forecast to validate the overall size of the business and identify improvement or slippage in market share. The macro forecast indicators should be monitored monthly for change.
3. Develop, document, update, and challenge the factors and assumptions supporting the demand plan.
4. Assist the sales, marketing, and brand/product organizations, including the demand review leader, in preparing for the demand consensus review meeting and executive sales and operations planning meeting.
5. Develop product mix forecasts as input for supply planning, based on the aggregate demand plan.
6. Develop demand plans for new products and/or new markets, working with product and marketing managers as appropriate.
7. Establish, maintain, and utilize forecasting and communications tools for accomplishing the above.
8. Assist in the development of marketing/manufacturing strategies and objectives, including customer service objectives, inventory targets, backlog/lead time objective, and decision points (time fences) for managing change.
9. Assist in the development of planning bills and product structures as needed.
10. Monitor the demand plan performance, providing detailed input to sales and marketing management for use in the demand consensus review and executive sales and operations planning meetings. Measure and report actual vs. planned performance overall, by market segment, sales territory, and product family, item, and mix.
11. Provide necessary training to internal personnel in all aspects of demand management, forecasting, order entry, etc. Develop and deliver communication/awareness sessions for external persons (customers and suppliers) on the concepts and practices of demand management and demand collaboration.
12. Serve as the technical expert in matters concerning the use of information systems for demand management, forecasting, order entry, and Internet or electronic data interchange interfacing.
13. Be the day-to-day point of contact for supply planning, including the master scheduler, to manage change and balance supply and demand to achieve the optimal balance of customer responsiveness and production stability. Assist in the resolution of issues involving order promising, deviations to planned finished goods inventory levels, establishment and utilization of safety stock, and customer delivery difficulties. Participate in the development and evaluation of what-if simulations to resolve demand/supply imbalances.
14. Play the lead role in developing customer linking and/or partnering processes with customers, utilizing best practices and available technology.

FIGURE 43   Demand Manager — Sample Position Description

Required
- Leader with superior analytical skills, exceptional oral and written communication skills, and can see the "big picture" while still paying attention to the detail.
- Possess the ability to work effectively in a collaborative team environment.
- Capable of presenting forecasts to all levels of management with supporting analysis and assumptions.

Responsibilities
- Facilitate the consensus process on a monthly basis between customer forecasts gathered by sales together with marketing forecasts developed by product managers.
- Document and challenge forecast assumptions based on the analysis of market data, industry statistics, and market dynamics.
- Incorporate product trends into forecast models and monthly forecast updates.
- Measure and report forecast accuracy at customer, market, and product levels.
- Participate in the development of the cause of error to ensure continuous improvement of the overall process.
- Maintain and use the forecast error data to quantify inventory strategies required to meet customer service targets.
- Manage the integration of information between various systems as well as ensuring that new product and discontinued product are added or removed from the system.
- Provide expertise for complex statistical modeling analysis.

FIGURE 44   Example of Position Advertising for Product Demand Manager (Source: International Business Forum, www.ibf.com)

of Internet postings for demand management positions. These examples show the prominence of the positions within organizations today.

One of the most hotly debated questions about the demand manager role is where the function should reside in the organization. Here is what the authors have found works best. When starting out to develop and operate the demand management process, the demand manager should reside in the organization that is responsible for the creation and execution of demand. That is to say, the demand manager should reside in the marketing and sales side of the business. There is a strong argument that initially the function should report to the sales organization. This serves two purposes:

1. It puts the demand manager closest to the customer, which helps to improve the demand plan accuracy.
2. It ensures that the sales organization is accountable for executing the demand plan.

When the sales organization is not actively involved in developing the demand plan, sales managers and salespeople do not feel ownership and respon-

Qualifications
- Five or more years direct experience managing forecasting activities for a retailer, consumer products, or apparel company.
- Strong ability to influence, must have a high level of personal credibility as a spokesperson for forecasting.
- Strong business knowledge/experience, especially with supply chain functions, critical knowledge of sales, retail, operations, finance, and merchandising.
- Must have excellent problem-solving skills across entire supply chain and customer service.
- Ability to make decisions regarding forecasting which directly impacts inventory strategies, on-time delivery, and order fill rates.
- Must demonstrate a complete understanding of quantitative/qualitative analysis.
- Ability to integrate the link between brand business processes and forecast, impact of forecast accuracy on business processes, systems, and supply chain clients.

Responsibilities
- Leads the development of strategy, processes, and tools for the company's key forecasting activities for its customers. Includes managing relationships and expectations/deliverables from sales, business planning, brand management, product management, finance, marketing, and market research to create accurate forecasts.
- Provides senior management with actionable decision support analysis to influence policy changes that result in improved profitability, volume growth, and achieved channel objectives.
- Manages the monthly consensus process, including reporting to senior management on forecasts, assumptions, risks, and opportunities.
- Establishes performance measures to support decision further down the supply chain.
- Represents the demand planning department in key cross-functional decisions, including short- and long-term strategy discussions, product initiatives, strategic business planning, and systems integration.
- Drives required team capabilities and objective setting for the department, leading to continuous improvement of the forecast process and adoption of best practices where possible.
- Acts as key representative of the company in contacts with customers related to the forecasting and replenishment functions.

FIGURE 45 Example of Position Advertising for Director, Forecasting for Multibillion-Dollar Consumer Brand (Source: Institute of Business Forecasting, Job Postings, www.ibforecast.com)

sibility for executing the plan. As a result, the demand management effort usually yields marginal results in the form of increased sales revenues, improved customer satisfaction and market share, inventory reductions, and increased profit margins. This should be the purpose of demand management and will be discussed in greater detail in Chapter 11 on performance measurements.

Once the participation of sales, marketing, and product/brand management in a multiview, collaborative process becomes institutionalized, it matters less where the demand manager resides in the organization. It is not unusual for companies to evolve to a supply chain management organizational structure, where both the demand manager and supply manager reside. For the demand management process to remain effective, however, the sales, marketing, and brand/product management organizations must continue to communicate their plans, assumptions, and market intelligence to the demand management function. They continue to be responsible for the four elements of demand management — plan, communicate, influence, and prioritize and manage. They continue to be responsible for creating and executing the demand plan. The demand management function simply provides a service to the demand organization.

When the demand manager resides in the supply chain organization, the position has a greater emphasis on demand coordination. The demand manager assimilates the multiple inputs from the demand organization into a proposed demand plan, which the demand organization then reviews and reaches consensus upon. The demand manager also coordinates use of the demand information throughout the supply chain, both inside the organization and with trading partners up and down the supply chain. When companies truly collaborate with trading partners and operate supply chain management effectively, the selling role changes as well. The roles involved in collaboration are covered in Chapter 13.

The role of the sales organization in the demand management process is to communicate its sales plans and assumptions as input into the demand plan, with or without collaboration with customers. Of course, this is not the only or primary responsibility of the sales organization. In defining the roles of the sales organization in the demand management process, The authors have found that the most effective companies have the following expectations of their sales force:

- The sales organization is responsible for direct contact with the customer. The sales force's primary job is to match the company's products to the customers' needs (and vice versa) and to book the business (sell).
- The sales organization is responsible not only for representing the company to the customer, but also for representing the customer to the company.
- The sales force is the live, real-time eyes and ears of the company in the marketplace. As such, the sales force is expected to communicate problems and market opportunities. This communication serves as key input for developing company strategies and tactics.
- The sales force is expected to provide some level of activity reporting as part of its administrative responsibilities.

■ Management prefers to have its sales force selling rather than doing administrative tasks. Therefore, the administrative processes are well designed to facilitate efficiency.

■ Sales planning (which involves identifying the timing and volume of sales), territory management, and account management are used to improve sales productivity.

■ There is value to the sales organization, and specifically sales management, in providing input into the demand planning process.

■ In the process of developing demand chain partners, the sales organization is responsible for negotiating the new process and rules by which the partners will conduct business. This role is clearly different than simply selling the company's products.

It is important to point out that the demand management function provides a vital role in looking at the sum of all the inputs from sales, marketing, brand/product managers, and other collaborators in the process. Someone must look at the whole picture when all the inputs are received from multiple parties. Otherwise, the total demand that is projected can be inaccurate, but will not be detected. This inaccuracy can be caused when one key sales territory fails to provide input into the demand plan. As a result, an inaccurate demand plan will be communicated to the demand, supply, and finance organizations.

Given the above, the specifics of how a sales organization supports demand planning varies by company, depending on the types and volume of products sold. Following are the most common approaches to providing sales input into the demand plan.

In companies that primarily serve customers that provide repeat business, the sales force is expected to provide visibility of anticipated purchases that each individual customer is expected to make. This visibility is usually accomplished through monthly updates of the sales plans for each individual customer. Often the customer can be persuaded to provide this input directly without additional administrative activities by the salesperson. The level of detail provided by customers will vary, depending on the type of product being sold, product availability, and delivery strategy.

In companies with a broad range of products and large number of customers, the sales force is typically expected to provide input every month on the anticipated product family or category demand in each territory. This information includes specific sales plans and activities that are expected to generate demand.

In companies that primarily sell project work, the sales force's primary responsibility is to communicate new project proposals and updates on project proposals awaiting customer acceptance. This is usually accomplished by communicating copies of all proposals and updates to the demand management function. The information communicated is structured to provide internally important "vital statistics," for example, probability that the project work will come to fruition, probability that the company will secure the project, the date the contract is expected to be booked, and dates when the products will be required. This information, along with product or scope changes, is typically updated once per month and more frequently when significant changes occur.

Bottom line: The selling organization's role in demand management is to make visible its plans and the resulting timing and volume of demand that these plans will generate.

The product or brand management organizations have a similar role (see Figure 46 for an overview of sales, marketing, and product/brand management roles). They, too, are responsible for communicating their plans and the expected timing and volume of demand resulting from those plans. The product or brand organization has an additional responsibility: to communicate the status of product launches, product and trade promotions, and the exit plans for products that will no longer be offered. For demand management, new product launches and the exit of products are frequently timing issues. If a new product launch is delayed, how the delay impacts products currently offered, and those on the chopping block, must be defined and communicated.

The role of marketing in demand management is broader. The marketing organization is responsible for looking outside the company and assessing the health of the economy, monitoring key indicators or drivers that influence demand, identifying market trends, evaluating the impact of competitors' activities on demand, and measuring market share. The marketing organization is also responsible for making visible its marketing strategies and tactics, including promotions, and their resulting impact on demand. In a classic push–pull marketing strategy, the marketing and brand organizations are influencing the consumers or end users to "pull" the demand, while the selling organization is responsible to sell, or "push," the product to customers and market channels.

When demand management processes are in their earliest stage of implementation, the demand organization may initially resist participating in the demand management process. As recounted in the last chapter, if people do not see the value in doing something, they usually will not do it. Or, if they do comply, it is halfheartedly.

This is where leadership comes in. Commitment to the process by senior management is the key to success. This is a business mantra that has been repeated so frequently that leaders in companies have almost become immune to the meaning of the statement. However, when senior leaders search for the reasons why business processes fail, the blame almost always lies at their feet.

The demand organization's leaders themselves play a significant role in the demand management process (see Figure 47 for an overview of their roles and

Sales	Marketing	Product/Brand Management
Role Make visible the sales plans and the resulting timing and volume of demand.	*Role* Communicate changes outside the company that impact demand. Make visible the marketing strategies and tactics and their resulting impact on demand.	*Role* Communicate product plans, including product launches and products that will be discontinued.
Responsibilities: ■ Once per month, communicate anticipated purchases that customers will make, including volume, timing, and degree of certainty, over the agreed upon planning horizon. ■ Once per month, communicate assumptions upon which the plans are based. ■ Communicate at least monthly market intelligence, including problems and opportunities. ■ Communicate any significant changes in demand (up or down) when the changes become known.	*Responsibilities* ■ Once per month, communicate the anticipated impact on demand from marketing strategies and tactics. ■ Once per month, communicate the assumptions upon which the strategies, tactics, and resulting demand are based. ■ Track, measure, and report every month the impact of external factors that impact demand, including economic indicators and competitors' actions.	*Responsibilities* ■ Once per month, update and communicate the product plans, including new product launches, product and trade promotions, and products that will be discontinued. ■ Communicate any delays in product launches or changes in product plans that will impact demand. ■ Communicate and update product life cycle plans and the assumptions behind those plans.

FIGURE 46 Overview of Roles and Responsibilities

responsibilities). People gauge the commitment of their leaders by how well they perform their roles and responsibilities in the process. People almost always follow their leaders' footsteps in this regard.

The senior leadership of the demand organization — sales, marketing, and product/brand management — is responsible for developing and assessing the comprehensive view of demand, or the big picture. Individual salespeople and district or regional sales managers see only their individual pieces of demand. Someone must compile the complete view, and that is the role of the senior leadership team.

Role
- Develop the comprehensive picture of demand.
- Ensure that the demand-related strategies, tactics, and execution are in place to deliver demand to meet the company's strategic and financial objectives.

Responsibilities
- Develop the comprehensive picture of demand to determine the overall status of demand and take appropriate actions as needed to achieve the company's strategic and financial objectives.
- Participate in the demand consensus review meeting, with the most senior executive in the demand organization leading the meeting. (This responsibility is not delegated.)
- Reach consensus on an updated demand plan every month.
- Provide leadership, oversight, and problem solving to ensure the execution of the demand plan.
- Ensure that the demand plan is integrated into and synchronized with the other company plans, including the supply plan and financial plan.
- Encourage and expect honesty and realism in developing strategic objectives, in providing input into the demand plan, and in the demand plan itself.
- Develop accountability for demand management through performance measures and feedback to the participants in the process.

FIGURE 47 Overview of Leadership Roles and Responsibilities

Day-to-day activities, however, frequently cloud senior managers' ability to analyze demand from the total company perspective. The role of the demand manager is to provide the information and analysis required to see the big picture. This way, the senior leadership team can determine the overall status of demand and take appropriate actions as needed to attain the company's strategic and financial objectives.

The senior leadership team also is responsible for participating in the demand consensus review. In fact, they "own" this meeting, and the meeting is chaired by the most senior executive in the demand organization. In some companies, the chairperson is the vice-president of sales. In other companies, it is the vice-president of marketing or the vice-president of marketing and sales. The conduct of this meeting is reviewed in Chapter 14. Looking at the complete picture of demand, the senior leadership team is responsible for reaching consensus on a demand plan every month and then providing oversight on the execution of the demand plan. This is a best practice.

The senior leadership team is also accountable for ensuring that the demand plan is integrated into and synchronized with the other company plans, principally the supply and financial plans. In companies that utilize best practices, this is accomplished through an integrated business management review process, known as sales and operations planning. Integration and synchronization of demand is reviewed in Chapter 14.

In leading the demand management process, the senior management team must create an environment that encourages realism. When people are criticized or penalized for communicating the truth, the quality of the demand information becomes less credible. Problems are buried, rather than exposed and acted upon.

Case in point: A company experienced a downturn in business near year end. The senior leadership team was caught by surprise. "We didn't see it coming," one executive lamented. The sales managers had a different perspective: "We tried to tell them, but they wouldn't listen. They actually became quite testy about it."

A demand management process was implemented the following year. The sales manager saw warning signs that business would decline significantly in Asia during the last half of the year. He communicated the information, and this time it was not ignored. The response was: What can we do about it? What actions need to take place? What is the decision point to change the demand plan?

"This process has given us a better compass as to what is coming ahead," a marketing manager observed. "The process allows us to challenge the demand plan in enough time to take action." He further observed that the demand management process caused the demand leadership to have a better, more realistic understanding of the marketplace. It made them more accountable for the decisions that were made about the demand plan and market strategies and tactics.

The demand management process also identified disconnects between marketing strategies and tactics and sales strategies and tactics. They were not synchronized. "We were going in different directions," a sales manager commented.

Healing the disconnect did not happen voluntarily. It occurred after the sales and marketing executives reviewed the demand information during the second demand consensus review meeting that the company conducted. The executives recognized that the sales and marketing organizations had different goals and objectives. They realized they had not paid enough attention to the tactics that were being executed to generate demand. They had been "too hands off," as the executive vice-president of marketing explained.

The demand consensus review meeting became the focal point for ensuring that the marketing strategy and sales plans dovetailed. Some of the demand consensus review meetings were painful for the participants. They were not used to having their strategies and tactics questioned. They also were not accustomed to having to report their execution performance every month. Surfacing problems every month was also new to them. So, too, was the assignment of actions (with due dates) to resolve the problems. The assigned actions were reviewed in every meeting for completion and resolution.

It took three months to resolve the major differences between the marketing strategy and the long-term sales plans. The entire demand team could see an improvement once the major differences were ironed out. They knew what they were expected to do and, by looking out in the planning horizon, they had time to act to deliver the demand. There were fewer surprises, and most of the surprises were positive ones, like additional business.

"Now we are looking at the marketing strategy and the long-term sales plan and asking ourselves whether we are doing the right things to meet the strategic objectives," the sales manager commented. "We are also talking to customers on a monthly basis, and it's making a difference in sales volume and revenue."

This turnaround started with leadership from senior management. They demonstrated their commitment to the process. In the demand consensus review meetings and one-on-one conversations, they explained the importance of the process. They instituted performance measurements that (1) reinforced the accountability for delivering the demand and (2) enabled people to see the improvements in their performance. And the leadership team did not delegate oversight and responsibility for the comprehensive view of demand to others lower in the organization. These are best leadership practices.

The senior management team exhibited what Larry Bossidy and Ram Charan, in *Execution: The Discipline of Getting Things Done,*[34] call the leader's essential behaviors:

1. Know your people and your business.
2. Insist on realism.
3. Set clear goals and priorities.
4. Follow through.
5. Reward the doers.
6. Expand people's capabilities.
7. Know yourself.

One question commonly asked by demand leaders is how to build competency in demand management. Developing the skills for demand management almost always involves what Bossidy and Charan call expanding people's capabilities.

Figure 48 illustrates an approach for developing competency in demand management as well as developing the demand management process itself.[35] It starts with awareness and understanding. This is a leadership role. First, the leaders of the demand organization must understand the potential of the process and create a vision of how the process should operate in their environment. As

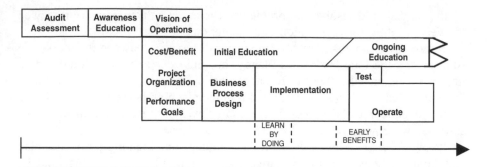

FIGURE 48   Proven Path Methodology for Process Development and Skill Development (Copyright Oliver Wight International)

part of creating the vision, the leaders assess the gaps between the vision and the current capability. These gaps include skills, process, and tools that enable the process.

Ancillary to creating the vision, an analysis of return on investment should be made. This analysis quantifies the benefits and the costs in developing competency in the process and in implementing the process.

The next phase involves the first steps in developing competency in demand management. The users of the process, particularly those users who tend to be agents of change within the organization, begin to work on a "to-be" model. During this work, they will need to gain an understanding of the best practices and techniques of demand management. They utilize this understanding to design the process. As they develop the process, they educate the other participants in the process on how the process works, the expectations of the process, their roles and responsibilities in supporting the process, and the best practices.

A transition point is shown in Figure 48 as learn by doing. This is an important step. The process needs to be put into practice as soon as possible — in months, not years. At this point, the leadership team should communicate that it does not expect the process to be perfect to start. Participants will gain skills and competency through implementation and experience.

The development of competency frequently stalls at this point of the implementation. Why? Because of a fear of failure. Change management expert James F. Huggett observes that fear of failure, not change itself, causes people to resist changes in their roles and responsibilities:

> What people really resist is the loss of control over their lives that they have fought so long and hard to create. When we say change, they think, "I used to have this job figured out; if it changes, will I know what to do? What if I fail?"[36]

Reassurance from the leadership team is needed to make it safe for people to risk performing their new roles. Competence is not ordained; it is developed over time. Thus, feedback through performance measurements is used to identify areas of weakness where additional education, coaching, and mentoring are needed to develop competency.

Performance measurements should also be used to demonstrate the early benefits and results of the demand management process. These measurements represent progress, and progress in the form of benefits and results should be communicated to the demand organization and the company at large. Measurement of progress demonstrates that the demand management participants are not failing at their roles and that they are making valuable contributions to the company.

As companies gain greater competence in demand management, the reliability of the sales, marketing, product/brand management plans — and the resulting demand plan — improves. When demand plan accuracy improves from 50 percent to consistently 90 percent, as occurred in the case of the company that worked to dovetail the marketing and sales strategies, the demand plan becomes more credible to the rest of the organization. Other functions, principally the supply and financial organizations, trust the demand plan and become willing to allow the demand plan to drive their plans. Credibility is the result of competence.

Despite the best efforts to develop the most reliable plans, there is always a degree of uncertainty in any plan. How uncertainty is managed is another competence that builds credibility. Managing uncertainty is the topic of the next chapter.

SUMMARY OF BEST PRACTICES
FOR THE HUMAN QUOTIENT

1. The company's leaders recognize the importance of people in the demand management process. The leaders value people's contributions to the process.
2. People's competency in demand management is considered the most important factor in developing an effective demand management process. Investment is made in developing competency.
3. The multifaceted role of the demand manager is recognized. The demand manager position is a full-time job.
4. The demand manager resides in the demand organization until such time as the sales, marketing, and product/brand management roles in the process are institutionalized and consistently performed.
5. The sales organization makes visible its plans and the resulting timing and volume of demand that its plans are expected to generate. This information

is updated and communicated to the demand manager at least monthly and more frequently when significant change occurs.

6. The marketing organization communicates changes in the economy, key indicators or drivers that influence demand, market trends, competitors' activities, and market share. This information is updated and communicated to the demand manager at least monthly and more frequently when significant change occurs.

7. The product/brand management organization makes visible its marketing strategies and tactics, including promotions, and their resulting impact on demand. This information is updated and communicated to the demand manager at least monthly and more frequently when significant change occurs.

8. The product or brand management organization communicates changes to planned new product launches, promotions, and the exit of products. If a new product launch is delayed, how the delay impacts the current product offering is defined and communicated. This information is updated and communicated to the demand manager at least monthly.

9. The senior leadership of the demand organization is responsible for developing and assessing the comprehensive picture of demand. This complete picture of demand is updated at least monthly.

10. The senior leadership team of the demand organization owns the demand consensus review meeting. The meeting is chaired by the most senior executive in the demand organization. Participation in this meeting is not delegated to those lower in the organization.

11. The senior leadership team of the demand organization is responsible for reaching consensus on a demand plan every month and then providing oversight on the execution of the demand plan.

12. The senior leadership team of the demand organization insists on realistic plans.

13. The senior leadership of the demand organization is accountable for ensuring that the demand plan is integrated into and synchronized with the other company plans. This is accomplished through an integrated business management (sales and operations planning) review process.

14. The senior leadership of the demand organization demonstrates its commitment to demand management through the execution of its roles and responsibilities in the process.

15. Performance measurements are used to provide feedback on execution, reinforce accountability, and demonstrate progress in improving people's skills and competency in demand management.

16. The senior leadership team of the demand organization creates the vision and expectation for demand management in the organization. It implements a process that builds competency in demand management.

17. The senior leadership team of the demand organization works to help people overcome their fear of failure when implementing the roles and responsibilities for demand management.
18. Competency in demand management is measured by the reliability of the sales, marketing, product/brand management plans — and the resulting demand plan.

QUESTIONS

1. Why are people the most critical element of demand management?
2. What are the roles and responsibilities of a demand manager?
3. What are the qualities a demand manager needs to be successful?
4. What are the roles and responsibilities of the sales organization?
5. What are the roles and responsibilities of the product/brand management organization?
6. What are the roles and responsibilities of the product/brand management organization?
7. What are the roles and responsibilities of the leaders in the demand organization?
8. What are the qualities the leaders in the demand organization need to be successful?
9. If you were the senior-most leader in the demand organization, how would you develop competency in your demand organization in demand manage-

10

PLANNING STRATEGIES FOR MANAGING UNCERTAINTY

Despite even the most intensive efforts at foresight, the best-laid plans of mice and men often go awry, as poet Robert Burns observed more than two centuries ago. So, too, with marketing, sales, and demand plans.

Why do plans go awry? Uncertainty is one reason. Despite the best efforts to obtain credible information upon which to base assumptions about demand, there is almost always some degree of uncertainty about markets, customers, competitors, and a company's own internal ability to execute.

Given this reality, methods are needed for managing uncertainty. Planning strategies for managing uncertainty are the focus of this chapter.

Company leaders respond to the potential for uncertainty in different ways. Some ignore it and then are surprised and disappointed when customers do not buy as planned. Others blame the person responsible for developing the demand plan, and the position of forecaster or demand manager becomes a revolving door. Others assign blame to the salesperson or marketing or brand manager.

More astute leaders recognize the inevitability of uncertainty. Instead of ignoring or resisting the fact that all plans (yes, even supply plans) are not perfect, they take a different tack. They *manage* uncertainty by:

- Identifying, clarifying, and reducing uncertainties about demand
- Deploying different planning strategies when uncertainties cannot be reduced or eliminated
- Developing demand scenarios to preplan contingencies

When company leaders manage uncertainty, they gain greater control over their company's destiny. Case in point: A company's sales and marketing executives reviewed the demand plan over the entire 18-month planning horizon during the monthly demand consensus review meeting. They focused a great deal of attention on the demand assumptions. The assumptions further out in the time horizon indicated that there would be few changes in the market and in customer buying behaviors.

The vice-president of sales and marketing, who chaired the demand consensus review, believed that demand in the future would not be stagnant. At least he hoped that future demand would grow. The industry as a whole had struggled with excess capacity, resulting in lower prices and profits than the industry really wanted. To increase demand, the company (as well as its competitors) was working to develop international markets for its products.

During the demand consensus review, the vice-president of sales and marketing peppered his managers with questions: Are you saying that our efforts to develop the Latin American market are going to result in the same demand next year as this year? Are you saying that the Latin American market is going to be stagnant? I thought we were supposed to be *growing* the market there.

His managers squirmed, and the room was silent. Finally, the marketing director for Latin America spoke up. He said that he was not certain when demand in Latin America would begin to grow, given the current state of its economy. He also was not sure when the selling and distribution channels would be fully in place in Argentina, Brazil, and Chile.

The vice-president of sales and marketing asked whether economic indicators and other data for Latin America were considered when developing the demand plan. He also wanted to know the company's market share compared to its competitors.

The marketing manager told him that the economic information was vague, based mostly on conversations with the people hired to set up the selling and distribution channels in Latin America. He did not have current market share figures. Lacking more definitive information, he thought it was prudent to anticipate continued flat demand over the next 18 months.

The vice-president of sales and marketing instructed his team to get information that would clarify the uncertainties about the economy in Latin America, including leading indicators if they were available. He asked for an update on market share figures. He also asked to review the plans for setting up the selling and distribution channels. He did not want to wait until the next demand consensus review to see this information. He scheduled a review in two weeks.

It turned out that the Latin American economy was not just flat but declining. The downturn was expected to continue over the next year. The company's market share in Latin America had actually slipped by five percentage points. Establishing selling channels and distribution centers was proving to be slower than anticipated; it would be another six to nine months before they were fully up and running.

While this was not news the vice-president of sales and marketing wanted to hear, learning it at this point in time was an advantage. The marketing and sales organizations had time to build sales revenue in other ways. The company could do little to influence Latin America's economy, but it could do something about market share and its selling channels and distribution centers. Changes were made to overcome the obstacles that had slowed setting up the selling relationships and distribution channels. The company reviewed and made changes to its marketing plans in Latin America. It would take time to see the impact from these actions, however. So the company accelerated plans to develop other international markets.

The company actually *reduced* the demand plan for Latin America, but reviewed the gaps between the annual business plan and the sales revenue the demand plan was expected to generate. The execution of activities to build demand in international markets was reviewed every month. This focus and attention helped to accelerate the penetration in other international markets.

The vice-president of sales and marketing commented later that if they had not clarified the uncertainties in the demand plan for Latin America, the financial impact would have been worse than just lower sales revenues than planned. They would have ended up building and possibly shipping inventory to Latin America, which would have further complicated the company's financial picture. They also would not have taken alternative action to increase sales revenues by accelerating plans to develop business in other international markets.

This experience represented a turning point for the company's demand management effort. Discussions during the demand consensus review meeting focused not just on the assumptions but on the degree of certainty — or uncertainty — of the assumptions over the entire planning horizon. This focus caused the marketing and sales managers to do a better job in developing assumptions. By identifying uncertainties over the longer term planning horizon, the company had time to clarify the uncertainties and then to take action if needed. This is a best practice.

To identify uncertainty, it is necessary to ask certain questions:

1. Is information, which enables making a precise enough decision about future demand, clearly known?
2. Is basic information lacking, as in the case example about the Latin American economy and market share, which makes it difficult to know the true demand picture with a high degree of certainty?
3. Is information known but additional detail required for greater clarity, as in the case example about when the Latin American sales and distribution channels would be fully operational?

4. Are there multiple factors whose outcomes are unknown and interdependent, which create such a high degree of ambiguity that it is extremely difficult to judge what will happen in the future?[37]

When uncertainty exists because basic information is lacking or greater clarity of existing information is needed, the response is easy — go get the information, as the Latin America director of marketing did in the case above. Even after obtaining the required information, some uncertainties may still exist, however. When the market situation is uncertain, and especially if there are ambiguities, one way to deal with the uncertainty is to develop different planning scenarios. This is a best practice.

Each scenario should show a different demand picture, which can then be evaluated by the demand, supply, and financial organizations. Factor analysis and forecasting techniques discussed in Chapter 8 can be used to develop the scenarios. The scenarios should highlight specific strategies and tactics required to generate the demand for each scenario.

Figure 49 is an example of scenario planning. It shows graphically the current demand plan as well as the demand plan for two different scenarios. The major assumptions for the current demand plan and both scenarios are included as well.

Scenario planning has several advantages:

■   It is possible to gauge the level of marketing and sales effort required to create the demand for each scenario.
■   It shows how changes in business factors or key drivers that impact demand.
■   The scenarios can serve as contingency plans.

When market conditions are uncertain, the scenarios are updated and reviewed each month during the demand consensus review meeting. This way, when conditions change, it is possible to implement a new demand plan very quickly based on one of the scenarios.

Another approach to managing uncertainty is to develop different planning strategies, based on the level of certainty or uncertainty for each product line. The demand for some products is more certain and thus easier to predict than other product demand. When products have a loyal customer base, steady volume, and there are good communications with customers on their buying intentions, the demand for these products is more certain.

The demand for other types of products can be less certain and, therefore, less predictable. The volume may be low and purchase of these products may be sporadic. Spare parts and replacement parts frequently fall into this category.

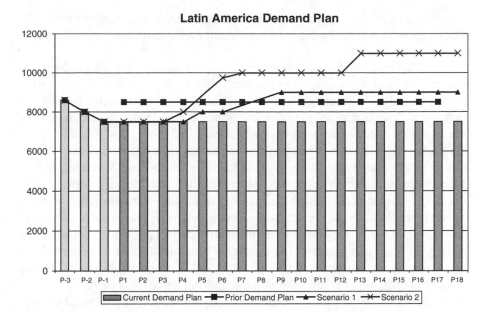

Major Assumptions

Current Plan
Economy declines or stays flat through P18.
CPI: Argentina +28.4, Brazil +7.8, Chile +2.0 expected to hold steady.
Interest rates: Argentina 44.5, Brazil 18.39, Chile 3.72.
Unknown when selling and distribution channels will be fully established.

Scenario 1
Sales and distribution channels will be in operation by P5. Ramp up in P5–P8 to 8500 P9–P18.

Marketing efforts will yield increase in market share beginning P9. Goal: Increase market share by 5%.

Economy stays steady in Chile and continues to decline in Argentina and Brazil; won't stabilize until P10.

Scenario 2
Establishing selling and distribution channels in Chile will be top priority and accomplished by P3.

Marketing efforts will increase market share in Chile beginning P7. Goal: Increase share by 10%.

Chile market will expand use of our type of products by 10% next year.

Selling and distribution channels will be established in Brazil by P6. Goal: Increase market share by 5%.

Selling and distribution channels will be established in Argentina by P9. Goal: Increase market share by 5%.

Use of our type of products will remain flat in Brazil and Argentina next year — unless interest rates decline.

FIGURE 49   Example of Scenario Planning

The purchase of these types of products is often based on an uncertainty itself. For example, when will a piece of equipment break down and require components to be replaced?

A pitfall to avoid is using the same planning strategy for all products, no matter their level of uncertainty or predictability. A generic approach will predict some demand quite accurately and other demand very inaccurately. To improve demand plan accuracy, unique planning strategies are needed based on level of certainty and predictability. This is a best practice.

So how do you know when different planning strategies are needed? A first step involves classifying products by demand volume versus variability in demand patterns. Some products will have relatively stable demand patterns. The demand for other products can be seasonal in nature. The seasonality itself is generally not variable, however, as it occurs regularly. (Note: some seasons will be earlier or later in the year, depending upon such variables as the weather and the timing of certain holidays, like Easter.) The demand for still other products can be highly inconsistent in a way that does not fit a repeatable pattern. In this case, it is difficult to predict the volume and timing for this demand.

Figure 50 illustrates the concept of classifying products by demand volume versus variability in demand patterns. High-volume products that exhibit relatively little variability in the demand patterns fall into quadrant A in Figure 50. Time series statistical forecasting methods, such as exponential smoothing or Box Jenkins ARIMA techniques, typically predict these products with a high degree of accuracy, as shown in Figure 51. While demand varies for the product shown in Figure 51, it does so in a consistent, seasonal pattern. Notice that the mean absolute percent error (MAPE) is 0.068259, or 6 percent. The adjusted R square statistic, an indicator of how well the forecast predicts the variability of demand, is 0.8443, or 84 percent, meaning that 84 percent of the demand variability is predicted by the forecast model.

For high-volume products with few variations in the pattern of demand, an effective planning strategy is to use the time series statistical forecast. With these types of products, many companies do not expect their sales and marketing organizations (as well as customers that provide their buying schedules or forecasts) to furnish demand numbers as part of their input into the demand plan. It is wasteful to do so because the statistical forecasting technique predicts demand with a great enough accuracy on which to base supply and financial plans.

Instead of communicating demand numbers, the input expected from the sales and marketing organization as well as customers involves the communication of expected changes. The marketing organization, for example, would be expected to communicate promotion plans that would significantly impact the volume and timing of demand. The sales organization would be expected to

High

D Challenge Why the Product Is Offered; Understand the Product Plan	**B** Input from Sales and Customers Is Critical
C Time Series Statistical Forecasting Methods Can Work Well, Augmented by Understanding the Product Marketing Plan	**A** Time Series Statistical Forecasting Methods Work Well

Variability

Low   Volume   High

FIGURE 50   Classification of Products by Volume versus Demand Variability (Copyright Oliver Wight International)

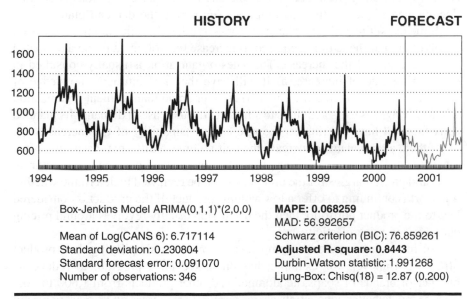

HISTORY   **FORECAST**

Box-Jenkins Model ARIMA(0,1,1)*(2,0,0)   **MAPE: 0.068259**
-          MAD: 56.992657
Mean of Log(CANS 6): 6.717114   Schwarz criterion (BIC): 76.859261
Standard deviation: 0.230804   **Adjusted R-square: 0.8443**
Standard forecast error: 0.091070   Durbin-Watson statistic: 1.991268
Number of observations: 346   Ljung-Box: Chisq(18) = 12.87 (0.200)

FIGURE 51   Statistical Forecast Example of High-Volume Product with Low Demand (Example Courtesy of Business Forecast Systems, Inc.)

communicate changes in its customers' buying plans as well as the addition of demand from new customers. Both the sales and marketing organizations would be expected to communicate information on competitors' activities that could significantly impact demand.

This planning strategy — relying on the statistical forecast with communication of significant changes from sales, marketing, and product or brand management — reduces the time required to provide input into the demand plan. It frees up the sales organization, in particular, to focus on those products and customers that are more difficult to predict and have a higher level of uncertainty.

For low-volume products with low variability in demand patterns, shown in quadrant C of Figure 50, time series statistical forecasting methods often can be very accurate as well, as demonstrated in Figure 52. The mean absolute percent error is 9 percent and the adjusted R square is 97 percent. The questions to answer for low-volume products with little variability in demand patterns are:

■   What volume do we want to achieve with this product?
■   Are there plans to increase the demand for this product?
■   Where is this product in its life cycle?

The product or brand management and marketing organizations are responsible for answering these questions. The answers to these questions should be documented as part of their assumptions supporting the demand plan.

If the marketing or brand plan calls for increasing the unit volume, discussion revolves around the actions required to increase the volume and the anticipated rate and timing of the increase. The sales organization is usually consulted in defining the rate of increase, as it will have the most intimate knowledge of customers' buying intentions. The marketing or brand management organization will add insight as to its activities to stimulate the increase in demand. Its planned activities will have bearing on the rate and sustainability of the increase.

If there are no plans to increase the unit volume, a different discussion often takes place. The discussion is about product rationalization. The manufacturing costs and profit margins for the product should be reviewed to determine whether it is worth continuing to offer a low-volume product. If the product is considered key to the product portfolio, then the discussion usually revolves around pricing changes and price elasticity.

An increasing number of companies see merit in simplifying their product offerings. Unilever, for example, has embarked on a program to reduce its number of brands of soaps, deodorants, and other products from 1,600 to 200. The reason: to better concentrate scarce corporate resources on its most powerful brands.[38]

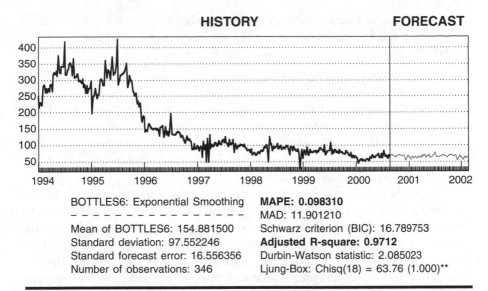

FIGURE 52 Statistical Forecast Example of Low-Volume Product with Low Demand Variability (Example Courtesy of Business Forecast Systems, Inc.)

Some companies, like Hewlett-Packard, address product simplification as part of the product development process. During the product development process for a new CD-RW device, an H-P team analyzed the supply chain costs to support the new product line. This analysis considered the inventory costs associated with keeping a buffer of stock for demand uncertainties. In the end, the company reduced the stockkeeping unit (SKU) count for the new product line, rather than quadrupling it as proposed by the marketing organization. This decision resulted in a 16 percent increase in profitability for the product line.[39]

Some companies take another approach to product rationalization. They perform a volume analysis to determine which products account for the vast majority of the unit volume. Using Pareto's rule, approximately 20 percent of the products will typically account for approximately 80 percent of the unit volume.

Using the Pareto approach, low-volume products (those products that account for 20 percent or less of the volume) come under scrutiny. The questions to answer about these products are:

- Are plans in place to increase the demand for these products?
- Should these products continue to be offered?
- What is the risk to customer retention by eliminating these low-volume products?

- What is the forecast accuracy for these products, and what are the inventory and/or lead time tactics as a buffer against demand uncertainty?
- What are the profit margins on these products?

We have been discussing planning strategies for products with low variability in demand patterns. Products with highly variable, inconsistent demand patterns present another challenge (see quadrants B and D in Figure 50). These products usually do not yield an accurate forecast using time series methods like exponential smoothing. Developing an accurate demand plan becomes highly dependent on information from the sales, marketing, and product or brand management organizations.

The example in Figure 53 illustrates the risk of basing the demand plan for products with highly variable demand solely on time series statistical forecasting methods. In this case, the demand volume for this product is low and the demand pattern is highly inconsistent. The mean absolute percent error of the time series statistical forecast is 90 percent! The adjusted R square value, which demonstrates how well the model predicts the variability in demand, is only 27 percent.

With this type of demand, the time series statistical forecast cannot be relied upon to yield an accurate demand plan. Information from the sales organization, including customer buying schedules, would strengthen the accuracy of the demand plan. So, too, would marketing and product plans for this product. Questions to answer in this case are:

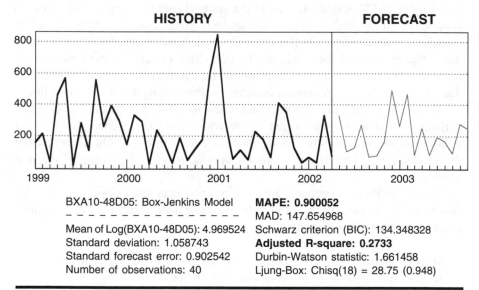

FIGURE 53   Statistical Forecast Example of Low-Volume Product with High Demand Variability

- Who are the customers that purchase this product, and are they willing to provide a schedule or forecast of their demand?
- What causes customers to purchase this product? Can another product be substituted?
- What are the consequences if we decide to no longer offer this product?
- What is the demand plan accuracy for these products, and what are the inventory and/or lead time tactics as a buffer against demand uncertainty?
- What are the profit margins on these products?

For products with low volume and highly variable demand (quadrant D in Figure 50), the product or brand management organization ought to rationalize why the product should continue to be offered. Of course, profitability, customer strategies, product life cycle, and market position should be considered in the product rationalization. A decision not to continue offering a product obviously should be based on more than demand variability alone.

Sometimes it is not possible to simply discontinue a product. Consider the aviation business, for example. To keep airplanes and helicopters flying, it is necessary to provide replacement parts long after the equipment is sold. Some Boeing 707 airplanes have been in service for more than 30 years.

When it is not feasible to discontinue a product with highly variable demand patterns, these products usually have a higher degree of planning error. The challenge is how the supply chain is managed to (1) ensure expected customer service and (2) maintain profits. This is a balancing act that, if not managed well, causes companies to either have too much slow-moving product on hand or to not meet customers' requested delivery dates.

Some companies choose to use a make-to-order, rather than a make-to-stock, strategy for slow-moving products with highly variable demand. In essence, this approach trades inventory risk for lead time and customer service risk. The effectiveness of a make-to-order strategy, of course, depends on whether materials can be purchased and the product can be made within a lead time that is acceptable to customers.

As a general rule, products with highly variable demand patterns require more attention from the sales organization to achieve improved accuracy of the demand plan. To accurately plan demand, the sales organization must communicate closely with customers about their purchasing plans. An industrial valve manufacturer, for example, provided replacement parts for its valves used in power generation plants. Repairs were usually performed on the valves during an annual maintenance shutdown. The time and duration of the shutdown varied year to year, depending on the scope of the maintenance work that was planned.

As planned maintenance shutdowns neared, the salespeople confirmed the machinery that was going to be involved in the maintenance and estimated how many valves would require the replacement of key components. This provided an estimate of the demand volume for the replacement parts. By keeping in close contact with each plant's maintenance superintendent, it was possible to pinpoint the timing of when the replacement parts would be required. The dilemma in this case example is that there can be many products in the product portfolio that are low volume with highly variable demand. Oftentimes, the sales organization cannot spend enough time to make the demand plans accurate. A balanced approach of supply chain tactics (inventory and lead time) versus demand planning effort must be employed.

High-volume products with highly variable demand patterns pose a different type of challenge than low-volume products with variable demand patterns. These products are typically not forecasted accurately using a time series statistical forecasting method, as shown in Figure 54. In this case example, the mean absolute percent error is 28 percent and the adjusted R square value is 61 percent.

Companies usually do not want to discontinue these products, however. Even though it is more difficult to predict the volume and timing of demand, these products still significantly contribute to sales revenues. The challenge is to reduce the uncertainty about the timing of when customers intend to buy these products.

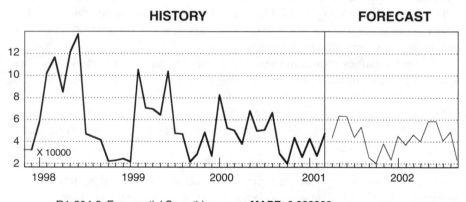

R1-204-3: Exponential Smoothing

Mean of R1-204-3: 54665.027344
Standard deviation: 30445.820313
Standard forecast error: 18971.30859
Number of observations: 41

MAPE: 0.283000
MAD: 13434.640625
Schwarz criterion (BIC): 20921.91601
Adjusted R-square: 0.6117
Durbin-Watson statistic: 2.002664
Ljung-Box: Chisq(18) = 17.51 (0.512)

FIGURE 54 Statistical Forecast Example of High-Volume Product with High Demand Variability (Example Courtesy of Business Forecast Systems, Inc.)

The sales organization is in the best position to know and communicate the timing of customers' purchases for products with highly variable demand patterns. High-volume products with variable demand are also ideal for engaging customers to communicate their buying schedules as another way of reducing uncertainty about the timing and volume of demand.

The good news is that high-volume products with high demand variability are often tied to specific programs or projects. Presumably, this is where the sales force is spending its critical time and effort. The sales force knows what is happening on these projects and programs. As a result, the sales force has the information needed to improve the demand plan accuracy. The task is to provide an efficient means for the sales force to communicate this information to the demand planning function.

Some types of businesses inherently have a greater level of uncertainty than others. It is typically much easier to determine the timing of demand for consumer packaged goods products, like laundry detergent, for example, than for products that are part of commercial construction projects, like the turbine generators for power plants. With project-based business, demand usually occurs in small unit volumes and the products typically require unique design configurations. Products of unique design configurations are usually dependent on the customer's engineering criteria and are capital intensive to produce and buy. Turbine generators, pumps, and satellites are some examples of project-based products.

The challenge in planning demand for these types of products is determining:

- The product design specifications that the customer wants to buy
- When the customer will place the order
- When the customer expects delivery of the product

A statistical forecast is rarely helpful in planning project type of demand. The timing of these purchases is usually dependent on some sort of facility construction or the replacement or retrofitting of current equipment. These projects are frequently delayed as they are at the mercy of construction timetables as well as the availability of capital to fund the projects. Consequently, the selling cycle can be quite long, up to a year or many years in some cases.

What is the best approach for planning project-based demand? The sales organization is the critical link. It has the best knowledge of the design specifications as well as the likelihood that the project will go forward. If the sales organization is doing its job properly, it will also be the first to know of changes in design specifications and the timing of the project. Therefore, it is essential to have in place a process for communicating updated information about each potential project and the products that will be purchased for each project.

Project Name and Number

Customer Name and Location

Customer's Project Nomenclature

Products and Services Being Offered

Date of Expected Booking (Receipt of Order)

Dates of Delivery Requirements (Required Delivery Dates)

Decision Point/Time Fence Dates (Time Points When the Supply Organization Needs to Take Action)

Probability of Customer Placing Order (Percent)

Probability of Customer Placing Order with Your Company (Percent)

Included in Demand Plan?   Yes or No

FIGURE 55   Project or Opportunity Database Information

Most companies involved in project-based business utilize a project or opportunity database to help manage the selling effort. The database contains specific details about all the projects in one place, which makes it easy to sort the information in a variety of ways for sales management and demand planning. The project or opportunity database typically contains, at a minimum, information shown in Figure 55. With a large number of projects, it may also be necessary to document the significance of the project as well as the probability of booking the business. This information is useful for determining which products to include in the demand plan.

Companies that use a disciplined strategic selling approach gather, document, and report the information shown in Figure 55 as part of their normal selling process.[40] Some companies utilize customer relationship management software to manage the project information. Whatever the database and software that is used, consistent communication about projects is needed. Access to this information should be easy for whoever needs to know it, including sales managers, the engineering organization, and the demand manager.

If a company's entire business is based on projects, it may be redundant to use a project or opportunity tracking approach. The company's proposal database may be sufficient to track and monitor project demand. The information documented about every project proposal, however, should include the information shown in Figure 55. This information should be updated at least monthly and should be accessible to the demand manager.

Most companies do not receive orders for all of the prospective projects. They may lose orders to competitors, and sometimes projects are canceled or delayed. To better manage the uncertainties of demand, the sales organization is responsible for communicating the percent of probability for each project and updating the database as the probability changes. Ideally, the probability should increase as the time draws near when the customer is expected to place the order. If the probability of booking the order does not increase over time, it is an indicator for the sales manager to determine what actions need to be taken to increase the probability of booking the project.

Because the probability of booking projects varies widely, it is necessary to determine which projects should be included in the demand plan. For example, is it prudent to include in the demand plan a project that is judged to have only a 10 percent probability of occurring?

One of the most common methods for developing a demand plan for products with a wide range of probability is shown in Figure 56. This approach works well for managing a large quantity of projects encompassing demand for similar products defined as a product group or family. In the example shown in Figure 56, the total demand potential is 9 units in April and 12 units in May. The probability of receiving individual orders for this total demand ranges from 15 to 100 percent. An average of the percent probability is calculated. In the example shown in Figure 56 for product 20-304 in April, the average probability is 64 percent. The average probability (64) is then multiplied by the total demand

Product 20-304

Customer	Quantity	Project #	Significance	Timing	% Probability
Customer MNO	1	135	1	April	100%
Customer DEF	1	125	3	April	90%
Customer GHI	2	130	2	April	60%
Customer JKL	3	132	2	April	40%
Customer ABC	2	122	1	April	30%

9	64%
Total Quantity	**Average Percentage**

Demand Based on Average Probability	5.76
(Total Quantity × Average Percentage)	

Customer	Quantity	Project #	Significance	Timing	% Probability
Customer MNO	2	135	1	May	100%
Customer DEF	3	125	1	May	70%
Customer JKL	3	132	3	May	50%
Customer ABC	2	122	1	May	20%
Customer GHI	2	130	2	May	15%

12	51%
Total Quantity	**Average Percentage**

Demand Based on Average Probability	6.12
(Total Quantity × Average Percentage)	

FIGURE 56   Example of Calculating Demand Volume by Probability

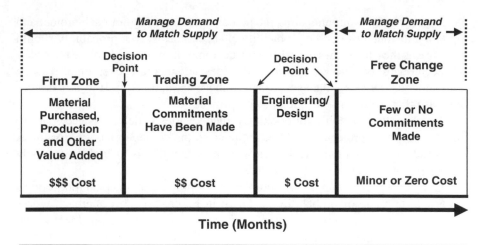

FIGURE 57 Example of Decision Points for Project-Based Business

potential (9) to determine the demand volume for each time period. The demand based on average probability in April is 5.76 units.

The result of this calculation should not be blindly accepted, however. This method for determining demand volume works well for the longer term planning horizon. It creates some risk in the time periods when resources must be committed to support that demand. To manage this risk, companies use decision points to determine whether or not to include the product in the demand plan. Use of decision points for project-based demand works as follows.

Decision points are established for the time point where engineering design is required, materials must be purchased, and production must begin, as shown in Figure 57. Rather than determine demand volume based on an average of probability, a go/no-go decision is made on a case-by-case basis (regardless of probability) as to whether the demand is in or out of the demand plan. The significance of the project to the organization often is a consideration when deciding which demand to include in the plan (see Figure 56).

When demand is excluded from the demand plan, this decision must be documented in the database. Communications are also needed with the customer so that the customer understands that its desired delivery date may not be met unless an order or specific engineering specifications are received by the decision point dates.

Decision points are also used by the sales organization to gain greater commitment from customers about their buying intentions. It is not unusual for the salesperson to create an equation for customers: If we receive your order by one of the time fence dates (such as when material must be purchased), we can give you a lead time of 12 weeks. Otherwise, the lead time may be up to 20 weeks. Companies also may increase the price of the product when customers book orders after the optimal lead time. The price increase covers higher costs associated with expediting procured material and additional resources required to design, build, and deliver the product to the customer's requested delivery date.

Use of decision points makes visible the risk involved with the demand. When the risk is known, it causes two courses of action. First, it stimulates actions by the sales organization to become more certain of the customers' buying intentions. Second, it causes the demand organization leaders to overtly consider the cost versus customer service risks in including or excluding demand from the plan. Decisions are made with forethought, rather than in a casual or cavalier manner.

If the demand organization decides to keep the demand for a low-probability project in the plan, it accepts the risk for any value that is added to the product, whether it is design, the purchase of materials, or production. If the order is not received, the demand organization is responsible for either generating another sale for the product or for inventory and other costs that are incurred. Discussions, therefore, at the demand review and consensus meeting revolve around risk:

- What will be the cost if we do not receive the order and we keep the demand in the plan?
- What will be the customer's reaction to a longer lead time if we decide to exclude the customer's demand from the demand plan?
- What are competitors' lead times compared to ours?

The same principles on decision points presented in Chapter 7 apply to managing and prioritizing demand for project-based business. In the time zones where value is being added to the product, demand is managed to match supply. In the time zone where little or no value is being added to the product, supply is managed to match demand (see Figure 57).

Once a decision is made to either include or exclude projects from the demand plan, risk management does not stop at that point. Every month, a risk assessment should be performed and the findings reviewed at the monthly demand consensus review. Some companies call this a risk and opportunity review. In essence, an opportunity is a project that was not included in the plan but still has a reasonable chance of the sale being booked. A risk is a project that is included in the plan but there is a reasonable chance that the project will be canceled, delayed, or the sale will be lost to a competitor.

Different demand scenarios are developed to determine the impact of deleting some projects from the plan and adding others to the plan. The factors that should be considered in these scenarios include engineering resources, supply constraints, and the financial impact of purchasing raw materials in advance of orders.

Another consideration when managing uncertainty, whether it involves high- or low-volume products, products with highly variable demand, or project-based demand, is how the planning of specific products can be simplified. Simplification often minimizes or negates inherent uncertainty. It may not be possible to predict demand with a high degree of accuracy at the item, or SKU, level, for example, but it may be possible to predict with a high degree of accuracy the demand for the entire product line or family. The question be-comes: When must we predict the item-level demand and communicate it to the supply organization?

Companies that employ lean manufacturing techniques compress procure-ment and manufacturing lead times. Shorter lead times help to reduce uncertainty about demand and improve the demand plan accuracy. Demand can be planned at an aggregate, or family, level without making a commitment to the product mix until later in time when there is greater certainty about the specific items that will be ordered. This is sometimes referred to as "postponement." Figure 58 illustrates this concept.

Let's say, for example, that a product family consists of five items. You sell 1,000 units per month of a product family. The number of specific items sold each month varies, however. Customers typically do not communicate their item-level purchase schedule until three weeks before they expect delivery. If your procurement and manufacturing process is three weeks or less, it is not necessary to communicate an item-level demand plan. Aggregate-level plans are almost always more accurate than detail-level plans. (Note: A forecast of product option mix may be required to ensure that raw materials are available to be configured to specific finished product SKUs. Forecasting the option mix, however, will be considerably more accurate than attempting to forecast the final SKU configurations.)

When manufacturing and procurement lead times are short, as in the case just described, the aggregate demand plan can be used to communicate total volume, and the specific items can be made to order. This eliminates the uncertainty of the item- or detail-level demand, as long as the family demand plan is accurate. No amount of adjustment at the detail level can make up for an error at the aggregate level.

Many companies do not have the luxury of short procurement and manufac-turing lead times. In these cases, decision points can be used to determine what level of detailed information needs to be communicated to the supply organi-zation and when. Sometimes, subfamily information can be communicated to

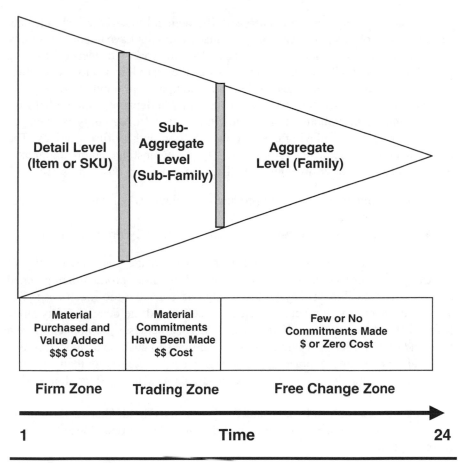

FIGURE 58 An Approach for Determining What Level of Detail to Plan

enable procurement, and the item-level information can be communicated at the point in time when production must begin (see Figure 58).

Planning demand at the aggregate level — and determining the detail-level demand plan at a later time when there are fewer uncertainties — is called risk pooling. This same approach can be used when planning the demand for products that are sold and distributed worldwide. A worldwide demand plan can be developed. Later on, as the demand by country becomes more certain, a country-specific demand plan can be communicated to facilitate supply planning at specific manufacturing and distribution locations.[41]

For this type of risk pooling to succeed, decision points need to be defined around manufacturing and transportation lead times for each manufacturing plant so that it is clear when country-specific demand must be communicated. The advantage of this planning strategy is that you do not have to commit supply resources until it is absolutely necessary. This approach to decision making provides greater flexibility in responding when there are lower sales than anticipated in one country and higher sales than anticipated in another country.

Even with the best efforts to reduce uncertainty in demand, there will always be some uncertainty about demand. How this residual uncertainty is managed becomes critical to achieving customer satisfaction and profit objectives. The most commonly used tactics for creating a buffer against demand being greater than planned are shown in Figure 59. The two most obvious tactics are:

- Carry inventory to ensure product is available when demand is greater than planned
- Vary customer lead times to ensure that delivery promises are met

Each of these tactics has advantages and disadvantages, as shown in Figure 59. Carrying safety stock as a hedge against selling more product than planned is not always feasible; it may be too costly and consume too much cash. The amount of inventory that accrues can increase beyond the desired safety stock level when less product is sold than planned. This increases the impact on cash flow and profitability. Varying customer lead times to cushion against accuracy errors also is not always practical. Customers may choose to buy their products from a competitor that has the product available to sell or offers shorter lead times.

Creating flexible production and design capacity is another tactic used to buffer against demand uncertainties and demand plan errors. Capacity can be flexed in two ways:

1. Sufficient capacity is available internally to cover peaks in demand.
2. Production and design work are outsourced to suppliers.

Reserving capacity in anticipation of demand is an effective tactic for products for which demand is sporadic in nature and difficult to predict, like replacement and spare parts. The upside to having sufficient capacity available to cover peak demand is higher levels of customer service and increased sales. Customer needs are fulfilled within their expected lead times. The downside to this tactic is that some capacity (equipment and people) will be idle when sufficient demand does not materialize to operate at full capacity. This results in higher operating costs.

Managing uncertainty always involves managing cost and risk. The decisions on how to manage risk will impact a company's financial performance. Cash flow, profitability, and sales revenues are at stake. Consequently, the decisions

Tactic	Pros	Cons
Vary customer lead time	Gives you time to produce without increasing cash outlays and resource outlays.	Customers may prefer competitors' shorter lead times and better product availability.
Carry inventory	More responsive to customers' delivery requirements.	Reduces cash flow and profitability. Can accumulate obsolete inventory.
Shorten process cycle times (e.g., order entry, engineering, material procurement, production, and shipping)	Have more time to reduce the uncertainty of demand without risking significant company resources. Can wait until later in the supply process to communicate a detailed demand plan.	Requires commitment from other functions within the company to reduce cycle times.
Flex design and manufacturing capacity	Sufficient capacity is available to accommodate peaks in demand, resulting in order fulfillment that meets customers' delivery expectations.	Capacity can go unused at times and/or arrangements must be made to outsource the work, which creates a more complicated supply chain.
Standardize and rationalize product lines	Greater commonality of components within product lines enables to plan at the aggregate level and delay the item-level demand plan until later in the supply process. Standardization can result in fewer products being offered, which reduces the number of products that must be planned.	Product offerings can be changed or discontinued; customers may choose to buy from a competitor with a more complete product offering.

FIGURE 59 Tactics for Managing Uncertainty of Demand

on risk management tactics should be made at the senior management level of the company. All too often, these decisions are made ad hoc by supply planners, distribution planners, and shipping and logistics people. The decisions on how to manage risk should be made in the integrated business review as part of a company's sales and operations planning process. This review involves all of the senior leaders in a company and is the subject of Chapter 14 on integration.

The degree of demand uncertainty is never static; it changes over time. As a result, the tactics used to manage uncertainty must change over time. Performance measurements are a useful indicator of uncertainty. When the demand plan accuracy for a product line is continually low, for example, it is a signal that more effort needs to be expended in creating greater certainty about the demand for that product line. It also is a signal to review the tactics for managing uncertainty and risk. Performance measurements are the subject of the next chapter.

SUMMARY OF BEST PRACTICES
FOR MANAGING UNCERTAINTY

1. The inevitability of uncertainty in demand is recognized and a process is in place for managing uncertainty.
2. Uncertainties are identified and actions are taken to reduce the uncertainty by acquiring additional information and clarifying existing information about demand.
3. As a way to manage uncertainty, scenarios are developed to determine demand plan options based on different marketing and sales tactics. The scenarios are used for contingency planning.
4. Planning strategies are developed for specific product lines based on demand volume versus demand variability.
5. Planning strategies consider what level of product detail must be communicated to the supply organization, recognizing the advantages of communicating detailed item-level demand as late as possible.
6. Product lines are rationalized and simplified whenever possible.
7. Fulfillment strategies are developed for every major product line. The strategies considered include make to order, assemble to order, and make to stock.
8. It is recognized that products with highly variable demand patterns typically are not forecasted accurately using time series statistical forecasting methods and require greater time and attention from the sales, marketing, and product/brand organizations in planning the demand.
9. Project-based businesses utilize a planning methodology that focuses on communicating and updating critical information about each project or opportunity. The information communicated by the sales organization includes product volume, when the order is expected to be booked and delivery is expected, and the probability of receiving the order.
10. For project-based business, a structured methodology is used to determine what products are included and excluded from the demand plan. The methodology includes go/no-go decisions at critical decision points.

11. Planning strategies are developed to pool risk and to ensure that decisions are not made until absolutely necessary to provide greater demand and supply flexibility.

12. Tactics are defined for buffering against uncertainty. These tactics include carrying safety inventory, varying customer lead time, and creating flexible production and design capacity.

13. It is recognized that managing uncertainty involves managing cost and risk. The decisions on how to best manage risk are made at the senior management level.

QUESTIONS

1. How would you determine the degree of uncertainty in demand for every product line?

2. What questions would you ask about the assumptions underlying the demand plan to determine the degree of certainty of the plan?

3. What is the value of scenario planning when demand is uncertain?

4. What are the advantages of simplifying product lines?

5. What questions should be asked and answered when rationalizing whether products should continue to be offered?

6. How would you approach planning demand for a project-based business?

7. What information should be included in a project or opportunity database to help better plan demand?

8. What calculation is used to determine the volume of demand when the probability of projects materializing varies?

9. How are decision points used in planning demand for project-based business?

10. What tactics can be used to buffer against demand uncertainty?

11. Who in the organization should make the decision on how to best manage the risk caused by demand uncertainty?

PERFORMANCE MEASUREMENTS

Some people believe that measuring demand plan accuracy is an exercise in futility. After all, demand plans are always wrong. So what is gained by measuring demand plan accuracy?

Those who most frequently express this sentiment have seen demand plan accuracy measurements used in a punitive way. Demand planners and demand managers are frequently criticized for demand plan errors. They take heat from the supply organization, sales and marketing managers, finance executives, and, all too often, the general manager or president.

Case in point: A client wanted to hire a demand manager from within the company. The management team believed it was important for the demand manager to understand the company's business, markets, customers, and products as well as to know the sales and marketing people. No one applied for the position. In response to the lack of applicants, the vice-president of sales and marketing worked with the human resources director to identify four candidates from within the company. All four candidates declined the offer.

One candidate most eloquently explained why he was not interested in the position: "Why would I want to take a job where every month I am criticized at the sales and operations planning meeting because the demand plan is wrong? It is embarrassing to be criticized by senior management, especially when you had little to do with creating the inaccuracy in the first place. The sales and marketing people should be called on the carpet. They're the ones who wait until the last minute to provide input for the demand plan, if they provide any at all. They're the ones who are late with their marketing programs or don't sell what they said they were going to sell. I like working for this company. Why should I jeopardize my career here by taking a position that is just a scapegoat for other people's nonperformance?"

The fellow hit the nail on the head. Focusing on the demand planner or demand manager alone as responsible for errors in the demand plan is unproductive. Demand plan accuracy, in actuality, is an indicator of the competence of the sales and marketing organization. It demonstrates how well the marketing, sales, and product/brand organizations plan, communicate, and execute. Blaming the demand manager for inaccuracies will do little to improve the marketing, sales, and product/brand management efforts. It also will not improve planning and execution by these organizations.

Remember, demand management does not consist solely of planning demand. It also involves influencing, communicating, managing, and prioritizing demand. The ultimate aim of demand management is to manage the level, timing, and composition of demand to achieve the company's goals in the most profitable manner. Performance measurements, therefore, should focus on the effectiveness of the demand management process, not just demand plan accuracy. What to measure and how to utilize the measurements to improve performance are the subjects of this chapter.

To truly understand the effectiveness of the demand management process, a series of performance metrics is needed. Figure 60 is one example of a performance metric dashboard. Measurements of the overall performance of the demand management process, like the ones shown in Figure 60, are typically addressed at the demand consensus review meeting.

The measurements on the left-hand side of Figure 60 address total demand plan accuracy, at the volume level and sales revenue level. Volume accuracy is shown for total demand as well as for each brand and sales region. Sales revenue accuracy is reported for total sales revenue as well as for each sales region.

The −3, −2, −1 indicate the performance three months ago, two months ago, and last month, respectively. A traffic signal approach is an effective way to display the metrics. Green means that the performance meets or exceeds the performance goal. Yellow warns that performance is less than the established goal. Red indicates that performance is significantly less than the standard goal and action is needed to rectify performance.

The criteria for green, yellow, and red designations for each metric are agreed upon by sales, marketing, and product/brand managers. Once a performance target is consistently achieved, the target should be changed to spur further improvement. This is a best practice.

In some companies, when the plan accuracy for a sales territory is in the red for three months in a row, that territory's performance becomes an agenda item

Demand Plan Accuracy — Unit Volume	-3	-2	-1
Total Demand Plan	70%	80%	90%
Brand A	95%	90%	92%
Brand B	75%	85%	90%
Brand C	65%	72%	74%
Brand D	80%	85%	90%

Demand Plan Accuracy — Sales Revenue	-3	-2	-1
Total Sales Revenue	85%	90%	95%
Sales Revenue Region A	92%	94%	98%
Sales Revenue Region B	98%	99%	99%
Sales Revenue Region C	94%	98%	98%

Demand Plan Accuracy — Unit Volume	-3	-2	-1
Unit Accuracy — Region A	85%	90%	95%
Unit Accuracy — Region B	92%	94%	98%
Unit Accuracy — Region C	98%	99%	99%

Metric	Actual	Strategic Goal
Total Market Share	48%	55%
Unit Volume	1,500,250	2,000,000
Number of Customers	10,000	12,000
Retained Customers	75%	90%
Lost Customers	1,000	200
New Customers	1,000	1,500
Unit Cost per Customer	$375	$420
Margin per Customer	50%	60%
Market Expense per Customer	$50	$40
Customer Complaints	350	300
On-Time Delivery	90%	98%
Return on Sales	40%	60%
Days of Inventory	10	10
Inventory Investment	$300,000	$300,000
Percent Profit Margin	58%	62%

Performance Issues for Discussion or Decision:

LEGEND: RED   YELLOW   GREEN

FIGURE 60   Overall Performance Measurement Dashboard

for the demand consensus review meeting. The territory sales manager explains the reasons for the inaccuracies and the actions being taken to improve performance. Some companies also require the brand manager to make the same kind of presentation when the demand plan accuracy for a brand is in the red for three months in a row.

This approach serves two purposes. First, it reinforces that the sales, marketing, and product/brand organizations are accountable for demand plan accuracy. Second, and just as important, it brings about a better understanding of sales and marketing conditions that prevent the company from executing its plans.

When the demand plan is inaccurate, the first course of action is to review the assumptions upon which the demand plan was based. This is a best practice. After all, the numbers in the plan are not wrong; the assumptions upon which the demand plan was based are the real culprit for the errors. Use of a formal method for documenting and updating assumptions, as discussed in Chapter 8, facilitates measuring the accuracy of assumptions. Assumption accuracy should be measured each month, as shown in Figure 61. This, too, is a best practice.

When assumptions are inaccurate, certain questions need to be asked and answered. These questions include:

- Is there a more accurate source of information upon which to base the assumption?
- Was bias involved in determining this assumption?
- What did we *not* consider in defining the assumptions that should be taken into account?
- What assumptions were neglected altogether and should be considered for the next demand plan?

It takes time, attention, and discipline to determine why demand plans are inaccurate each month. This is time well spent, however. Ascertaining why the demand plan was inaccurate and which assumptions were wrong has a primary benefit. It improves the understanding of the markets, customers, competitors, internal sales and marketing capability, and other factors that influence demand. With better understanding comes better judgment as to the demand plan, and demand plan accuracy increases over time.

Case in point: A client company's total demand plan accuracy was consistently around 70 to 75 percent. For those sales regions where accuracy was less than 80 percent, the vice-president of sales called the regional sales managers and told each that their region's performance was on the agenda for the upcoming demand consensus review meeting. The sales managers were asked to explain why their regions had not executed the demand plan.

The reasons varied. Some managers reported delays in the timing of customer orders. Other managers explained that they lost orders to competitors for two reasons: price and the company's poor on-time delivery record. One manager candidly admitted that he had spent very little time developing input into the demand plan and had not engaged his salespeople in the process.

The vice-president of sales continued to require the sales managers to make formal presentations at the demand consensus review meeting whenever they missed the plan target three months in a row. Some interesting findings emerged from this process:

- Gaps in the sales organization's knowledge about its customers and their buying intentions
- Bias, particularly overoptimism
- Difficulty in accurately pinpointing the timing of orders
- The practice of requesting more product than was really needed in anticipation of supply shortages
- The influence of pricing tactics on demand

The sales managers were tasked with bringing more credible information and better judgment to the demand planning process. To develop more credible information, the sales managers realized that their salespeople had to become more engaged with their customers. They needed to better identify who the economic buyers, technical buyers, and decision makers were in their customers' buying process.[42] They also needed more frequent communication with customers to gain earlier knowledge of when customers' buying intentions were changing.

As one sales manager observed, "We're becoming less transaction oriented and more focused on understanding the longer term needs and objectives of our customers. This process is really causing us to do our jobs better." Within four months, this company improved its total demand plan accuracy at the unit volume level to consistently 90 percent or higher.

Demand plan accuracy is one view of the effectiveness of a demand management process. The metrics on the right-hand side of Figure 60 provide another view. These metrics address how well the demand organization is achieving the company's strategic goals in the most profitable manner. Remember that the goal of demand management is not revenue growth alone, but *profitable* growth.[43] The strategic metrics, at a minimum, include:

- Market share
- Customer retention and new customer acquisition
- Cost and profit per customer

Assumption Management

Product Family: Date:	Degree of Control		Last Period	This Period	Period 3	Period 6	Period 12	Period 15	Period 18
Marketing Assumptions									
Population of users	Some	Assumed	20,000	20,000	20,000	22,000	25,000	28,000	32,000
		Actual	20,000						
Economic trend	None	Assumed	-0.5%	-0.5%	-1.0%	0.0%	0.0%	1.0%	2.0%
		Actual	-1.00%						
Volume from new products	Full	Assumed	10,000	8,000	8,000	12,000	15,000	10,000	8,000
		Actual	6,000						
Revenue from new products	Full	Assumed	$500,000	$400,000	$400,000	$600,000	$750,000	$1,000,000	$400,000
		Actual	$300,000						
Rate of new product introductions	Full	Assumed	1			1			
		Actual	1						
Lift from planned promotions	Full	Assumed	8,000	4,000	2,000	8,000	10,000		
		Actual	6,000						
Competitor activity	None	Assumed	Price discounts	Price discounts	Price discounts	New product & promotions	Promotion		
		Actual	Price discounts						
Market price movement	Some	Assumed	-5%	-0.25%	-3%	-5%	-5%	0%	0%
		Actual	-0.25%						
Market share	Full	Assumed	25%	25%	25%	27%	27%	30%	30%
		Actual	21%						
Profit	Full	Assumed	30%	30%	30%	33%	33%	33%	33%
		Actual	28%						

Sales Assumptions

			$200,000	$250,000	$75,000	$250,000	$300,000	$100,000	$50,000
Revenue from new customers	Full	Assured	$200,000	$250,000	$75,000	$250,000	$300,000	$100,000	$50,000
		Actual	$125,000						
Volume from new customers	Full	Assumed	400	500	150	500	600	200	10
		Actual	250						
Customer retention rate	Full	Assumed	98%	98%	98%	95%	95%	98%	98%
		Actual	95%						
Volume from new products	Full	Assumed	6,000	9,000	10,000	14,000	15,000	12,000	10,000
		Actual	6,000						
Changes in buying patterns	Some	Assumed	None	Wait for new products	Wait for new products	Increased buying	Increased buying	Freer spending	Freer spending
		Actua	Delaying purchases						
Price discounts	Full	Assured	5%	5%	5%	0%	0%	0%	5%
		Actua	5%						

Product/Brand Management Assumptions

			$200,000	$250,000	$75,000	$250,000	$300,000	$100,000	$50,000
New product launches	Full	Assumed	1			1			
		Actual	1						
Launch delays	Full	Assumed	0	0	0	0	0	0	0
		Actual	0						
New product sales volumes	Full	Assumed	10,000	8,000	8,000	12,000	15,000	10,000	8,000
		Actual	6,000						
New product samples for sales	Full	Assumed	0	0	1,000	0	0	0	0
		Actual	0						

☐ Inaccurate Assumption   ▨ Disagreement on Assumption

FIGURE 61   Assumption Accuracy Measurement Example (Copyright Oliver Wight International)

- Customer satisfaction as measured by on-time delivery and the number of customer complaints
- Return on sales
- Inventory metrics, such as number of turns, days/weeks on hand, and dollar investment
- Overall profit margin

Comparing the current performance to the strategic goal shows gaps in meeting the strategic objectives. When there are gaps, it should trigger discussion about why the strategic goal is not being met — and what can be done about it. Sometimes, the required actions revolve around improving execution. Frequently, the gaps are caused by not being in sync with market and customer needs.[44] Other times, the strategic objectives themselves need to be reviewed to determine whether they are still feasible or whether they need to be revised given the current market situation.

Another useful measurement approach is to correlate demand plan accuracy with some of the metrics above. Figure 62 shows an example of comparing demand plan accuracy to inventory turns per month. The correlation of demand

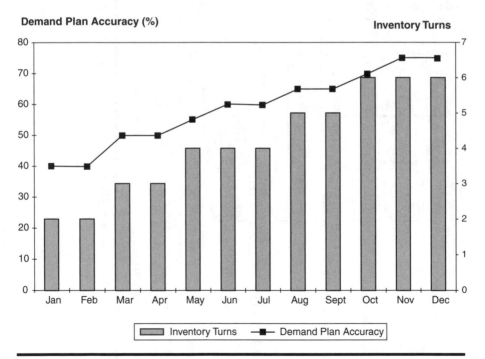

FIGURE 62   Correlation of Demand Plan Accuracy to Inventory Turns

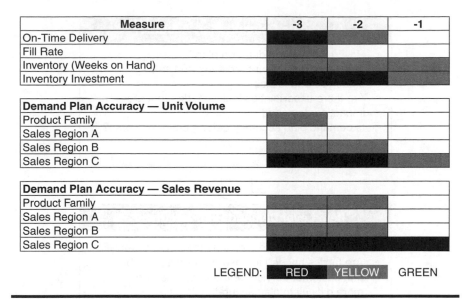

Measure	-3	-2	-1
On-Time Delivery			
Fill Rate			
Inventory (Weeks on Hand)			
Inventory Investment			

Demand Plan Accuracy — Unit Volume			
Product Family			
Sales Region A			
Sales Region B			
Sales Region C			

Demand Plan Accuracy — Sales Revenue			
Product Family			
Sales Region A			
Sales Region B			
Sales Region C			

LEGEND: RED   YELLOW   GREEN

FIGURE 63   Product Family Performance Measurements

plan accuracy with other metrics, particularly financial-related measurements, shows the value of an accurate demand plan and effective demand management process. It enables people to understand how their efforts to develop an effective demand management process contribute to the overall performance of the company. They can see that the time and attention spent on improving the demand management process are worthwhile.

So far, we have focused on measuring the performance of the overall demand management process. Performance measurements by product family are also needed and are a best practice. Figure 63 illustrates product family measures. In addition to demand plan accuracy, other pertinent product family measures include:

■ Inventory metrics, like inventory investment and number of days or weeks on hand

■ Customer-service-related measurements, like on-time delivery and fill rate

These measures are usually included on a dashboard that shows a graphic of the demand plan and a summary of assumptions (see Figure 19 in Chapter 5).

There are three types of product-related plan accuracy measurements: aggregate accuracy, item accuracy, and mix accuracy. The primary purpose of these measurements is to determine how well the demand plan was executed. To put

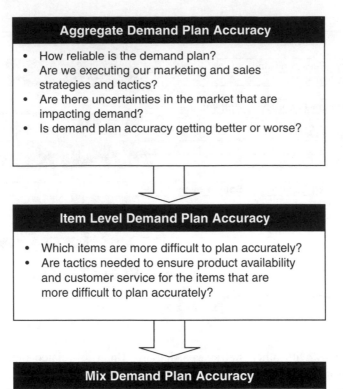

Aggregate Demand Plan Accuracy

- How reliable is the demand plan?
- Are we executing our marketing and sales strategies and tactics?
- Are there uncertainties in the market that are impacting demand?
- Is demand plan accuracy getting better or worse?

Item Level Demand Plan Accuracy

- Which items are more difficult to plan accurately?
- Are tactics needed to ensure product availability and customer service for the items that are more difficult to plan accurately?

Mix Demand Plan Accuracy

- Are we planning the right mix of product demand?
- What changes in mix demand are occurring?
- Do these changes fit with our product portfolio strategy and tactics?

FIGURE 64 Summary of the Reasons for Aggregate, Item, and Mix Measures

it another way: How well did we do what we said we were going to do? Making these measurements routinely, at least monthly, shows whether (1) greater time and attention are needed to improve the sales and marketing effort and (2) certain products have a high enough level of uncertainty and inaccuracy to require special tactics to ensure adequate customer service.

Each of these three measurements has a specific purpose (see Figure 64). The measurements should be made for both unit volume and sales revenue at both the aggregate and item level.

How to mathematically calculate these measurements is shown in Figure 65. Note that the measurements can be calculated as error, percent error, and percent

		Month		
Aggregate		-3	-2	-1
Family 1	Plan	238	221	245
	Actual	232	206	219
	Error	-6	-15	-26
	Error %	-3	-7	-11
	Accuracy %	97	93	89
Items				
Item 1	Plan	55	60	65
	Actual	49	48	52
	Error	-6	-12	-13
	Error %	-11	-20	-20
	Accuracy %	89	80	80
Item 2	Plan	102	90	98
	Actual	93	89	91
	Error	-9	-1	-7
	Error %	-9	-1	-7
	Accuracy %	91	99	93
Item 3	Plan	15	18	22
	Actual	24	16	19
	Error	9	-2	-3
	Error %	60	-11	-14
	Accuracy %	40	89	86
Item 4	Plan	56	48	52
	Actual	61	50	53
	Error	5	2	1
	Error %	9	4	2
	Accuracy %	91	96	98
Item 5	Plan	10	5	8
	Actual	5	3	4
	Error	-5	-2	-4
	Error %	-50	-40	-50
	Accuracy %	50	60	50
Mix	Sum of Absolute Deviations	34	19	28

Error Calculation:
= +Actual − Plan

Error % Calculation:
= (+Actual − Plan)/Plan
Note: Express the result as a percentage

Accuracy % Calculation:
100 − ABS(Error%)
Note: ABS means absolute value

Sum of Absolute Deviations Calculation:
For all items, add the absolute value of variances between the forecast and actual

FIGURE 65 Demand Plan Accuracy Calculations — Aggregate and Item

accuracy. The error and percent error measurements show whether the error was over (+) or under (−) the plan. The percent accuracy measurement does not show whether actual demand was over or under the plan.

The measure of demand plan accuracy at the aggregate level helps to answer several questions:

- Is the demand plan reliable?
- Are there uncertain market conditions that make it difficult to predict aggregate demand?
- Is the demand plan accuracy getting better or worse?

		Month					
		-6	-5	-4	-3	-2	-1
Item 3	Plan	9	12	14	15	18	22
	Actual	11	7	9	24	16	19
	Error	2	-5	-5	9	-2	-3
	Error %	22	-42	-36	60	-11	-14
	Accuracy %	78	58	64	40	89	86

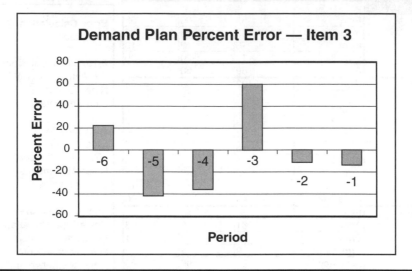

FIGURE 66   Display of Item Accuracy (Percent Error) Over Six Months

To better understand why the demand plan is inaccurate at the aggregate level, it is necessary to know which items within the family are more difficult to plan accurately. Item-level accuracy should be measured at least monthly for every product family, as, ultimately, improvements in the demand plan accuracy must be made at the individual item level. Many companies monitor demand plan accuracy at the item level every week to find any significant errors early. How to calculate item-level accuracy is shown in Figure 65.

A method of charting the percent error over time for an item is displayed in Figure 66. This presentation allows for identifying bias and seeing improvement over time, beginning with six months ago (–6) through last month (–1).

To avoid having to review the accuracy measurement for all items (a time-consuming and laborious process), many companies generate an exception report. The exception report lists those items that did not meet the accuracy target. Items that are consistently below the accuracy target require tactics to ensure product availability, customer service, and profitability.

It is possible for the aggregate plan accuracy to be within the tolerance or goal yet the organization to still struggle with demand plan errors. The product mix is the problem. Measuring only aggregate plan accuracy gives a false sense of assurance that the demand management process is effective. This is because the aggregate accuracy measurement is an arithmetic comparison of the total demand versus the total items planned. For some of the items, there will have been more demand than planned. This is frequently called being "over" the plan. For other items, there will be less demand than planned. This is typically called being "under" the plan.

In summing the actual demand to determine aggregate demand accuracy, the "overs and unders" tend to cancel each other out. The demand plan, as a result, may appear very accurate when, in fact, there are considerable deviations at the item level. These deviations may or may not be significant for financial planning, but the inaccuracies certainly cause problems for the supply organization.

Figure 67 illustrates the problem. If the sum of deviations is used to calculate demand plan accuracy, it appears that there was a variance of 6 units in the

Items		Month -3	Deviation	Absolute Deviation
Item 1	Plan	55	-6	6
	Actual	49		
Item 2	Plan	102	-9	9
	Actual	93		
Item 3	Plan	15	9	9
	Actual	24		
Item 4	Plan	56	5	5
	Actual	61		
Item 5	Plan	10	-5	5
	Actual	5		
Mix		Sum	-6	34

Aggregate	Plan	238
	Actual	232
Mix Percent Error		14.3
Mix Percent Accuracy		85.7

Sum of Absolute Deviations Calculation:
For all items, add the absolute value of the variances between the forecast and actual

Mix Percent Error Calculation:
Sum of Absolute Deviations/Aggregate Plan * 100
Note: Express as a percentage

Mix Percent Accuracy Calculation:
100 – ABS(Mix Percent Error)
Note: Express as a percentage

FIGURE 67   Product Mix Accuracy Calculation

aggregate demand plan. This is because the pluses and minuses (overs and unders) cancel each other out. In reality, there was a variance of 34 units in the demand plan for individual items, as the sum of absolute deviations calculation shows. The sum of absolute deviations ignores the pluses and minuses in making the calculation to determine the mix accuracy.

The mix accuracy measure indicates the magnitude of the accuracy errors in the demand plan at the item level. Understanding the magnitude of the error guides the demand organization as to where to focus its time and attention in improving the demand plan accuracy. It also causes the marketing and product/brand organizations to review the product mix strategy and tactics.

Demand plan errors are a reality. The demand plan is based on the best knowledge currently available about efforts to generate demand and market conditions that influence demand. This knowledge will never be perfect, however. There almost always will be variation in actual customer demand, in either product quantity, timing of orders, or both.

Given this reality, tactics are needed to deal with these variations. As a rule, the greater the demand plan error, the greater the amount of tactics needed to manage the impact of the inaccuracy (see Figure 68).[45] Most companies utilize a combination of the following tactics to dampen the impact of demand plan errors:

- Carry a buffer inventory, or safety stock
- Vary delivery lead time
- Maintain the ability to flex capacity
- Manage and prioritize demand

FIGURE 68   Scope of Tactics Required for Demand Plan Inaccuracies (Copyright Oliver Wight International)

The purpose of these tactics is to ensure customer satisfaction and protect profit margins as much as possible. The specific tactics used should not be left to chance or be casually determined by the shipping clerk or production scheduler. The tactics have too much impact on cost, resource requirements, customer service, and financial performance for casual decision making.

The tactics should be agreed upon through a managed process. This is a best practice. The managed process many companies utilize is the integrated management review as part of the sales and operations planning process, which will be the subject of Chapter 14.

A common question about measuring demand plan accuracy is when accuracy should be measured. In theory, demand plan accuracy would be 100 percent if the plan were updated continuously as actual customer orders are received. Obviously, this is impractical and adds little value.

The objective of demand planning is to provide sufficient information in sufficient detail in sufficient time to economically respond to the demand. By measuring demand plan accuracy at key decision points, knowledge is gained about the degree of demand uncertainty at these critical points in time. This knowledge, in turn, should trigger efforts to reduce the uncertainty of demand and improve demand plan accuracy.

Case in point: A pharmaceutical company's products were based upon biological material that had procurement lead times averaging six months or longer. The cost of purchasing this material was millions of dollars. Thus, the company wanted as accurate a demand plan as possible at the point in time when purchasing commitments for the biological material were required. The company measured aggregate demand plan accuracy at the point in time when material procurement commitments were made (see Figure 69). Initially, the aggregate demand plan accuracy at this critical point was less than 50 percent. Over two years of time and effort, the plan accuracy improved to 90 percent.

As discussed in the last chapter, one purpose of lean manufacturing techniques is to reduce the cycle times for manufacturing and procurement. As these times shorten, the time zones can be compressed without sacrificing the ability to economically respond to changes in demand in sufficient time to meet customer delivery expectations. Compression of the time zones also reduces the need to plan demand accurately at the item level as far out in the future. The item-level demand can be communicated later when additional, more accurate information is available. Reducing cycle times to improve responsiveness and to facilitate demand plan accuracy is a best practice.

A multitude of accuracy measures can be made. The question is which measures will provide the most insight to improve the effectiveness of the demand management process. Each measurement should have a specific purpose and use, as the measures described above do. Care should be taken not to

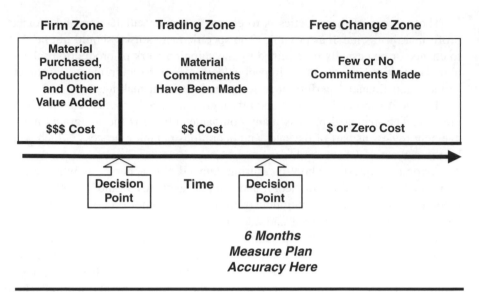

FIGURE 69   Demand Plan Accuracy Measurements at Key Points in Time (Copyright Oliver Wight International)

overwhelm the demand management process with too many measurements that do not provide significant insight.

Two other accuracy measures are commonly used to gain greater insight on the reliability of the demand plan. One is the measurement of the overall quality of the demand plan. The other is plan accuracy by product classification. These measurements work as follows.

The quality measurement is based on the accuracy at the item level. A chart can be created to show the number of items that were over and under the demand plan accuracy objective — and the degree of the error (see Figure 70).

This measurement reveals bias. If the distribution of the forecast errors is left or right of zero, there is bias in the demand plan. An unbiased demand plan shows errors centered closely around zero.

By monitoring the quality measurement month to month, it is easy to see if demand plan accuracy is getting better or worse. As the overall accuracy of the demand plan improves, the distribution of the errors will move closer to zero. The percentage of the items closer to zero will also increase.

When products are consistently over or under plan, bias exists. The challenge is to determine why the demand plan is biased. Sometimes the reason for the bias is purely judgment. Other times, bias is caused by wanting to avoid delivering bad news. Bias can also be caused by the desire to manipulate the internal

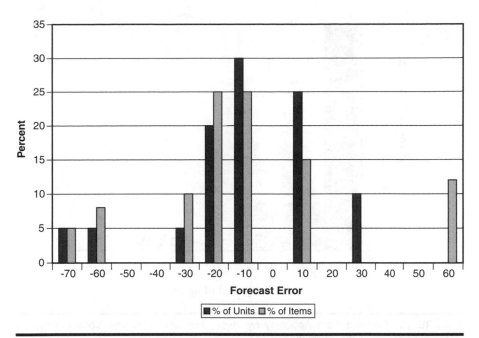

FIGURE 70 Demand Plan Quality Measurement (Courtesy of Demand Solutions of Demand Management, Inc.)

reward system, particularly when the reward system is based on exceeding the demand plan. Whatever the cause, bias must be rooted out of the demand plan.

Operating with a biased demand plan always causes resource problems. Either there will be too much resource (capacity, labor, and raw materials) for the demand, causing higher costs, or there will be insufficient resources to fulfill the demand, causing missed deliveries, lost revenue, and poor customer service.

Measuring accuracy at a product classification level provides a different viewpoint. It shows how effectively demand is being planned and managed for a company's most significant products. Products are classified, using Pareto analysis techniques, into high, medium, and low sales revenue categories. High-revenue products are considered A items, medium-revenue products B items, and low-revenue products C items.

Demand plan accuracy is measured for each classification, as shown in Figure 71. Hence the term ABC demand plan accuracy measurement. The greatest time and attention should be spent on improving the demand management techniques and plan accuracy for high sales revenue products and/or high-margin products — those 15 to 20 percent of products that account for approximately 80 percent of the sales revenue. This does not mean that the items in the

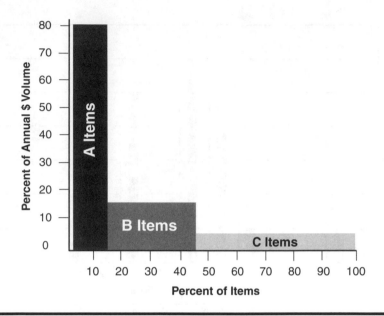

FIGURE 71   Demand Plan Accuracy by High-, Medium-, and Low-Volume Products (Copyright Oliver Wight International)

B and C categories can be ignored. The B and C items should be reviewed monthly to determine the reasons for demand plan errors and to develop appropriate tactics to deal with demand plan errors at the item level.

Two of the most frequently asked questions are: What should our demand plan accuracy be? Is there an industry standard for demand plan accuracy? Unfortunately, the answer to the first question is not simple, and there is no industry standard for demand plan accuracy.

Demand plan accuracy depends on the type of product, its volume, and demand variability, as well as the degree of uncertainty in the marketplace. As a result, there is no best practice standard for demand plan accuracy. The lack of a standard does not mean that demand plan accuracy should not be measured, however. While it is not realistic to expect demand plan accuracy to be 100 percent, it is realistic to expect accuracy to be continuously improving.

Here are some general guidelines for demand plan accuracy:

- Measure demand plan accuracy, and other marketing and sales performance measurements, as outlined above. The first time you make these measurements, consider them baseline and determine performance objectives. Measure monthly and take action to continuously improve.

Aggregate		Month			Rolling 3-Months
		-3	-2	-1	
Family 1	Plan	238	221	245	704
	Actual	232	206	219	657
	Error	-6	-15	-26	-47
	Accuracy %	97.5	93.2	89.4	93.3
	Error %	2.5	6.8	10.6	-6.7

Rolling 3-Month Average Calculation:
Sum the total demand planned for 3 months.
Sum the actual demand for 3 months.

Accuracy % Calculation:
100 – ABS(Error)
Note: ABS means Absolute Value

Error % Calculation:
= (+Actual – Plan)/Plan
Note: Express the result as a percentage

FIGURE 72   Family Demand Plan Accuracy — Rolling Three-Month Calculation

- A realistic goal should be accuracy of 95+ percent at the family level. Utilizing a rolling three-month measurement at the family level minimizes the impact of order timing on the measurements. It is very common to accurately predict the sales volume but not accurately predict the timing of customer orders. How to make the rolling measurement is shown in Figure 72. The rolling measure provides an average measure of demand plan accuracy. The rolling average accuracy over three months in this example is 93 percent. Month-to-month accuracy ranged from a low of 89 percent to a high of 97 percent. This method of measurement provides a better perspective of performance overall, recognizing that it can be more difficult to predict the timing of orders than the total volume of demand.
- Set demand plan accuracy objectives for the A, B, and C products. It is realistic to expect accuracy of 80 to 100 percent for the A items and 65 to 100 percent for the B items. The accuracy of the C items, especially if orders are infrequent, can vary widely month to month, both over and under the plan. It is not unusual for C item accuracy to range from 0 to 250 percent, depending largely upon volume, order quantity,

and order frequency. For C items that have infrequent orders, it may be more useful to use a rolling three-month average measurement, as shown in Figure 72.

■ Set a total mix plan accuracy objective. Total mix plan accuracy of all items within a family (A, B, and C) can typically vary from 70 to 100 percent.[46]

The above guidelines are intended to provide a basis for determining demand plan accuracy targets. What targets are best for your company will depend on the number and types of products produced, the number of new products introduced (it is always more difficult to plan accurately in the early phase of the product life cycle), customer buying patterns, and market uncertainties.

Chronic inaccuracy should always be a concern, and actions should be taken to reduce the inaccuracies. One common cause of chronic inaccuracy is basing the demand plan on executive wishes rather than marketplace reality. It is all too common for the senior leaders in companies to autocratically force the demand plan to equal the business plan or financial numbers communicated to Wall Street. This practice ultimately undermines a company's financial performance as it causes companies to utilize highly unprofitable techniques in an attempt to achieve the business plan goal or Wall Street targets.

Case in point: Lucent Technologies' sales revenues increased over three years from 18 to 49 percent. The telecommunications equipment maker's growth was spurred largely by federal legislation that allowed other telephone carriers to compete with local phone monopolies. The expanded market opportunity had an upside and a downside, however: new competitors that focused on local phone company business, taking market share away from Lucent. As its market share slipped, Lucent offered incentives to customers in order to hit its sales revenue targets. These incentives involved financing of customer deals as well as discounts.

The discounts helped Lucent achieve its short-term sales revenue targets, but with the following consequences:

■ The discounts lowered profit margins on the goods sold.
■ Customers bought earlier than originally planned, reducing future sales that could have resulted in higher profit margins.

The practice of motivating customers to buy early is frequently called "mortgaging the future." When companies mortgage their future, they are playing a game of charades with their shareholders, Wall Street, and themselves. Eventually, they can no longer sustain the charade. No matter what they do, they are unable to achieve the sales revenue and profit plan. Customers either become tapped out, believing it unwise to carry the additional inventory, or they become very well trained to wait for the price discount, resulting in lower profit margins for the selling company. The selling company's financial performance suffers, and eventually the stock price declines. In the case of Lucent, its stock price peaked at $138 and eventually plunged to below $2 as the telecommunications industry as a whole suffered during the economic downturn of 2001–2002.

The Lucent case has another twist. The executive responsible for North American sales was asked to retire after she refused to comply with the chief executive officer's order to change her sales plan to match the sales growth target. The sales executive believed that promised future discounts made it impossible to achieve the sales growth goal. This case gained widespread media attention when the sales executive filed suit against Lucent for her forced retirement.[47]

The moral of this case example: Forcing the demand plan to equal the business plan or Wall Street target is unwise. It causes tactics to stimulate demand that reduce profits and jeopardize future sales. It causes increased inventory when sales do not materialize and production rates are based on the unrealistic plan. It can also create supply chain glitches when enough product cannot be produced to satisfy the early orders. Financial performance suffers and, in turn, causes a reduction in stock price. As discussed in Chapter 3, supply chain glitches result in an average stock price reduction of 18.5 percent.

Lucent is not alone in the practice of arbitrarily changing the demand plan to meet the annual business plan or Wall Street target. This practice is widespread throughout the manufacturing industry. It takes discipline and fortitude not to mortgage the future. A more fruitful approach is to redefine the marketing strategies and determine a different, more realistic course for achieving the corporate goals.

Sometimes it may not be possible to attain the business plan goals even with a change in strategy. This typically occurs when external factors, like downturns in the economy and competitors' moves, are too powerful to overcome. Then it is a matter of following the discipline of communicating bad news early (which is better than delivering bad news late) and developing a realistic demand plan.

This is exactly what a biotechnology client did. The vice-president of sales and marketing astutely recognized early in the year that the company would not achieve its sales revenue targets. The company was underbid on a major account that would have significantly increased sales revenues. The vice-president of sales and marketing resisted the temptation to lower the sales price to win the account. To do so would put the company dangerously close to not realizing profit from the sale. The vice-president of sales and marketing understood that the objective was *profitable* sales, not just achieving a sales target.

Through the sales and operations planning process, the company adjusted the demand plan, and production and inventory plans, accordingly. Every month, the company also reviewed the gap between the sales revenue target and the sales revenue the demand plan was expected to generate. Actions were taken to shrink the gap, although the gap was never entirely closed. At the end of the year, the company won the major account when its competitor could not deliver the expected product quality. By taking a longer term approach to managing the business, in the end the company was poised to increase sales revenues the following year and continue to achieve excellent profit margins.

The key in this case example was operating to a realistic demand plan. When companies do so, they minimize building unneeded product, which will only increase inventory and reduce cash flow and profit margins.

The Coca-Cola company set a precedent in December 2002 by announcing that it would no longer communicate quarterly sales projections to Wall Street. The company will no longer try to predict to the penny, and create expectations of, how much money it will earn every quarter. The abandonment of this practice will enable Coca-Cola to focus on long-term growth, rather than managing only to Wall Street's short-term expectations.[48]

It is hoped that other companies will follow Coca-Cola's leadership. By doing so, companies can focus on influencing real customer demand, rather than on short-term manipulations to meet quarterly projections or business plan numbers. This, in turn, promotes open and honest communication within the company and provides for improved communication of demand and the realities of the marketplace. In the end, executives will do what they ought to be doing — managing the business, not managing the numbers.

Companies, in search of an accurate demand plan, often seek the Holy Grail that will eliminate all problems in predicting demand accurately. All too often, technology is seen as the solution. Those who focus on technology as the answer are frequently disappointed, however. Technology alone does not improve demand plan accuracy or the effectiveness of the demand management process. Technology is a process enabler and is the focus of the next chapter.

SUMMARY OF BEST PRACTICES
FOR PERFORMANCE MEASUREMENTS

1. The purpose of performance measurements is to determine the effectiveness of the demand management process, which includes planning, communicating, influencing, and prioritizing and managing demand.
2. The demand plan accuracy measurement is an indicator of the competence of the sales, marketing, and product/brand management organizations.

3. When demand plans are inaccurate, the first course of action is to determine the assumptions that were incorrect.
4. Correlating demand plan accuracy with other financial-related measurements demonstrates how an effective demand management process contributes to a company's financial performance.
5. Improved demand plan accuracy allows a company to operate with fewer buffer resources like inventory, thus lowering operating costs.
6. Demand plan accuracy is measured at the aggregate, item, and mix levels, in both unit volume and sales revenue.
7. It is recognized that there will always be some degree of demand plan error, and tactics are needed to minimize the impact of the errors. The tactics are determined through a managed process.
8. There is no industry standard for demand plan accuracy. Accuracy metrics are used for continuous improvement. An objective is established. Once it is met, a tougher metric is instituted.
9. Demand is classified in A, B, and C categories according to sales volume. Different plan accuracy objectives are set for each category, with the most time and attention spent on improving the plan accuracy for the A items.
10. The demand plan is not arbitrarily forced to match the annual business plan or sales revenue plan, as this practice ultimately compromises a company's financial performance.
11. When the demand plan does not match the annual business plan or sales revenue target, the company's strategies are reviewed to determine how a change in strategy and supporting tactics will increase demand.

QUESTIONS

1. You are the vice-president of sales and marketing. What performance metrics would you want to review each month? Why?
2. You are the brand/product manager. What performance metrics would you want to review each month? Why?
3. You are the demand manager. What performance metrics would you want to review each month? Why?
4. What questions should be asked when there are differences between market metric performance and the strategic objective? Why are these metrics important?
5. How is correlating demand plan accuracy with inventory and financial measures useful?
6. When the demand plan accuracy is under the target three months in a row, what should the leader of the demand organization's response do to understand the reasons for the inaccuracy?

7. When the demand plan accuracy is below the target, what should be reviewed — the numbers in the demand plan or the assumptions upon which the plan is based? Why?
8. What questions should be asked about the assumptions when demand plan accuracy is below the target?
9. How is demand plan accuracy at the aggregate level calculated?
10. What questions does the measure of demand plan accuracy at the aggregate level help to answer?
11. How is demand plan accuracy at the item level calculated?
12. Why is it necessary to measure demand plan accuracy at the item level?
13. How is mix accuracy calculated?

ROLE OF TECHNOLOGY

An interesting phenomenon occurs with information technology. Companies invest millions of dollars in computer hardware and application software. Technology users, however, eschew these powerful tools for the spreadsheet — technology in one of its simplest and least expensive forms. Executives are disappointed that the anticipated performance improvements and financial benefits from their technology investments are not achieved.

One cause of the phenomenon is that executives all too often are looking for the Holy Grail — a one-step solution to their companies' performance problems. They look to technology more than people and processes for the solution. Once the technology is implemented, executives expect people and processes to fall in place.

In reality, it does not work that way. Technology users are looking for software that is easy to use and supports how they currently get their work done. If it does not, they find ways to work around the technology. The end result? Disappointment all around.

The situation described above is not isolated to companies of a specific size or industry. It is widespread throughout business today. A study by AMR Research on implementations of customer relationship management technology showed that 47 percent of the projects were in jeopardy of failing. Why? The needs of end users (employees, partners, and customers) were not considered in defining the technology requirements.[49]

Technology fails for other reasons as well. Some prime examples: After spending $120 million on planning technology, software incompatibility problems caused candy-maker Hershey Foods to miss or delay shipments during the Halloween season. The company lost an estimated $120 million in sales. Nike invested $400 million in technology that allowed retailers to order directly from the shoe and apparel maker, only to have software glitches cause overstocks for some shoes and shortages for others. The problems contributed to eroding profits for Nike.[50]

Does this mean that companies should avoid implementing information technology? Would corporate life and profits be better without it? The answer is no. Information technology, deployed well, enables better decision making and improved execution. The trick is to select, implement, and deploy technology appropriately, which is the subject of this chapter.

Without information technology, it would not be possible to plan demand for hundreds and thousands of product items and communicate the demand plan to the supply organization, let alone collaborate with customers on a demand plan. Few companies performed demand management 30 years ago. It simply was too time consuming to gather information on customers' buying intentions, integrate this information with marketing and sales plans, and perform statistical forecasting. Most of this work had to be performed manually, without the aid of even spreadsheets.

Computer technology, in the words of cultural anthropologists James Burke and Robert Ornstein, has "the power to change the world with unexpected speed and in unprecedented detail."[51] Speed and detailed information are just what is needed for demand management. Today, software applications can statistically forecast hundreds of items in minutes. Sales orders and demand schedules can be communicated via electronic data interchange and the Internet in real time. Retail companies can share point-of-sale information with their trading partners — daily, if desired. Salespeople can sit in their customers' offices and look up product availability, specifications, and pricing on their companies' information systems, using handheld devices known as personal data acquisition tools.

This is the upside of technology. The downside of technology is that it will not make poor business processes perform better. It will not make decisions for decision makers. If processes are not in place to act upon demand information, the communication of point-of-sale data, demand schedules, sales and marketing plans, and statistical forecasts is futile. If processes are not in place to reach consensus on a demand plan, synchronize demand and supply, and make tactical decisions when demand is uncertain, no software application will enable fulfilling sales orders on time.

This lesson is driven home every Christmas holiday season in the United States when companies selling their goods on the Internet have difficulty fulfilling orders. According to a study by Jupiter Media Metrics, 53 percent of

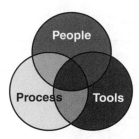

FIGURE 73   Integration of People, Processes, and Tools (Copyright Oliver Wight International)

holiday shoppers in 1999 did not receive their orders when promised. Less than one-third of these shoppers were notified that their orders would be late. The result? Disappointed customers and tarnished company reputations.

Industry experts observe that despite the disappointing performance, few companies had taken the required action to better serve customers in the future. According to one report:

> Fulfillment and customer service execution was critical. But many companies still lack processes and integrated systems to avoid disappointing numerous consumers.[52]

The most successful companies in deploying technology, in the authors' observation, recognize the interdependence of people, processes, and tools (Figure 73). Technology is a tool; it is not a substitute for processes and people. Success in deploying technology is predicated on how well people, processes, and tools are integrated. Stated another way, you can have the best hammer in the world, but it does not necessarily make you a good carpenter.

So how do you integrate people, processes, and tools? Years ago, the Oliver Wight Companies studied the difference between successful and failed implementations that involved business processes, people, and information systems. Common traits of success and failure were found and led to documenting what is known as the Proven Path methodology (Figure 74).

Following are the key findings embodied in the Proven Path methodology and considered best practices. These findings have been validated repeatedly over the years by the Oliver Wight Companies as well as numerous other consulting firms, technology firms, and practitioners.

Successful implementations start with senior executive involvement to build awareness of and to understand:

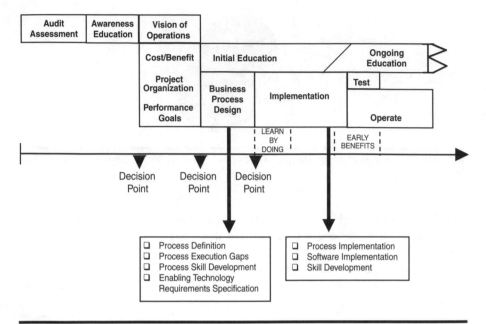

FIGURE 74 Proven Path Implementation Methodology (Copyright Oliver Wight International)

- Critical business problems and opportunities
- Effectiveness of current processes in solving the business problems and leveraging business opportunities
- Current skills of people in operating the business processes
- Effectiveness of current technology in supporting the business processes and enabling people to perform their work
- Industry best practices and the impact of these best practices on competitive positioning and financial performance

Once the above is understood, a high-level definition is developed for how the company intends to operate and the changes that need to be made in processes, people development, and technology to operate in the defined manner. This high-level definition is frequently called a vision of operations.

In conjunction with developing a vision of operations, the benefits of operating with this new vision are defined. The benefits include operational and financial performance improvements. A deployment plan is also created, outlining the major milestones, the steps in implementing the vision of operations, and the cost for the next phase (process redesign).

The understanding and awareness phase of the Proven Path approach gives executives the ability to determine whether the proposed new vision of operations is worthwhile — *before spending a dime on process improvement and technology.* Executives have the information needed to decide whether the investment makes business sense. The criteria for determining the business case should be whether the investment will better position the company to improve customer service, competitive position, and financial performance.

Once a commitment is made by the executive team to implement the vision of operations, redesign of the business processes is the next phase (Figure 74). Redesign efforts involve end users in determining the detailed changes to make in the business processes.

Involving end users in the process redesign has several advantages. They are experienced experts on the strengths and weaknesses of the current business processes. They know in a very practical sense what it will take to execute the new vision of operations.

The retailer Wal-Mart is known for developing and leveraging technology better than almost any company in the world. Wal-Mart currently employs a technology staff of more than 2,000 people. Wal-Mart's technology executives insist that their software developers are "retailers first" and "programmers second," according to Ron Ireland, a former Wal-Mart technology manager. Technology developers are required to work in Wal-Mart stores and distribution centers every year to stay current on the company's frontline business needs. Knowledge of business needs is critical for designing technology that works effectively for employees at Wal-Mart stores and distribution centers.

End-user participation in the process redesign has an additional benefit. The end users become experts on the newly designed processes and, thus, are influential as agents of change. They help the organization to more quickly adopt the new way of doing work. This leads to faster performance improvements, which shortens the time to achieve the desired return on investment.

The best technology testimonial is when the end users say, "This is my system." As AMR Research points out in its study findings of customer relationship management implementation failures, "Corporations can only achieve benefits from CRM software if end users see an application as a blessing rather than a curse."[53] The same is true with demand management software and just about any form of technology, in the authors' experience.

In the Proven Path methodology, technology requirements are not addressed until after the new business processes are defined. The business process definition drives the technology specifications, not the other way around.

When business process redesign is not addressed first, companies frequently end up wasting their technology investment. As noted earlier, process users work around the technology when it does not meet their needs. Companies also buy technology that is not useful, as was shown in a study by Morgan Stanley. The investment banking firm found that U.S. companies spent $130 billion on unneeded software and other technology during a two-year period.[54]

By defining the business processes first, a more accurate technology specification can be created. The understanding has been developed to determine the technology functionality needed to support the vision of operations and defined business processes. This puts the buyer in greater control of the technology selection. Otherwise, people end up making a "best guess" at what is needed (much like kicking tires when buying a car). Or they focus on which application has the most bells and whistles (when many of the bells and whistles are not needed). In other cases, companies end up buying subpar technology.

Many technology tools come with standard functionality that supports best process practices. When companies opt not to design their business processes first, they frequently overlook these more robust tools and end up investing needlessly in customized software to beef up their software application of choice.

The virtue of defining the vision of operations and business processes first is supported by experts from technology firms interviewed in the course of writing this book. All the people interviewed noted what Marc Bergeron of Verticalnet calls "huge gaps in process development." What companies need to do, according to Bergeron and others, is educate first, design the business processes second, and then buy the technology. This is a best practice.

The definition of technology requirements should also address whether the proposed technology is aligned with the company's current technology infrastructure and strategy. More companies, for example, are moving away from buying suites of enterprise-wide software from the same vendor. They desire instead to purchase best-of-class software applications and link them together. As a result, the integration readiness of software is becoming a more critical technology requirement.

This trend has some experts calling for industry standards that facilitate integration. An industry standard would prevent the kinds of problems that Hershey Foods and other companies have experienced with software incompatibility. The development of an industry standard could take years to accomplish, however. While waiting for an industry-standard application server, experts recommend investing in infrastructure technologies that enable integration with existing technology. These technologies include private trading exchange, single-portal framework, integration bus framework, and single analytical data model.[55]

After the technology requirements have been defined, including integration requirements and alignment with technology strategy, the next step is implementation. Implementation focuses on developing the skills required to operate the new business processes and tools as well as learning by doing.

All too often, companies attempt to shortcut skill development. Why? When implementations are behind schedule, they choose not to change the schedule and instead compress the time available for training. Other times, the technology investment has exceeded the original budget, and companies trim training expenses from their budgets.

Whatever the reason for truncating skill development, it is an unwise decision. Ultimately, it slows the implementation. It takes longer for end users to operate the business processes and tools effectively — if they ever do at all. When users choose spreadsheets over new technology, it frequently is a symptom of lack of training. They do not understand how to use the new technology tools and choose to use the tools they know best. They do not recognize the importance of using the new tools to support communication and integration with other business processes and end users.

As a result, cutting the investment (in time and money) in skill development inevitably extends the amount of time it takes to achieve the desired performance and financial improvements. Some companies never achieve the expected benefits. Companies end up with process users operating in individual silos with individual spreadsheets. Companies miss the opportunity to achieve untold millions of dollars in benefits, and executives blame the new technology for the failure.

In introducing clients to the Proven Path approach, they frequently ask how long it takes to educate, redesign the business processes, and buy the technology. The time it takes is dependent upon the resources and time committed to the effort. Some companies make a concerted effort over a short period of time. In these cases, the definition of the vision of operations can be completed in less than one month. The redesign and software specification phase can be completed in two to three months. Other companies take a committee approach, meeting several times per month. In these cases, it can take up to six months to define the vision of operations and complete the process redesign and technology specifications.

Using an approach like the Proven Path is time well spent, however. It prevents mistakes in buying inadequate or wrong technology. Decision points are also defined, as shown in Figure 74, which helps executives make better decisions and an informed commitment to the project. At certain milestones, executives review the status of the project and the required investment in resources, time, and money for the next phase. The purpose of the review is to make a go/no-go decision about whether to:

■   Proceed to the next phase
■   Fine-tune the requirements and budget for the next phase
■   Abandon the effort altogether

The go/no-go decision is based on achieving the vision of operations and the defined return on investment. The use of decision points has the effect of not forcing executives to commit the company's resources all at once. It provides flexibility to change, if change is needed, to ensure a successful implementation. It also creates a well-defined expectation of what work must be performed and information made available to executives before they will invest in the next phase.

Using this approach gives senior executives greater control over the technology investment. Senior executives are routinely blamed for technology failures. Lack of senior executive commitment is widely cited as the most common reason why technology (and process improvement) implementations fail.

In the authors' experience, executives want to make the right choices, but often lack the information and understanding to make informed decisions. The Proven Path approach enables executives to listen, understand the issues and opportunities, review the financial and resource commitments, and then commit to the project. It also causes executives to create realistic expectations of technology as an *enabler* rather than as the *solution* to a company's business problems and opportunities.

In the area of demand management, technology enablers continue to improve. Several tiers of tools are available:

- Stand-alone statistical forecasting applications
- Demand planning packages that integrate statistical forecasting, promotions forecasting, forecasting of product life cycles, and sales planning information
- Sales planning and customer relationship management packages
- Collaborative planning packages that enable customers to communicate their planned promotions, buying schedules, and forecasts, as well as end user or consumer point-of-sale information
- Suites of the above capabilities as part of enterprise resource planning and supply chain management software

Which of the above approaches is best for a company depends on its vision of operations, business process design, and technology strategy. It is not unusual for companies to initially purchase a stand-alone statistical forecasting package. Stand-alone packages usually can be implemented very quickly, in a few days or less. Applications that are part of an enterprise-wide software suite can take a year or longer to become operational. The cost of stand-alone statistical forecasting tools ranges from $1,500 to $50,000, making them an affordable near-term option. Companies frequently use the stand-alone tool until a full-scale software suite is implemented.

Whatever statistical forecasting tool is selected, stand-alone or part of a suite of applications, most of the tools today include a variety of modeling techniques or algorithms for generating the statistical forecast. This approach was pioneered by Demand Solutions of Demand Management, Inc. and Forecast Pro of Business Forecast Systems in the mid-1980s. With these tools, users do not have to determine the most accurate forecasting technique by trial and error. The tool makes the selection for the user, using what is widely called the expert selection mode. Users also have the option of manually selecting any of the forecasting techniques.

Some companies opt to continue to use the stand-alone package even after enterprise resource planning software with statistical forecasting capabilities is implemented. Some (not all) enterprise resource planning suites have only rudimentary statistical forecasting tools. The stand-alone applications yield more accurate statistical forecasts. Figure 75 shows the minimum requirements for statistical forecasting tools, whether they are stand-alone applications or part of an enterprise or supply-chain-wide system.

A second tier of technology offers a more comprehensive approach to demand planning. These tools utilize a database to capture and decompose demand information — by individual customer, by sales territory, market segment, and by product category, family, and item. The database approach enables developing multiple views of demand — the sales view, product/brand view, customer view, and statistical forecast view. These tools also track and forecast promotions and include algorithms for determining product life cycles. The minimum requirements for demand planning software packages are shown in Figure 75.

For companies with a large number of products, complex business environment, and large customer base, the demand planning tools are advantageous in the long run. The effectiveness of the tools is dependent on the ability to capture demand information by customer, sales territory, market segment, and product. This data capture typically requires integration with sales planning, customer relationship management, and enterprise resource planning software. As a result, it takes more forethought in developing the data capture process and stronger technology infrastructure to utilize demand planning technology to its fullest capability. These tools also take longer to implement.

As more companies develop collaborative relationships with trading partners for demand planning, the need for supporting technology tools has emerged. The earliest efforts at collaboration utilized faxes and electronic data interchange for communicating demand information. These tools work effectively when collaborating with a few trading partners, but are inefficient when dealing with many trading partners.

As we will see in the next chapter, trading partner collaboration is a process, not a technology. The process is dependent on the visibility of demand information, and that is the critical supporting role that technology plays.

Minimum Software Requirements

Statistical Forecasting	Demand Planning	Collaboration
■ Multiple modeling techniques, including simple exponential smoothing, Holt, Winters, Box Jenkins (ARIMA), Croston, and multiple and linear regression	■ Multidimensional database that enables the capture and decomposition of demand information: by customer, sales territory, market segment, and by product category, family, subfamily, and item	■ Multidimensional database that enables the capture and decomposition of demand information: by buyer, seller, marketing plan, and product category, family, and item
■ Statistical forecast decomposition: base level, trend, and seasonality	■ Capability to plan by customer, product, sales territory, category, and market segment	■ Display the demand information by base, promotion, and total (base + promotion)
■ Top-down and bottom-up forecasting	■ Capability to document assumptions and qualitative information	■ Display the difference between the buyer plan and seller plan (by percent and units)
■ Statistical output of forecast error: mean absolute error, mean absolute deviation, mean absolute percent error, and adjusted R square	■ Statistical forecasting capabilities (see minimum requirements)	■ Capability to document assumptions, qualitative information, and other pertinent notes
■ Automated or expert selection based on the lowest mean absolute percent error	■ What-if scenario planning	■ Capture historical demand information and performance measurements
■ Manual overrides of the statistical forecast (based on volume and percent)	■ Customization (slicing and dicing) of information for planning, analysis, and measuring performance; filtering and sorting of information	

- Event modeling that allows adjusting for events like promotions, inconsistent holidays (Easter and Rosh Hashanah), and one-time occurrences like strikes and work outages
- Batch forecasting of hundreds of items at the same time
- Graphical presentation of the demand history and statistical forecast
- Numeric output of the statistical forecast in spreadsheet format
- Ease of use — ability to learn how to operate the application in a few days' time

- Graphical and numeric displays to enable analysis and decision making
- Real-time reporting capability, including exception management reports
- ABC analysis and planning
- Forecasting accuracy measurement, reporting, and archiving
- Real-time conversion of demand data (currency, unit of measure, etc.)
- Financial planning, including revenue planning, pricing analysis, and average selling price data
- Integration with enterprise resource planning, supply chain planning, sales planning and customer relationship management, and financial planning systems

- Communicate point-of-sale information and graphically display comparisons of the demand plan and historical point-of-sale data
- Plan replenishment and communicate replenishment schedules to trading partners
- Graphical and numeric displays to enable analysis and decision making
- Real-time reporting capability, including exception management reports
- Real-time conversion of demand data (currency, unit of measure, etc.)
- Sharing of data via the Internet and private exchanges
- Integration with demand planning, enterprise resource planning, supply chain planning, sales planning and customer relationship management, and financial planning system
- Secure Web-based environment

FIGURE 75 Minimum Requirements — Software Applications

The technology tools have developed more quickly than effective collaboration processes, in most cases. Technology is now available for sharing demand information and demand plans with trading partners via electronic data interchange and Web-based exchanges. Product movement information at retail stores and distribution centers can be made visible to trading partners, using a shared system. Access by trading partners to this shared system is accomplished through private exchanges.

Collaboration demand planning software provides multiple demand views, showing the seller's plan, buyer's plan, marketing plan, and the collaborated (agreed upon) plan (see Figure 76). By highlighting differences in the buyer and seller views by time period, these differences can be resolved through collaboration.

Collaboration demand planning software on the market today can communicate promotions planned by trading partners and the historical performance of promotions in generating demand. Point-of-sale information can be communicated and compared to the demand plan by product item. Today's software can also be used to plan replenishment and communicate replenishment schedules. The minimum requirements for collaboration demand planning software are detailed in Figure 75.

Despite these technology advances, as of this writing, trading partner collaboration has not reached critical mass, nor has it achieved the expectations of the early collaboration pioneers. It is proving to be much easier to install collaboration hardware and software than to develop the business processes and people skills to perform collaboration. What it takes to successfully collaborate is the subject of the next chapter.

As we will see in the next two chapters, there is no autopilot when it comes to managing the business. Technology makes information visible to enable better decision making. The critical success factors for demand management, including collaboration with trading partners on demand plans, are people, process, and technology, in that order.

SUMMARY OF BEST PRACTICES
FOR USE OF TECHNOLOGY

1. The interdependence of people, processes, and technology tools is recognized.
2. Successful deployment of technology requires the integration of people, processes, and technology.
3. Senior management is responsible for developing a vision of operations and understanding how people, processes, and technology will enable achieving the vision of operations.

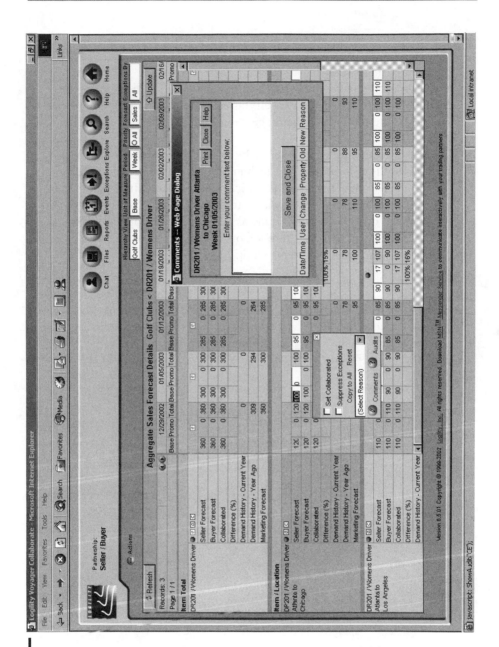

FIGURE 76
Example of
Collaboration
Software
(Courtesy of
Logility, Inc.)

4. A cost/benefit analysis of the vision of operations is developed and approved by senior management prior to implementing process design and buying technology tools.
5. Deployment of technology involves education first, redesigning business processes second, and then specifying and buying the technology.
6. End users are involved in the process redesign and technology specification and selection.
7. The specification of technology includes addressing whether the new technology is aligned with current technology infrastructure and strategy.
8. Training of technology users is critical to the successful operation of the processes and technology. Lack of training extends the time required to achieve the operational and financial performance improvements.
9. Technology is not seen as a cure-all, but as an enabler of business processes and people in performing their work.

QUESTIONS

1. You are the president of a manufacturing company. What process would you use to decide whether or not to invest in technology for demand management?
2. Why is it advantageous to develop a vision of operations before investing in technology?
3. What approach should be used to ensure that technology investment is not wasted?
4. What are the reasons for educating first, redesigning business processes second, and then buying technology?
5. What are the advantages of involving process users in process redesign and technology specification?
6. Why are go/no-go decision points utilized?

This book has free materials available for download from the
Web Added Value™ Resource Center at www.jrosspub.com.

PART III:
COLLABORATION, CONSENSUS, AND INTEGRATION

13

DEMAND
COLLABORATION

Demand collaboration makes such good sense. If demand information can be communicated throughout the entire supply chain, each trading partner would know how much product to have available and when. Less inventory would be needed as a hedge against uncertainty. Lead times could be shortened as less unneeded product would be made, freeing up production capacity. Sales would increase because the right amount of product would be available at the right points of consumption. As a result, all trading partners in the supply chain would reduce the cost of goods sold and increase their profits.

That is the potential, which has been validated by the relatively few companies that have successfully implemented demand collaboration processes. So why are more companies not doing it? And of the companies that have attempted demand collaboration, why are many of them disappointed by the results?

Here are the most common reasons why demand collaboration has not realized its potential:

- The pace of adopting new ways of doing business is slow.
- Demand information supplied by customers is not put to use in trading partners' own demand, supply, logistics, and corporate planning in an integrated manner.
- Demand management and supply management processes are not integrated, and sales and operations planning is not utilized to synchronize demand and supply.
- Lack of trust among trading partners to share pertinent information and collaborate on decision making.

- The desire to partner but not commit to executing the communicated plans.
- A common view that demand collaboration is a technology solution, and the current technology is too complex.

This chapter addresses these issues, the principles of demand collaboration, and what it takes to partner successfully.

Just because demand collaboration is not yet used widely does not mean that it is not worthwhile. The pace of adopting any new way of doing business is at work here. Case example: The earliest implementation of sales and operations planning occurred in the early 1980s. Widespread effort in implementing sales and operations planning did not occur until the mid-1990s. It takes a minimum of ten years, according to the authors' experience, for fundamental changes in business practices to become widely adopted. It takes another five to ten years for these changes to become a routine way of doing business for the majority of companies.

At this writing, the use of demand collaboration is in the early adopter phase. Innovators, like Procter & Gamble, Wal-Mart, Warner-Lambert, Kimberly Clark, Nabisco, Wegmans, and Sara Lee, proved that collaborating to plan demand and replenishment strips costs from the supply chain — for all trading partners' financial benefit. Now early adopters are following the leadership of these pioneers.

Some of the earliest efforts in demand collaboration have occurred in the consumer goods industry. Wal-Mart pioneered the effort. Two of its supply chain executives, Robert Bruce and Ron Ireland, first articulated the process of collaborative forecasting and replenishment and worked to develop industry-wide interest in the process. Based on early experiences with the process, a consumer goods industry guideline called CPFR® (Collaborative Planning, Forecasting, and Replenishment) was adopted in 1996 by the Voluntary Inter-industry Commerce Standards (VICS). The guideline promotes best practices and helps companies avoid pitfalls that the pioneers encountered in implementing collaborative trading partner relationships.[56]

The success of demand collaboration and the more extensive collaborative planning, forecasting, and replenishment process hinges on sharing demand information. Demand drives the value chain. When demand information is visible throughout the value chain, it reduces uncertainty about the volume and timing of demand. With less uncertainty, order quantities throughout the value chain more closely resemble true demand. There is less need for tactics, like safety stock, as a hedge against the unknown, which in turn reduces the costly bullwhip effect throughout the supply chain.

The bullwhip effect (see Figure 77) occurs when each trading partner along

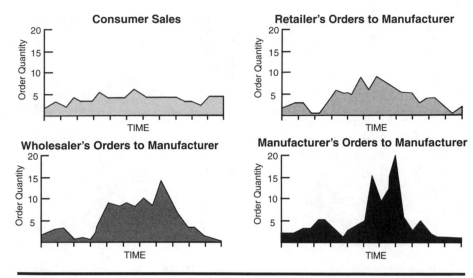

FIGURE 77   Bullwhip Effect

the value chain places orders against uncertainty and the unknown. The volume of the orders is typically amplified at each trading partner point along the value chain. The largest distortion of demand usually occurs with trading partners that are the farthest removed from the end user or consumer. These trading partners typically have the least visibility of true demand.[57]

With the bullwhip effect, the ordering of unneeded product and material creates a buildup of inventory throughout the value chain. The retail industry alone is estimated to be carrying $1.1 trillion in inventory against retail sales of $3.2 trillion, according to a study based on U.S. Commerce Department sales and inventory reports.[58]

One objective of demand collaboration is to dampen the bullwhip effect and strip inventory from the value chain. The fundamental principle is to substitute demand information for inventory (see Figure 78). Early implementers of CPFR in Europe showed this was possible. Companies piloting CPFR in Europe reduced inventory 30 to 50 percent and cut supply chain costs 15 to 25 percent without sacrificing customer service. Customer service actually improved by 5 to 10 percent.[59]

Increased sales is another benefit from dampening the bullwhip effect. Pilot efforts in CPFR have shown a 5 to 20 percent gain in sales. Wal-Mart and Warner-Lambert's CPFR pilot implementation, for example, resulted in an $8.5 million increase in Listerine sales.[60]

Despite this potential, most companies have not been beating down the door to collaborate with their customers. According to one survey, only 41 percent

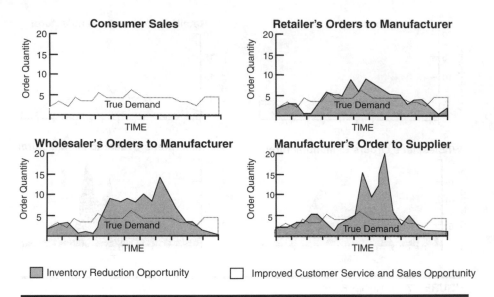

FIGURE 78 Inventory and Customer Service Opportunity When Bullwhip Effect Is Minimized

of consumer goods companies and 25 percent of retailers indicated they would implement any part of CPFR by 2003.[61] This lack of momentum has left some retailers frustrated to the point of mandating that their major suppliers implement the VICS CPFR guidelines by a certain date in the future.

Suppliers argue, and sometimes rightfully so, that the approach of their customers in a demand collaboration relationship is not win–win. Some suppliers, in fact, say that their customers' philosophy is, in the words of CPFR pioneer Ron Ireland: "I win, and you'll have to figure out how to win on your own." The major points of dissension between customer and supplier are:

- When a customer has spent the time and resources to communicate demand information to its suppliers, it expects product to be available when it said it wanted it.
- Suppliers contend that customers communicate demand information, but then do not buy in the volume and timing that were communicated, leaving the supplier on the hook for the inventory or to absorb the additional costs of filling last-minute orders of unplanned demand.

Both parties are correct. The solution is not to throw the baby out with the bathwater, however. Rather, both parties require a more formalized approach to the trading partner relationship that defines the operating rules or parameters and mutual expectations.

The most successful demand collaboration relationships are not brokered at the buyer–salesperson level, but at the senior executive level of the trading partner organizations. Case in point: H.J. Heinz Ltd. in Canada and Oshawa Foods developed one of the earliest (and successful) collaborative relationships in the mid-1990s. The senior executives of both companies championed the collaboration effort. Prior to collaborating, they met to agree on:

- The vision of how a collaborative effort would benefit both companies
- The expectations of each company in a trading partner relationship
- The demand and inventory information that needed to be communicated and how it would be acted upon
- The execution performance required to ensure that both companies would achieve the desired financial gains

Managers of the sales, marketing, purchasing, distribution, and supply chain functions in both companies were assigned to implement the agreement. The financial managers reported the financial results, and key functional managers reviewed the operational and financial performance measures every month. The company presidents met periodically to review the results and address issues that threatened the success of the relationship.

This approach, as depicted in Figure 79, gave the collaborative effort a *business* focus, rather than a *transaction* focus. Decisions were based on operational effectiveness and what was needed to enable both companies to strengthen their financial performance. This is a best practice for developing trading partner relationships for demand collaboration.

Once a trading partnership for demand collaboration is agreed upon, all too often companies leap into designing the transaction — the act of trading information — rather than developing the demand management process for the collaborative environment. In actuality, demand collaboration is an extension of the demand management process — outside the walls of a single business entity (see Figure 80). As such, the basic principles of demand management still apply and, in fact, are essential to partnering effectively.

The fundamental elements of demand planning must be in place, and operating well, in a demand collaboration process. Those elements are planning, communicating, influencing, and prioritizing and managing demand. The principles and best practices of these elements, covered in Chapters 4 through 7, are just as important in a demand collaboration process as in a company's internal demand management process.

The demand management process for any trading partner is enhanced by regularly and routinely receiving information on customer and end-user or consumer demand. Wal-Mart fostered frequent access to demand information by

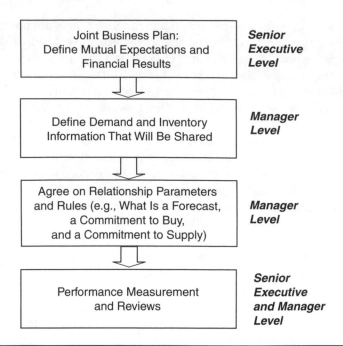

FIGURE 79   Business Focus in Developing Trading Partner Relationship for Demand Collaboration

giving the information to its suppliers rather than expecting suppliers to buy the information from services like AC Nielsen. Wal-Mart founder Sam Walton explained his company's philosophy on sharing information with trading partners in his autobiography:

> Communicate everything you possibly can to your partners. The more they know, the more they'll understand. The more they understand, the more they'll care. Once they care, there's no stopping them.[62]

When customers make visible demand information, it in turn fosters improved communication between trading partners. With better communication, companies begin to collaborate on influencing demand. Together, they develop marketing strategies and tactics to stimulate greater demand and more profitable sales. Done well, a demand management process drives companies — jointly and individually — to improve and enhance their marketing effort.

At a minimum, demand collaboration provides suppliers with another view for their demand planning process, as shown in Figure 81. One of the key

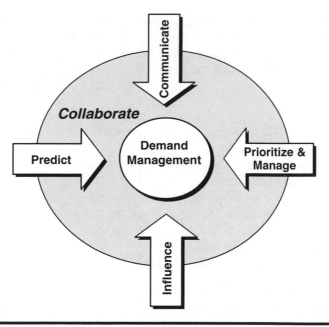

FIGURE 80   Elements of Demand Management in a Collaborative Environment

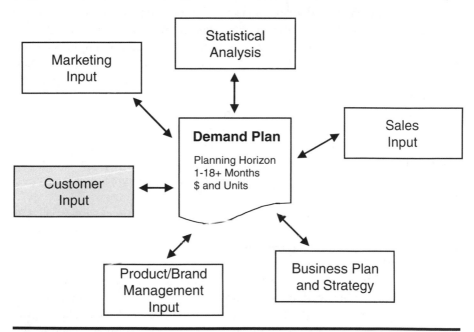

FIGURE 81   Multiple-View Demand Planning in a Collaborative Environment (Copyright Oliver Wight International)

questions to address in establishing a trading partnership for demand collaboration is: What customer, end-user, or consumer information will be useful for the supplier? Care must be taken not to overwhelm the process with information, but to communicate vital information that is pertinent to good judgment and decision making. Useful information communicated by customers typically includes:

- Item-level demand plan for the short term and the assumptions upon which the plan is based
- Aggregate demand plan over the longer term and the assumptions upon which the plan is based
- Sales history, including end-user or consumer sales data
- Planned promotions, pricing changes, and other activities that will influence the timing and volume of demand in the future
- Current inventory by location
- Desired inventory levels by location

Demand information communicated by customers should not be taken at face value. It should be treated as another perspective of demand and another input in developing a consensus plan. 3M of Post-it® note fame established one of the earliest demand collaboration processes in the late 1980s. When 3M's demand manager consolidated the demand plans from all of its customers for a particular product, he found that the combined plans equaled more than 200 percent of the total market potential. This experience reinforces the need for suppliers to look beyond individual trading partners and develop a composite picture of demand based on customer, sales, marketing, and brand/product management input. This is a best practice.

Customer demand information requires evaluation and analysis to put it in the proper business context. Correlation of the customer's end-user or consumer point-of-sale data with the supplier's sales history to the customer can be quite informative. It causes companies to re-evaluate their marketing and sales tactics and better understand end-user or consumer buying behavior, as the case example in Figure 82 illustrates.

A client in the consumer goods industry compared its customer sales to consumer point-of-sales data. Sales to customers rarely coincided with sales to consumers. In determining the reasons for the spikes in sales, it became obvious that the supplier's marketing tactics were at cross-purposes with good business sense. Most of the spikes, followed by steep declines, in customer sales were caused by the supplier loading customers with product at a discounted price to meet midyear and year-end sales revenue goals. The announcement of price increases also caused a less severe peak in demand as customers opted to buy product early to obtain the lower price.

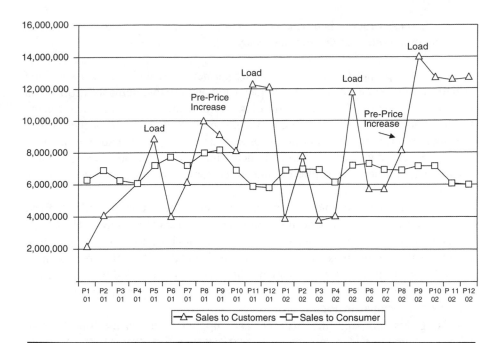

FIGURE 82 Comparison of Sales to Customers and Sales to Consumer

Loading and price discounting practices are the antithesis of effective demand management and supply chain management. These practices cause both supplier and customer to consume capital needlessly. In the case example above, the supplier had to invest in material and production before they were really needed. Customers were enticed to spend early and incur costs to warehouse and manage inventory.

Discipline and managing for the long-term financial health of trading partners — rather than for short-term gains — are required among partners. By sharing demand information and having the discipline to eliminate or marginalize the bullwhip effect, trading partners require less capital to operate their businesses. This is where the true win–win is realized from demand collaboration.

With demand collaboration, selling relationships and marketing tactics change. A study, conducted jointly by Canada's grocery-related trade organizations, focused on continuous replenishment practices and trading partner relationships. The practitioners, who conducted the study, predicted in a report on their findings:

> The most attractive merchandise strategies and tactics will be driven
> by valid information. Information itself, such as on-hand inventory

balances, order schedules, point-of-sale data, and forecasts, will become sought-after commodities.[63]

The value proposition between trading partners should change with demand collaboration. When a customer provides valid and reliable demand information to a trading partner, this information has the potential to reduce costs for the trading partner. When a customer does not provide demand information to a trading partner, the trading partner's costs are usually higher because of the need to build safety stock against demand uncertainty and to respond to last-minute, unanticipated orders. Thus, the pricing for customers should not necessarily be the same.

Many suppliers complain, however, that customers that provide demand information do not order what they communicate in their forecasts. Thus, suppliers do not realize the benefits from demand collaboration. One approach to resolving this problem is agreeing on when demand information represents a commitment to buy and when demand information is provided as future guidance only. This agreement can be based on a time zone and decision point approach, as shown in Figure 83.

Using this approach, the customer and supplier agree on the time horizon when the communicated demand plan or forecast is a firm order. In the example shown in Figure 83, this time zone is zero to three weeks. For this time horizon, the customer agrees to communicate an order plan by quantities and daily timing

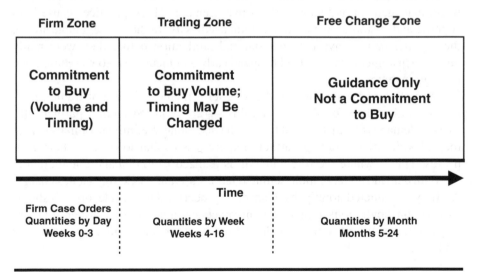

FIGURE 83 Time Zone Approach to Managing Demand Collaboration Relationships (Copyright Oliver Wight International)

for delivery. In weeks 4 to 16 in the planning horizon, the customer agrees to communicate quantities for delivery each week. The customer commits to ordering the volume in this time zone, but has flexibility to change the timing of the delivery. Beyond four months, the demand plan or forecast is for guidance purposes only and does not represent a commitment to buy.

The time zones and decision points that are agreed upon will vary company by company and industry by industry. The time zones are dependent upon customer and supplier lead times as well as the degree of flexibility desired by both trading partners. Time zone parameters typically can be negotiated between the supplier's selling organization and the customer's purchasing organization. The agreement, however, should be approved by the trading partners' senior executive teams so that both companies' leadership teams understand and support the commitment. This is a best practice.

In the authors' opinion, the majority of suppliers will not embrace demand collaboration until their customers commit to buying what they forecast over some agreed upon planning horizon, even if only measured in days. Suppliers require demand stability, at least over the short term, to optimize their production and procurement processes. This stability is the basis for the supplier to gain financial benefits from demand collaboration. Without a commitment from customers to create some form of demand plan stability, suppliers will remain reluctant to commit to a process that is not truly win–win in nature.

One of the criticisms of current demand collaboration practices is the short-term focus. As discussed throughout the book, a longer term planning horizon has many virtues. Chief among the virtues is the ability to respond economically to demand. A planning structure based upon time zones creates a longer term focus and injects greater stability into the demand plan. The full potential of demand collaboration will not be realized until, as Ernest R. Lazor, chief information officer at Prestone Products Corp., observes:

> If everybody can agree on a forecast and stick to it, you don't have to be changing your production schedules back and forth. That's the way to get better margins.[64]

To agree on a forecast and stick to it requires communication between trading partners. The customer may communicate a forecast or demand plan, which upon review by the supplier may be questionable. Some demand collaboration software applications have a feature that automatically alerts the supplier when customer forecasts are over or under a pre-established tolerance. In CPFR parlance, this is called error checking.

The customer and supplier must have the ability to clarify, review, and challenge one another's assumptions. These discussions improve the accuracy of the demand plan. Companies that collaborate on demand have seen improvements in demand plan accuracy. According to a study by AMR Research, 35 percent of customers and 20 percent of suppliers reported improved forecast accuracy as a result of demand collaboration.[65]

Another way to improve the accuracy of collaborative demand plans is to update the plans at least monthly and more frequently as needed. As companies develop more automated customer–supplier linkages, the frequency of update becomes at least weekly and in many cases daily. This brings suppliers closer to real-time updates of demand.

A shortcoming cited in the AMR Research study was that both buyer and seller organizations operate from different forecast numbers that are updated at inconsistent times. For example, customer and supplier organizations may both employ people to collaborate on forecasts that are updated weekly. These forecasts, which tend to focus on the short term, are usually not communicated to other pertinent functions within each organization, such as the supplier's sales organization and demand manager or the customer's purchasing management. Thus, these functions operate with different forecasts of demand.

Some people involved in the weekly forecasting process between trading partners claim that they attempt to communicate the updated demand plan to their respective organizations. The plans are not integrated into their companies' planning processes, however. Whichever the case, companies end up operating with multiple demand forecasts or plans, which is counterproductive to achieving financial benefits from demand collaboration. With proper integration of demand and supply processes at suppliers, this problem can be reduced. Reaching consensus on a single demand plan that is used by both the customer and supplier organizations to drive supply management and financial planning is a best practice and is the subject of the next chapter.

Trust is at issue here. Today, demand plans communicated between trading partners are usually just numbers. The assumptions that explain the numbers are communicated either sporadically or not at all. As a result, the demand plans are not well understood and thus lack credibility. The adoption of demand planning best practices, including communicating assumptions, by both customer and supplier helps to overcome the trust issue.

At heart of the trust issue is credibility. From the supplier's point of view, its trading partner's credibility erodes when it does not buy what was in the forecast. From the customer's point of view, its trading partner's credibility erodes when orders are not delivered on time and in the requested volume.

To regularly and routinely fulfill customer orders on time, suppliers' own internal supply chain management processes must operate effectively. An integrated business management process is needed as well. An AMR Research study cites four critical success factors for demand collaboration:

- An integrated forecast (demand planning) organization
- Single-number demand planning process
- Formal sales and operations planning process
- Performance measurements[65]

Many supplier companies opt to get their own internal house in order before embarking on demand collaboration. This involves implementing best practices for demand management and an integrated business management review, known as sales and operations planning, for synchronizing supply and demand on a monthly basis. Improving internal operational competence also involves operating supply chain management processes, such as enterprise resource planning and distribution resource planning, at best practice levels. The Oliver Wight Companies publishes an industry-recognized standard, the *Oliver Wight ABCD Checklist for Operational Excellence*, which is widely used to assess companies' performance to these best practice standards.[66]

As suppliers become better prepared for demand collaboration, the question becomes: Should we partner with selected customers or all of our customers? Our recommendation is to pilot first with your most forgiving customers, then extend out to strategic customers where partnering has the best opportunity to increase sales and reduce supply chain costs.

Procter & Gamble has demonstrated that partnering with Wal-Mart, a strategic customer, pays big dividends. Procter & Gamble increased sales to Wal-Mart from $350 million in 1988 to an estimated $4 billion in 1999, while tripling product turns in Wal-Mart stores, according to industry experts.[67] Procter & Gamble's path to partnering with Wal-Mart began by developing best practices for demand management, sales and operations planning, enterprise resource planning, and distribution resource planning. This capability created the backbone of Procter & Gamble's success.

As demand collaboration with trading partners matures, the question becomes: Which partner has the best capability to most accurately predict demand? A model (Figure 84), presented by Scott Williams of Procter & Gamble at a Supply Chain Council conference, addressed this issue. One Procter & Gamble business division found that 30 percent of its customers accounted for 80 percent of the variability in demand. For the 70 percent of customers with little variability in demand, Procter & Gamble could develop the demand forecast with a high degree of accuracy. Procter & Gamble did not request forecast numbers from these customers. Procter & Gamble asked those customers with the greatest variability of demand to communicate time-phased schedules of demand for a 14- to 90-day planning horizon. All customers were expected to communicate a firm order schedule over a 1- to 14-day planning horizon.[68]

As trading partners build greater credibility with one another, they will be

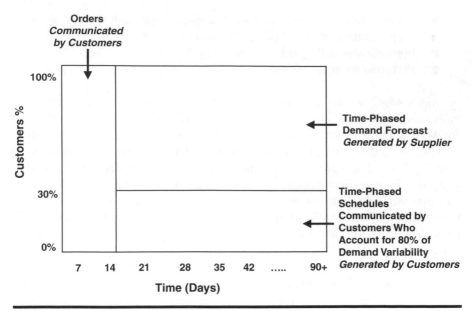

FIGURE 84   Model for Who Develops the Demand Plan in a Collaborative Environment (Source: Supply Chain Council Conference, May 1998)

positioned to determine who in the value chain has the best demand planning capability. Enough trust will have been developed to allow that party to generate the demand plan. This does not mean that the other trading partners relinquish their demand planning role. They will still need to communicate sales and marketing assumptions and end-user or consumer point-of-sale information. The level of detail that they communicate will be simplified, however.

Collaboration will still be required, and communication will remain essential, to fine-tune the demand plan day to day, week to week, month to month, and year to year. These communications, even with the aid of technology, will be people-to-people oriented. The challenge is to ensure that the right people are talking to create an effective collaboration process.

Technology certainly facilitates the exchange of demand information between trading partners. Sophisticated computer software, however, is not a prerequisite for demand collaboration. Many companies exchange information via fax, e-mail messages, and electronic data interchange.

One of the most common criticisms of the current technology for demand collaboration is its complexity. Many technology providers have patterned their software applications after the VICS CPFR guideline. Many users, however, are looking for simple, uncomplicated technology solutions, according to an AMR Research study.[69]

Just as demand collaboration practices will evolve over time, so too will the software applications that support these practices. While technology is not essential to support demand collaboration, it becomes more critical when a company desires to collaborate with a large number of trading partners. An automated tool is needed to facilitate the exchange of demand, inventory, and replenishment information in a timely manner.

Demand collaboration will be commonplace 20 years from now, just as consensus demand planning and sales and operations planning are becoming commonplace in industry today. What is taking place today with demand collaboration is a natural phase of the evolution of any new way of doing business. It starts with understanding the potential and recognizing why this potential is beneficial. Then, business process models are developed, tried, and refined, and technology is created to support the new business processes. This is all taking place today and heralds a new dimension for demand management, developing the most attractive value propositions, and determining how trading partners best work together to generate sales and profits.

The next chapter addresses the first steps many companies take to prepare for this new way of doing business. Those first steps involve reaching consensus internally on a demand plan and synchronizing demand and supply.

SUMMARY OF BEST PRACTICES FOR DEMAND COLLABORATION

1. The dangers of the bullwhip effect are recognized and measures are taken to minimize it.
2. A formalized approach is taken with demand collaboration. Expectations for trading partners are defined, operating rules and parameters are agreed upon, and performance metrics are agreed upon.
3. The senior leaders of companies are involved in agreeing to a trading partnership for demand collaboration and defining the mutual expectations.
4. The demand collaboration process is driven by a business focus, rather than a transaction focus.
5. The principles of demand management — planning, communicating, influencing, and prioritizing and managing demand — are utilized in a demand collaboration partnership.
6. Demand information provided by customers is clarified, reviewed, and challenged to validate the plan and improve plan accuracy.

7. Demand information provided by customers is considered another view in a multiple-view demand planning process. It is not taken at face value.

8. Trading partners agree upon the demand information to communicate. The information that is communicated is vital to good judgment and decision making. Care is taken not to overwhelm the process with information.

9. Customer demand information is evaluated and analyzed to put it in the proper business context for the supplier.

10. Customer and supplier agree on time zones when a forecast or demand plan represents a firm order and the time zone when the forecast or demand plan is communicated for guidance purposes only.

11. Suppliers recognize that customers expect on-time, complete order delivery when they communicate their forecasts or demand plans.

12. Trading partners use discipline to manage for the long-term financial health of each partner and the value chain. Trading partners recognize that the true win–win is realized when less capital for all trading partners is needed to operate the value chain.

QUESTIONS

1. What are the major points of dissension between customer and supplier in establishing successful trading partnerships for demand collaboration?

2. What can the customer do to overcome the supplier's point of dissension?

3. What can the supplier do to overcome the customer's point of dissension?

4. What is the bullwhip effect?

5. How does the bullwhip effect add costs to a value chain?

6. What steps are involved in establishing a business focus for demand collaboration between partners?

7. What is the role of the senior leadership team in establishing trading partnerships for demand collaboration?

8. What demand information is typically communicated as part of a partnership for demand collaboration?

9. Why should customer demand information not be taken at face value?

10. What elements of demand management are employed in a trading partnership for demand collaboration?

11. Should a customer that communicates demand information to its supplier receive different pricing than a customer that does not? Why or why not?

12. What are the advantages of agreeing on time zone parameters for demand information?

13. How can trust among trading partners be fostered?

14. What are the four critical success factors for demand collaboration?

15. What is the role of technology in demand collaboration?

DEMAND CONSENSUS AND INTEGRATION

How often does the following occur in your company? The sales organization sells a particular product mix to a different customer base than what the marketing or product/brand management organization is targeting. Or a new product is set to launch, and the product or brand management organization communicates a demand plan that has a much steeper ramp up of demand than how the sales organization believes the new product will sell. And the statistical forecast, if you have this capability in place, differs from what all three organizations say the demand will be.

Rarely do the sales, marketing, and product/brand management organizations agree on the demand plan numbers. When you add customer demand plans to the mix, they also do not often coincide with the demand organization's plans. It is not bad that the demand numbers are not in agreement; it is to be expected. After all, each demand organization has a different view of and experience with the marketplace.

What is bad is not reconciling the different views. What happens when consensus on the demand plan is not reached? It is the genesis of companies operating with multiple plans or numbers. The following typically occurs.

Sales, marketing, and product/brand management organizations operate to their own individual numbers. The supply and finance organizations are not sure which demand numbers to use to drive their plans. The finance organization opts to use its own set of financial numbers, which are dissimilar to all of the various demand numbers. The supply organization does not trust any of the demand numbers, or the financial numbers for that matter, and plugs in its own demand numbers to drive the company's supply planning process. This causes the supply organization to jerk itself and its suppliers around when actual demand is different from its self-imposed demand numbers. It's no wonder that the company's suppliers do not trust the procurement plan and choose to operate from their own set of numbers.

In this scenario, you end up with the bullwhip effect and an endless struggle to fulfill customer demand in the volume and timing that customers want it. Sales are lost, customers are disgruntled, and profits are diminished.

This is not an unusual scenario. In fact, it is typical. In studying supply chains, Ron Ireland, a pioneer on collaborative forecasting and replenishment and an Oliver Wight colleague, finds that *most supply chains operate with 14 to 25 different demand forecasts.*

Not all companies operate in a multiple-number environment, however. Companies that use a single set of operational numbers are usually among the top performers in their industries. They are almost always profitable.

What is their secret? It is really not a secret at all. Companies that operate with a single set of numbers usually have the following in common:

- They reach consensus on the demand plan over at least an 18-month planning horizon, using a monthly demand consensus review meeting as the forum for reaching consensus.
- They utilize an integrated business management review process, known as sales and operations planning, to synchronize the demand, supply, and financial plans every month.

This chapter discusses the demand consensus review meeting and how to conduct it using best practice principles. It also provides an overview of sales and operations planning and why it is essential to the demand side of the business and the overall financial health of a company and value chain.

First of all, what is a single set of numbers? The practice of using a single set of numbers was conceived in the late 1970s with the express purpose of ensuring that sales, marketing, manufacturing, distribution, and finance plans were synchronized, or as Andrew White of Logility, Inc. describes, "singing from the same book."[70] The effort first started within manufacturing to synchronize production and procurement schedules. It soon became apparent that synchronization of manufacturing plans alone did not solve customer service and inventory problems. In the 1980s, the practice of synchronizing demand and supply became a best practice. This meant the sales, marketing, and brand/product management had to agree on a demand plan.

The development of a single set of numbers begins with reaching consensus on a demand plan. The monthly demand consensus review meeting is the forum

- Performance reviews (demand plan accuracy, customer service, sales plan performance, market share, and other sales and marketing metrics)
- Review of total demand plan, over a minimum 18-month planning horizon
- Review of proposed product family demand plans, over a minimum 18-month planning horizon, with focus on:
  1. What has changed since last month's demand plan, including the impact of new product plans
  2. Review of significant assumptions supporting each product family demand plan
  3. Review of opportunities and risks
  4. Review of performance metrics for each product family
- Approved changes to the proposed family demand plans
- Review of major demand opportunities for the business
- Review of vulnerabilities and risks (market/economic conditions, competitor activities, potential new competitive entrants/exits, substitute products, etc.) that could impact the business overall
- Alternate demand plan review with assumptions ("what-if" analysis)
- Identification of issues and decisions:
  1. To communicate to the supply and finance organizations
  2. For discussion and decision at the sales and operations planning meeting
- Review of outstanding action items from previous meetings
- Review of decisions and action items assigned during the meeting

FIGURE 85   Best Practice Agenda — Demand Review and Consensus Meeting

for agreeing on a single demand plan. Consensus is reached by reviewing the comprehensive picture of demand — the total composite demand plan as well as the aggregate demand plan for each product family, supported by the most significant assumptions. These plans are reviewed in unit volume and the resulting sales revenue and profit margin over at least an 18-month planning horizon. The objective of the review is to gain consensus on a volume plan to communicate to the supply organization and the resulting sales revenue and profit plans to communicate to the financial organization.

The demand consensus review meeting should not be a long-winded affair. In best practice environments, the meeting generally takes no longer than two hours per month (see Figure 85 for a typical meeting agenda), unless specific unanticipated events dictate a longer session. The information for the meeting should be prepared in advance in a dashboard graphical format (see Figures 86 and 87). This graphical approach facilitates an easy grasp of whether there are issues to address regarding the volume and timing of demand as well as the resulting sales revenue and profit margin plans. The demand consensus review meeting is not the time to review the demand numbers in detail. Any detailed review should occur prior to the meeting. These are best practices.

Demand Dashboard

BU: COMM   Family: XXX
Inventory Strategy: _____
Lead Time Strategy: _____

Demand Plan

History   Future

■ Demand   ▭ Orders   ◆ Bookings

Performance Measures

Measure	-3	-2	-1
On-Time Delivery	90%	85%	85%
Plan vs. Actual	80%	80%	70%
Territory A	98%	95%	95%
Territory B	70%	60%	70%
Territory C	80%	75%	85%
Territory D	50%	60%	50%

- **Assumptions/Internal**
  Will add 1 salesperson in period 5. Promotion planned in periods 6 through 9.

- **Assumptions/External**
  Competitor will introduce a competing product in period 7.

- **Vulnerabilities/Risks**
  Product introduction delayed 3 months.

- **Opportunities**
  Customer A is increasing its volume by 20%.

- **Issues/Decisions**
  Resources for completing new product.

- **Occurrences/Internal**
  Shipment delayed in period 2 — quality problems.

- **Occurrences/External**
  Softening of economy in last quarter.

FIGURE 86 Sample Dashboard for Family Demand

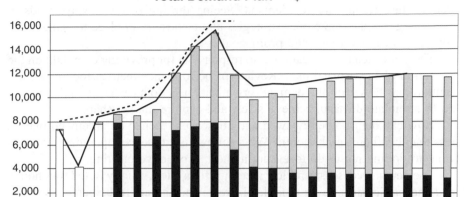

Metric	Actual	Strategic Goal
Total Market Share	48%	55%
Marketing Expense per Customer	$45	$40
Percent Profit Margin	58%	62%

- **Changes Since Last Month**
- **Issues/Decisions**
- **Assumptions**

FIGURE 87   Sample Dashboard for Total Demand

One misconception about the demand consensus review is that the demand manager chairs the meeting. The demand consensus review is the leadership meeting for the demand organization. The highest level person in the demand organization, typically the vice-president of sales or marketing, owns and chairs the meeting. The meeting is also not large. The participants are the direct reports to the vice-presidents of sales and marketing. These, too, are best practices.

Why should the meeting participants be the most senior people in the demand organization? *Because they are ultimately accountable for making demand happen.* If they do not or cannot reach consensus on a demand plan, the people who work for them will be working at cross-purposes. The most senior leaders in the demand organization also have the authority to establish or change strategic and tactical direction. Reviewing the demand plan in composite gives the senior leaders the "big picture" of demand. Seeing the big picture always leads to examining whether the proper strategies and tactics are in place to achieve the company's sales revenue and profit goals.

The senior leadership team is also responsible for providing oversight on the execution of the demand plan. Review of performance metrics focuses on execution and how well the demand organization is doing what it said it would do to stimulate demand, achieve sales, and capture market share.

How can demand be reviewed and consensus reached on a demand plan in less than two hours each month? What follows is a case example that illustrates what to do and not to do to ensure a short, productive meeting.

The demand consensus review meetings for a client usually lasted four hours, and the participants never completely reviewed the entire demand plan. The vice-presidents of sales and marketing always left the meeting frustrated and believing they had wasted their time. "I never know how we truly stand with demand," the vice-president of sales complained.

The complaint was legitimate. The demand plan was presented at a subfamily level, which meant that demand for 21 subfamilies had to be reviewed. Instead of showing graphs of the demand, the plan was presented in spreadsheets of numbers. No assumptions accompanied the plan. The meeting participants attempted to go over every number for every period in the 24-period planning horizon for all 21 subfamilies. The vice-presidents of sales and marketing never received a composite picture of demand or the assumptions behind the plan.

To develop a meaningful demand consensus review, the consensus and review process was restructured. The following changes were made:

■ The vice-president of sales chairs the meeting, rather than the demand manager.

■ Instead of four product managers, three demand planners, and six sales managers attending the meeting, only the vice-president of sales, vice-president of marketing, directors of sales and marketing, and the demand manager participate in the meeting.

■ A higher aggregation of demand was established, and product demand was rolled into 9 product families for review rather than 21 subfamilies. Demand by subfamilies and at times the item level is reviewed on an exception basis — only when there are significant demand and performance issues.

■ The vice-presidents of sales and marketing worked together to develop a standing agenda for the meeting. This agenda is heavily tilted toward: (1) reviewing what has changed in the aggregate demand plans and total demand plan since the previous month, (2) validating the significant

Demand Manager's Role

PRODUCT FAMILY/BRAND A

Period	Statistical Forecast	Sales Plan	Customer Forecasts	Marketing Plan	New Product Plans	Proposed New Demand Plan	Previous Month's Approved Demand Plan	Annual Budget
1	1000	1500	2000			1000	1000	1500
2	2500	3000	3500			2500	2500	3000
3	4500	5000	5500			4500	4500	5000
4	1000	500	1000			1000	1000	1000
5	1000	500	1000			1000	1000	1000
6	1000	500	1000		10000	1000	1000	1000
7	3000	4000	5000	10000	10000	3000	4000	5000
8	3000	4000	5000	10000	10000	5000	4000	5000
9	4500	5500	6500	2500	10000	6000	5500	5000
10	6500	7500	8500	2500	5000	7000	7500	8000
11	7500	8500	9500			8000	8500	8000
12	5000	3000	4000			5000	3000	4000
13	1100	1725	2000			1100	1100	
14	2750	3450	3500			2750	2750	
15	4950	5750	5500			4950	4950	
16	1100	575	1000			1100	1100	
17	1100	575	1000			1100	1100	
18	1100	575	1000			1100	1100	

FIGURE 88   Consolidating Multiple Views into a Proposed Plan

assumptions, (3) reviewing performance metrics, and (4) determining what strategies, tactics, and actions are needed to narrow any gap between the sales revenue plan and financial goal.

- The demand manager was tasked with creating and updating graphical dashboards of demand information, rather than spreadsheets of numbers, for review at the meeting.
- The demand manager became responsible for developing a proposed demand plan prior to the meeting (see Figure 88), based on the multiple inputs from sales, marketing, and product management.
- The demand manager was made responsible for interacting with the appropriate sales, marketing, and product managers when the proposed demand plan differed significantly from their input. If the sales or marketing managers disagree with the proposed plan, they are responsible for taking the issue to the appropriate sales or marketing director.

- The directors of sales and marketing became responsible for presenting their teams' view at the monthly meeting when there is a lack of consensus on the demand plan.
- The demand manager was made responsible for reviewing demand and working with the supply manager to keep demand and supply in balance on a daily and weekly basis.

These process changes greatly enhanced the demand consensus review process. The meeting is now focused on exceptions — what is different from last month's approved plan, where consensus is lacking, and what problems and opportunities must be addressed. By looking at the exceptions, rather than trying to validate every single demand number, the meeting quickly gets at the heart of the issues facing the demand organization.

Addressing the issues is also enhanced. The decision makers participate in the meeting each month. Decisions are now made, rather than issues either never surfacing or never being brought to the attention of the appropriate decision makers. Demand problems and sales opportunities are recognized early by reviewing the demand plan over the entire 24-period planning horizon. This allows the demand organization sufficient time to plan and execute the most advantageous response to the problems and opportunities. Sales and marketing strategies are reviewed, particularly the habit of offering discounts to meet quarterly revenue objectives. Seeing the negative impact of this practice on profit margins, the focus has shifted to developing new customers and penetrating new market segments to meet sales revenue goals.

The first three meetings under the new structure lasted longer than two hours. The leadership team, for the first time, received a composite picture of demand and identified problems that needed to be addressed. For the first time, the leaders from sales and marketing saw how their actions sometimes were at cross-purposes, which created some lengthy discussions and consensus building.

After the third meeting, most of the problems were either resolved or actions were being taken to resolve them. The focus of the meeting shifted from problem solving to problem prevention over the long-term planning horizon.

In reaching consensus on the demand plan every month, the vice-presidents of sales and marketing challenged the meeting participants with a question: Is this the product we really want the supply organization to produce on our behalf and our customers' behalf? They observed the behavior rule that silence is approval.

Use of the "silence is approval" approach serves two purposes. First, it encourages people to speak out when they disagree with the demand plan. Second, it reinforces the expectation that once consensus is reached on the demand plan, the demand organization is accountable for executing the plan.

As the demand leadership team became more comfortable with the process, it began to see the value of updating and reaching consensus on a demand plan every month, or what is known as replanning. A replanning process encourages consensus.

Here is how a replanning process works. Let's say there is uncertainty or disagreement about the demand plan in months 9 to 12. The demand leadership team agrees to a demand number for that time period with a caveat. The caveat is that during the next month, the meeting participants will clarify the demand for that period and the issues will be revisited during next month's meeting. Actions are assigned to meeting participants to ensure that information is gathered and discussions ensue during the month so that consensus can be reached at the meeting.

Review of performance metrics is also part of the monthly demand consensus review meeting. The purpose of the performance review is to:

■ Determine how well the demand organization is executing the demand plan
■ Identify whether the demand organization's goals for sales growth, profits, market share, and other key objectives are being accomplished

When the performance goals are not achieved three months in a row for any specific product family, key account, or key metric, it is a common practice to discuss the reasons for the subpar performance and the actions being taken to correct the situation. This review reinforces accountability for execution. It also triggers evaluating whether different strategies and tactics are needed to accomplish the demand organization's goals. And, when the demand plan accuracy is consistently under- or overachieved, it indicates that the request for product (demand plan) may need to be changed.

Once consensus is reached on the demand plan each month, it does not mean that the demand plan is approved at this point. Two questions remain to be asked and answered:

■ Can the supply organization produce the product in the quantity and timing needed to fulfill the demand plan?
■ Is the demand plan in the best financial interest of the company?

The demand plan is a request for product. As such, it is a request for the company to utilize its capital (time, money, and labor) to ensure that product will be available in the volume and timing that are indicated in the demand plan. It may not always be possible to fulfill the volume and timing of the demand plan, however. The supply organization may have production constraints, or the demand may outstrip a supplier's capability to produce raw material or components in sufficient quantity. If it is not possible to fulfill the demand, it is better to recognize the situation early so that there is time to develop supply alternatives or, in the worst case, so that false promises are not made to customers if supply alternatives are not feasible.

The need to synchronize demand and supply on a monthly basis was the driving force behind the advent of sales and operations planning. Sales and operations planning is a monthly process in which the senior executives of a company meet to review and approve the demand, supply, and financial plans. The purpose of the review is to make sure the plans are synchronized and that execution of the plans will generate the desired sales revenue and profits.

Some executives call sales and operations planning a truth process. For many executives, implementation of sales and operations planning enabled them for the first time to truly understand the company's plans and capabilities and whether or not the company would be able to attain its financial and strategic objectives. Sales and operations planning gives executives more control over the business. In just a few hours every month, they get a reliable picture of their company's current capabilities and what changes need to be made to achieve the company's goals and objectives.

The demand consensus review meeting is a step in the sales and operations planning process (see Figure 89). The process starts with an update of new product activities and other corporate initiatives, like the implementation of a new planning system, that consume significant capital and company resources. The update of new product activities is vital to the demand organization. It informs the demand organization whether the development of new products is proceeding on time or is delayed. This information enables the marketing and sales organizations to adjust their activities for introducing new products and change the demand plan accordingly.

FIGURE 89   Sales and Operations Planning Process (Copyright Oliver Wight International)

After consensus is reached on a demand plan, the proposed demand plan is communicated to the supply organization. The supply organization prepares a supply plan based on the demand plan (see Figure 90). The purpose of this planning step is to determine whether demand and supply (including inventory) can be synchronized.

When demand and supply cannot be synchronized, the supply organization develops alternative supply plans for fulfilling the demand plan. These alternative supply plans may propose any of the following alternatives: building product early to fulfill future demand, extending delivery lead times, working overtime, hiring additional labor, acquiring additional production equipment, outsourcing production, or, as a last resource, reducing the demand plan. In proposing alternative supply plans, the costs and risks associated with each alternative are identified from a demand, supply, and financial perspective.

Even if the demand and supply organizations agree on a plan that synchronizes demand and supply, consensus has not yet been attained. The financial organization reviews both the demand plan and supply plan (including any alternate proposed plans). The purpose of this review is to determine the impact of the plans on the company's financial performance, including revenue, profits, cash flow, and capital investments. When alternative plans are proposed, the financial organization is expected to weigh in on which plan makes the best financial sense for the company.

After the demand, supply, and financial reviews are completed, the executive sales and operations planning meeting takes place. This monthly meeting is chaired by the general manager or president of the company and is attended by his or her direct reports. The purpose of the meeting is to:

- Reach consensus on a synchronized demand, supply, and financial plan
- Review a "balanced scorecard" of key performance metrics[71]
- Validate that the company's plans will enable the company to achieve its strategic and financial objectives

To accomplish the above, discussion at the executive sales and operations planning meeting focuses on answering the questions shown in Figure 91.[72]

Once the demand, supply, and financial plans are approved, they are communicated throughout the organization so that everyone is operating to the agreed upon plan and expectations. This is what is meant by the term integration or what Andrew White describes as "singing from the same book."

The demand plan drives the sales and operations planning process. The supply plans and financial plans are derived from the demand plan. This is critical to operating with a single set of operational numbers and is a best practice.

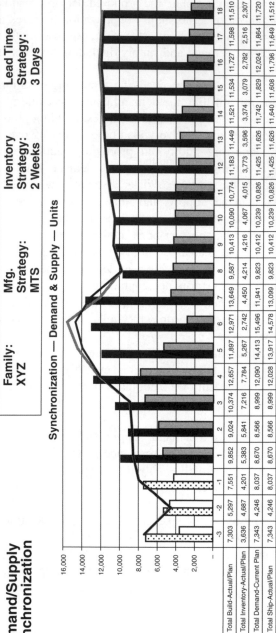

Demand/Supply Synchronization

	Family: XYZ		Mfg. Strategy: MTS		Inventory Strategy: 2 Weeks		Lead Time Strategy: 3 Days

Synchronization — Demand & Supply — Units

	-3	-2	-1	1	2	3	4	5	6	7	8	9	10	11	12	13	14	15	16	17	18
Total Build-Actual/Plan	7,303	5,297	7,551	9,852	9,024	10,374	12,657	11,897	12,971	13,649	9,587	10,413	10,090	10,774	11,183	11,449	11,521	11,534	11,727	11,598	11,510
Total Inventory-Actual/Plan	3,636	4,687	4,201	5,383	5,841	7,216	7,784	5,267	2,742	4,450	4,214	4,216	4,067	4,015	3,773	3,596	3,374	3,079	2,782	2,516	2,307
Total Demand-Current Plan	7,343	4,246	8,037	8,670	8,566	8,999	12,090	14,413	15,496	11,941	9,823	10,412	10,239	10,826	11,425	11,626	11,742	11,829	12,024	11,864	11,720
Total Ship-Actual/Plan	7,343	4,246	8,037	8,670	8,566	8,999	12,028	13,917	14,578	13,099	9,823	10,412	10,239	10,826	11,425	11,626	11,640	11,608	11,796	11,649	11,512

	To Plan
Demand	
Supply	
Inventory	

- **Assumptions**
  Plant maintenance in period 5.
  Supplier quality problems will be resolved in period 2.

- **Opportunities**
  Improve output 10% on machine 6 during maintenance.

- **Occurrences**
  Supplier quality issues in period 2.

- **Vulnerabilities/Risks**
  Completion of planned maintenance on time.

- **Issues/Decisions**
  Imbalance periods 5–6. Delay planned maintenance? Or increase inventory build prior to shutdown.

FIGURE 90 Demand/Supply Synchronization Plan

- What has changed since last month?
- What decisions need to be made or approved during this month's executive sales and operations planning meeting?
- Are we comfortable with the synchronized demand, supply, and financial plans across the entire planning horizon?
- Are we on plan financially?
- How are we performing to our company's goals and key performance indicators, that is, the "balanced scorecard" of performance measurements?
- What new or different risks should we understand and consider?
- What decisions will we be compelled to make during the next few months?
- How are the individual product families or aggregate groupings performing?
- Are we on schedule, on cost, on scope with our product development efforts?
- How are we performing to company initiatives? Are we on scope, on schedule, on cost?
- Do we have any resource constraints, and how well are we utilizing our key resources?
- Is there any reason to re-evaluate our strategic plans or company goals?

FIGURE 91 Questions to Answer in the Executive Sales and Operations Planning Meeting

When companies collaborate with trading partners, the approved plans should be communicated as appropriate. For example, the supply organization would communicate an updated procurement schedule for both the near- and long-term planning horizon to its supplier trading partners. The demand organization would communicate its company's capabilities to fulfill the demand that customers have requested in their demand plans for the near- and long-term planning horizon. When the needs and expectations of trading partners are not synchronized, discussions should take place about how to best synchronize demand and supply and who assumes the risk. This is sometimes called joint business planning.

In reality today, little joint business planning and synchronization take place between trading partners. That is because most trading partner relationships for demand collaboration efforts focus on the very near term, for example the next four weeks. A longer term focus and involvement by the executives of trading partner companies are needed to truly synchronize demand and supply and integrate plans across the value chain. Joint business planning needs to expand in the following ways:

- Near-term synchronization of demand and supply on at least a weekly basis
- Monthly synchronization of demand and supply at the aggregate level across a minimum 18-month planning horizon
- Synchronization of strategies and tactics for increasing sales to end users or consumers and reducing costs in the value chain. This should occur at least twice per year and more frequently when market dynamics and trading partner capabilities significantly change.
- Agreed upon performance metrics to monitor execution and the financial benefits from collaboration.

The customer's supply manager and the supplier's demand manager should be responsible for integrating demand and supply plans over the near-term planning horizon. Synchronization of demand and supply across an 18+-month planning horizon should be led by supply executives for the customer and the sales and marketing executives for the supplier. The trading partner company presidents, supported by their executive leadership teams, should lead the synchronization of strategies and tactics over the long-term planning horizon.

While this model of value chain integration is not yet widely used, the authors predict that companies will move toward this approach in the future. Once companies effectively integrate their internal processes, they will see what is lacking by not collaborating with their trading partners. Once they begin to collaborate, they will realize that integration of plans and execution are required to realize optimum financial benefits.

Demand drives integration — whether integration takes place inside a single company or throughout a value chain. It all starts with demand and the following questions: What are customers and end users or consumers interested in buying? How can we best entice them to buy our products and services? What are they willing to pay for our products and services, and how much profit can we generate from the sales? What quantities will customers, end users, or consumers buy at that price?

To integrate well, companies are implementing best practices in demand management. This has put greater pressure on the demand organization to do the best it possibly can to plan, communicate, influence, and prioritize and manage demand. As a result, there is a greater awareness than ever before that the demand organization truly matters. And not only does it matter, but other functions within the business enterprise and enterprises in the value chain are dependent upon the demand organization's competency. Companies and value chains cannot attain their full potential without excellence in demand management.

SUMMARY OF BEST PRACTICES
FOR DEMAND CONSENSUS AND INTEGRATION

1. The business entity operates with a single set of operational numbers (demand, supply, and financial) that is driven by the demand plan.
2. A monthly demand consensus review meeting is conducted, led by the highest ranking person in sales and/or marketing and attended by the direct reports of the highest ranking demand organization executive.
3. Consensus is reached on the demand plan by reviewing the total demand plan and the aggregate (family) plans and assumptions over a minimum 18-month planning horizon.
4. Demand information is presented in a graphical manner that enables easy grasp of demand issues.
5. The demand manager proposes a demand plan, based on multiple inputs from sales, marketing, and brand/product management, that is reviewed for consensus at the monthly demand consensus review meeting.
6. "Silence is approval" behavioral rules are in place, and the demand organization understands that silence means acceptance of the demand plan and commitment to execute it.
7. Performance metrics are reviewed every month at the demand consensus review meeting.
8. When performance goals are not achieved three months in a row, the reasons for subpar performance and actions being taken to correct the situation are reviewed at the monthly demand consensus review meeting. Demand plans are also adjusted accordingly.
9. It is understood that once consensus is reached on the demand plan, it must be reviewed and approved at the executive sales and operations planning meeting.
10. The demand plan is used to determine whether the supply organization can produce the product in the timing and quantity needed to fulfill the demand plan.
11. The demand plan is used as the basis for the company's sales revenue plan.
12. The demand, supply, and financial plans are synchronized every month through the sales and operations planning process.
13. The executive sales and operations planning meeting is used to reach consensus on a synchronized demand, supply, and financial plan as well as to review a balanced scorecard of key performance metrics.
14. The approved, synchronized plans are communicated throughout the organization to ensure that all functions are operating from the same single set of numbers.

15. When collaborating with trading partners, the demand and supply plans are communicated, as appropriate, to trading partners to facilitate the synchronization of plans between trading partners.
16. When collaborating with trading partners, demand and supply are synchronized over the near term on at least a weekly basis. The customer's supply manager and supplier's demand manager are responsible for near-term synchronization.
17. When collaborating with trading partners, demand and supply at the aggregate level are synchronized across a minimum 18-month planning horizon. This synchronization is led by the supply executives for the customer and the sales and marketing executives for the supplier.
18. When collaborating with trading partners, strategies and tactics for increasing sales to end users or consumers and reducing costs in the value chain are synchronized at least twice per year and more frequently as needed. The trading partner company presidents, supported by their executive leadership teams, are responsible for synchronizing strategies and tactics.

QUESTIONS

1. What are the advantages of operating with a single set of numbers?
2. What is the role of the demand plan in developing a single set of numbers?
3. If you were the vice-president of sales and marketing, what would be the agenda for your monthly demand consensus review meeting?
4. Who should participate in the demand consensus review meeting?
5. What is the purpose of the demand consensus review meeting?
6. What are the reasons for operating with a "silence is approval" philosophy?
7. What are the steps in the sales and operations planning process?
8. What is the purpose of the executive sales and operations planning meeting?
9. What questions should be asked and answered during the executive sales and operations planning meeting?
10. What is one future model for integrating trading partners' plans throughout the value chain?
11. Who needs to be involved in trading partner collaboration from each trading partner business entity? What are their roles?

REFERENCES

1. Lalonde, Bud, Better to Hang Together, *Supply Chain Management Review,* January/February 2002, p. 9.
2. Verity, John, Clearing the Cobwebs from the Stockroom: New Internet Software May Make Forecasting a Snap, *Business Week,* October 21, 1996.
3. Kotler, Philip, *Kotler on Marketing: How to Create, Win, and Dominate Markets*, The Free Press, 1999, p. 46.
4. Kotler, Philip, *Marketing Management: Analysis, Planning, Implementation, and Control,* Ninth Edition, Prentice Hall, 1997, pp. 15, 134.
5. Cox III, James F., Blackstone, Jr., John H., *APICS Dictionary, 9th Edition,* APICS—The Educational Society for Resource Management, 1998.
6. Drucker, Peter F., The Guru's Guru: A Lively Conversation with Peter Drucker, Dean of the Deep Thinkers, *Business 2.0,* October 2001, pp. 70–71.
7. Peck, Michael, Stone Apparel Spells Success: E-R-P, *Consumer Goods Technology*, March 2001, p. 17.
8. *Inventory Reduction Report* is published by the Institute of Management & Administration, Inc.
9. Perry, Daphne, Ross, Dale, et al., *Roadmap to Continuous Replenishment: A Canadian Perspective,* Joint Canadian ECR Initiative, 1995, p 71.
10. Ibid., p. 70.
11. Serwer, Andy Firnt Glut Check, *Fortune,* May 14, 2001, pp. 105–112.
12. Fairfield, Daren K., CPFR and the Collaborative Economy — Are You Ready, *Consumer Goods Technology,* February 2001, p. 12.
13. Singhal, Vinod R., Hendricks, Kevin B., How Supply Chain Glitches Torpedo Shareholder Value, *Supply Chain Management Review*, January/February 2002, pp. 18–24.
14. *Webster's Encyclopedic Unabridged Dictionary of the English Language*, Random House Value Publishing, 1996, p. 1523.
15. Drucker, Peter F., *The Executive in Action*, Harper Business, 1996, p. 185.

16. Palmatier, George E. with Crum, Colleen, *Enterprise Sales and Operations Planning: Synchronizing Demand, Supply and Resources for Peak Performance*, J. Ross Publishing, 2002.
17. Proud, John, *Master Scheduling, A Practical Guide to Competitive Manufacturing*, John Wiley & Sons, 1994, pp. 439–441.
18. Norton, Rob, The Motley Crew That Hates Rate Increases, *Fortune,* January 24, 2000, p. 72.
19. Quote of the Day, *New York Times,* May 24, 2002, p. 2.
20. Wurman, Richard Saul, *Information Anxiety 2,* Que, 2001, p. 14.
21. Wriston, Walter B., *The Twilight of Sovereignty: How the Information Revolution Is Transforming Our World,* Charles Scribner's Sons, 1992, p. 115.
22. Kotler, Philip, *Kotler on Marketing: How to Create, Win, and Dominate Markets,* The Free Press, 1999, p. 46.
23. Ibid, p. 18.
24. Lautenborn, Robert, New Marketing Litany: 4 P's Passé; C-Words Take Over, *Advertising Age,* October 1, 1990, p. 26.
25. Best, Roger J., *Market-Based Management: Strategies for Growing Customer Value and Profitability,* Prentice Hall, 2000, p. 347.
26. Kotler, Philip, *Kotler on Marketing: How to Create, Win, and Dominate Markets,* The Free Press, 1999, p. xiii.
27. Kurt Salmon Associates, Inc., *Efficient Consumer Response: Enhancing Customer Value in the Grocery Industry,* Food Marketing Institute, 1993, pp. 82–83.
28. Kopczak, Laura Rock, Designing Supply Chains for the "Click-and-Mortar" Economy, *Supply Chain Management Review,* January/February 2001, p. 66.
29. Singhal, Vinod, Hendricks, Kevin, How Supply Chain Glitches Torpedo Shareholder Value, *Supply Chain Management Review,* January/February 2002, p. 20.
30. Swann, Don, Out with the Old Truths and In with the New, *APICS—The Performance Advantage,* January 2002, p. 44.
31. Brentnall, Gareth, Managing the Uncertainty in Customer Demand, *Control,* June 2001, p. 10.
32. Crosby, John V., *Cycles, Trends, and Turning,* NTC Business Books, 1999, p. 199.
33. An excellent resource is Hanke, John E., Rietsch, Arthur G., *Business Forecasting,* Sixth Edition, Prentice Hall, 1998, pp. 193–222.
34. Bossidy, Larry, Charan, Ram, *Execution: The Discipline of Getting Things Done,* Crown Business, 2002, p. 57.
35. Palmatier, George E. with Crum, Colleen, *Enterprise Sales and Operations Planning: Synchronizing Demand, Supply and Resources for Peak Performance,* J. Ross Publishing, 2002, p. 32.
36. Huggett, James F., When Cultures Resist Change, *Quality Progress,* March 1999, pp. 35–39.
37. Courtney, Hugh, Kirkland, Jane, Viguerie, Patrick, *Strategy Under Uncertainty, Harvard Business Review on Managing Uncertainty,* Harvard Business Review Paperback Series, 1999, pp. 5–11.
38. Elliott, Stuart, At an Industry Gathering, The Emphasis Is on Reasserting the Power of Brand-Name Products, *New York Times,* October 14, 2002, p. C8.

39. Cargille, Brian, Bliss, Robert, How Supply Chain Analysis Enhances Product Design, *Supply Chain Management Review,* September/October 2001, pp. 64–74.
40. Miller, Robert B., Heiman, Stephen E., *Strategic Selling,* Miller Heiman, 1987, pp. 34–42.
41. Cargille, Brian, Bliss, Robert, How Supply Chain Analysis Enhances Product Design, *Supply Chain Management Review,* September/October 2001, p. 68.
42. Miller, Robert B., Heiman, Stephen E., *Strategic Selling,* Miller Heiman, 1987, pp. 69–99.
43. Kotler, Philip, *Kotler on Marketing: How to Create, Win, and Dominate Markets,* The Free Press, 1999, p. 19.
44. Best, Roger J., *Market-Based Management: Strategies for Growing Customer Value and Profitability,* Prentice Hall, 2000, pp. 39–42.
45. Palmatier, George E. with Crum, Colleen, *Enterprise Sales and Operations Planning: Synchronizing Demand, Supply and Resources for Peak Performance,* J. Ross Publishing, 2002, p. 199.
46. Palmatier, George, *Forecast Measurement and Evaluation,* The Oliver Wight Companies, 1994.
47. Mehta, Stephanie N., Lessons from the Lucent Debacle, *Fortune,* February 5, 2001, pp. 143–148.
48. Coke to Stop Giving Guidance, Reuters, December 13, 2002.
49. CRM: Inflicting Pain or Profit? *AMR Research,* December 2002.
50. Hopkins, Jim, Kessler, Michelle, Companies Squander Billions on Tech, *USA Today,* May 19, 2002.
51. Burke, James, Ornstein, Robert, *The Axemaker's Gift,* G.P. Putnam's Sons, 1995, p. 176.
52. Consumer-Centric Benchmarks for 2001 and Beyond, *Consumer Goods Technology Supplement,* 2001, p. 30.
53. CRM: Inflicting Pain or Profit? *AMR Research,* December 2002.
54. Hopkins, Jim, Kessler, Michelle, Companies Squander Billions on Tech, *USA Today,* May 19, 2002.
55. Travis, Lance, Johnson, Rod, Parker, Bob, Shepherd, Jim, The End of the Enterprise Application Era, *AMR Research,* February 5, 2002.
56. Andraski, Joseph C., *CPFR Emerges as the Next Movement in Supply Chain Management, Collaborative Planning, Forecasting and Replenishment,* Galileo Business, 2002, pp. 75–78.
57. Lee, Hau L., Creating Value Through Supply Chain Integration, *Supply Chain Management Review,* September/October 2000, p. 33.
58. Ireland, Ron, Bruce, Robert, CPFR: Only the Beginning of Collaboration, *Supply Chain Management Review,* September/October 2000, p. 83.
59. Koch, Christian, Hausruckinger, Gerhard, On the Road to the Network Economy: Developing an e-Transformation Roadmap for Profitable Growth in the Consumer Goods Industry, *Collaborative Planning, Forecasting and Replenishment,* Galileo Business, 2002, p. 263.
60. Bruce, Robert, Ireland, Ron, Retail Planning Week Presentation, CPFR® Institute, Orlando, Florida, November 13–14, 2002.

61. Emerging Practices in Collaborative Planning and Forecasting, *Bridging the Customer Divide 2002: A New Look at Value Chain Collaboration,* A.T. Kearney, 2002, p. 14.

62. Walton, Sam, Huey, John, *Made in America: My Story,* Doubleday, 1992, p. 247.

63. *Roadmap to Continuous Improvement: A Canadian ECR Enabler,* The Canadian Efficient Consumer Response Steering Committee, 1995, p. 7.

64. Verity, John, Clearing the Cobwebs from the Stockroom: New Internet Software May Make Forecasting a Snap, *Business Week,* October 21, 1996.

65. O'Marah, Kevin, Best Practices for Collaborative Forecasting, *AMR Research Report,* March 2002.

66. Oliver Wight Companies, *Oliver Wight ABCD Checklist for Operational Excellence,* John Wiley & Sons, 2001.

67. Robinson, Alan, Is That Circle Broken, *Food Logistics,* June 15, 1999, p. 48.

68. Williams, Scott, Forecasting Panel, Supply Chain Council Conference, New Orleans, Louisiana, May 14, 1998.

69. O'Marah, Kevin, Best Practices for Collaborative Forecasting, *AMR Research Report,* March 2002.

70. White, Andrew, *The Value Equation: Value Chain Management, Collaboration, and the Internet,* Logility, Inc., 1999.

71. Kaplan, Robert S., Norton, David P., *The Balanced Scorecard: Translating Strategy into Action,* Harvard Business School Press, 1996.

72. Palmatier, George E. with Crum, Colleen, *Enterprise Sales and Operations Planning: Synchronizing Demand, Supply and Resources for Peak Performance,* J. Ross Publishing, 2003, p. 151.

INDEX